THE LAST SECONDS

The tension had mounted. They knew that the "eels," as they called the torpedoes, would be leaving the submarine's bow and, gliding invisibly under water, would strike the hull of the enemy ship and explode, causing a deadly wound. On the big ship facing them, gradually coming into the spider-lines of the sighting gear, behind thin steel plates there were men and women happy to be returning home, children sleeping peacefully. Poor wretches, they didn't know . . .

THE BANTAM WAR BOOK SERIES

This is a series of books about a world on fire.

These carefully chosen volumes cover the full dramatic sweep of World War II. Many are eyewitness accounts by the men who fought in this global conflict in which the future of the civilized world hung in balance. Fighter pilots, tank commanders and infantry commanders, among others, recount exploits of individual courage in the midst of the large-scale terrors of war. They present portraits of brave men and true stories of gallantry and cowardice in action, moving sagas of survival and tragedies of untimely death. Some of the stories are told from the enemy viewpoint to give the reader an immediate sense of the incredible life and death struggle of both sides of the battle.

Through these books we begin to discover what it was like to be there, a participant in an epic war for freedom.

Each of the books in the Bantam War Book series contains illustrations specially commissioned for each title to give the reader a deeper understanding of the roles played by the men and machines of World War II.

THE LACONIA
AFFAIR

Léonce Peillard

**Translated from the French by
Oliver Coburn**

BANTAM BOOKS
TORONTO · NEW YORK · LONDON · SYDNEY

THE LACONIA AFFAIR

*A Bantam Book / published by arrangement with
The Putnam Publishing Group*

PRINTING HISTORY

Putnam's edition published October 1963

Originally published in France under the title L'Afaire du Laconia

*This translation was published in England under the title
U-Boats to the Rescue.*

Bantam edition / March 1983

*Drawings by Greg Beecham and Tom Beecham.
Maps by Alan and William McKnight.*

In memory of two sailors
Lieutenant-Commander Werner Hartenstein
and
Captain Rudolph Sharp

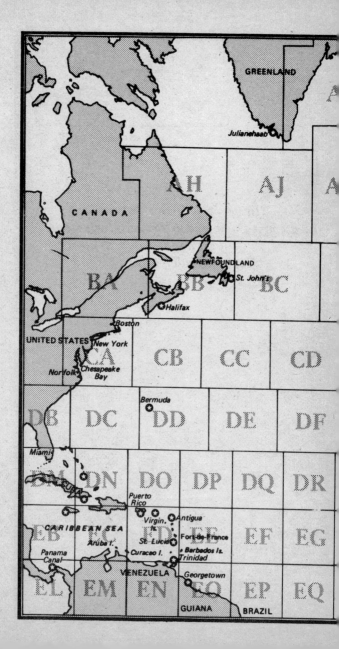

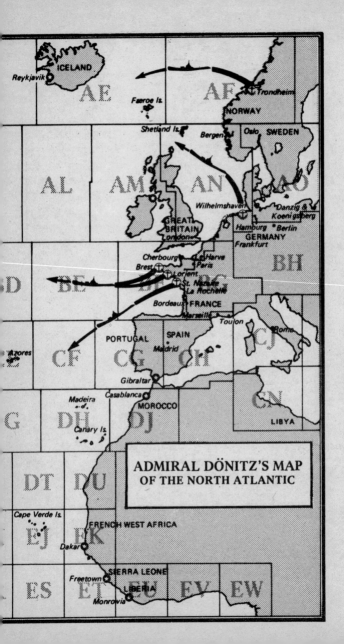

ADMIRAL DÖNITZ'S MAP
OF THE NORTH ATLANTIC

CONTENTS

PREFACE

On September 12th, 1942, a German submarine, U-156, torpedoed in mid-Atlantic the *Laconia*, a British liner, crammed with British soldiers, their wives and children, Italian prisoners of war and their Polish guards.

Before trying to recreate the story of that day and the days that followed, I should like to say a word about my own background and approach to these events.

My father was a sailor, an engineer in the French Navy. As a small boy I lived mostly in one or other of the French Channel ports, so that I was encouraged to learn English. At thirteen, shortly before the first World War, I was sent to boarding-school in England, to St Mary's, Dover.

At first I was rather lost in my strange surroundings. More particularly I was shocked by the history lessons and the textbooks we studied, where I found that French victories were minimized or even passed over in silence. Trafalgar and Waterloo were clearly *the* victories of the era, and the glories of Nelson and Wellington far outshone those of my hero Napoleon. He indeed was presented as a bandit, and was commonly referred to by the boys as "old Boney." This shattered my faith in historical truth, or at least gave me an early revelation of how relative a thing it is. My boyish disillusion has now faded, but the lesson it taught me has remained. It has helped to make me scrupulously careful in my search for the truth about this drama of the sea, in which the protagonists were the British and the Germans, with minor roles played by Italians, French and a few Poles, and a small but vital part performed by unknown Americans.

I have tried very hard to get as near to the truth as possible, visiting survivors among the British and Italians and the German submarine crews involved, and obtaining personal accounts wherever I could. Details may vary with the different circumstances, languages and temperaments, but the synthesis of these accounts reveals a spirit of humanity and self-sacrifice, mingling with much that is horrible and some acts of cowardice and brutality.

Through a notice in the *Leinen los*, the magazine for German old sailors, I first found some of the survivors from the U-boats involved. All these submarines were sunk with their commanders and crews on voyages later than the torpedoing of the *Laconia;* but some among the crews were saved by chance factors such as illness, leave, training courses or drafting to other ships.

I went to call on them at Mannheim, Bochum, Hamburg and Kiel, knowing nothing of their present lives, uneasy and yet rather moved to be meeting former enemies. They were very reserved at first, and if in the end they were ready to confide their memories to me, it was largely because I was an old sailor myself. We were united across frontiers by the sea. A word, an expression, a way of dressing, walking, standing, all sorts of trivial signs enable the "great family of old salts" to recognize each other.

One of them insisted on taking me through the port of Hamburg till we reached a quay where a British cruiser was tied up. We stayed there some time, and I saw the wistful look in his eyes as he gazed at the grey ship and the sailors moving about cheerfully on board. Few of these men are still sailors, but all retain a deep nostalgia for the sea, for the wonderful days of their twenties, with the mortal dangers and the comradeship they felt with their "old men"—the submarine commanders, who were barely thirty themselves.

With all these former submariners I talked about the *Laconia*'s torpedoing by U-156 and the rescue operation which Hartenstein, the submarine commander, ordered afterwards. They were proud of his act of humanity, and we recalled the naval tradition which existed well before Dunant and before the Geneva Convention (August 22nd, 1864): the tradition that once an engagement was over, the survivors of a shipwreck should be rescued.

"The finest decoration for a sailor is the life-saving medal," ex-Grand Admiral Karl Dönitz told me, during my visit to his house near Hamburg; I had gone there to discuss the

Laconia incident. We had no point in common except that we had both sailed in the same waters. He opened the door to me himself, looked me straight in the face with his grey eyes, and held out his hand to me as if he were receiving me at the gangway of his ship. Frau Dönitz stood behind him. We went into a huge library-cum-study. I was impressed by this haughty-looking but courteous admiral, a fairly tall man who was nearly seventy but looked ten years less. He had lost the lean hardness of his features I had expected from war-time photographs. He replied to my questions in French, with Frau Dönitz kindly helping him out now and then. By tacit consent we avoided politics. The man who had commanded all the German submarines from 1936 to 1945, who for twenty days succeeded Hitler as head of the German government, who served a ten-year prison sentence at Spandau, explained his ideas to me, told me of his doubts and fears, gave me the reasons for his orders. I had read in full detail the indictment, the speeches for the defence, the ex-admiral's testimony, at the Nuremberg trials. He soon saw from my precise and searching questions that I knew everything he had then said with reference to the sinking of the *Laconia* and what followed.

"Once Hartenstein had begun the rescue operation," he said, "I couldn't have given him the order to break it off. The morale of my men was very high, and to give them an order contrary to the laws of humanity would have destroyed it utterly... Then came the bombing of U-156 by an American Liberator. So, from a military point of view I was wrong; yet I ordered the rescue operation to be continued till the French arrived. My general staff did not agree with me. I remember one officer thumping on the table red with fury."

"And your chief of operations, Commander Günther Hessler?" This was his son-in-law, whom I had seen the evening before in a Ruhr town.

"Hessler was in charge of operations. His task was to organize the destruction of enemy ships and crews. So he wanted this operation broken off. I refused point blank. 'We can't throw these people back into the sea,' I told him."

All this happened in 1942 at the German U-boat Command in Paris. I could imagine the scene: the admiral opposed by his officers, perhaps not too sure of himself and apprehensive of Hitler's anger.

At the end of the book I have given some extracts from

the section in the Nuremberg trials dealing with the *Laconia* incident, and the reader can form his own judgment on Dönitz's behaviour. In fact the admiral was not condemned at Nuremberg as Submarine Commander-in-Chief, but on political grounds. He never gave me the impression of bearing any resentment, and remarked: "Ten years—I had plenty of time to think, to meditate."

Hessler was an American prisoner of war for a year, and *he* told me: "I don't regret that year. I came out of it a different man, happier. I see life differently now. Since then I've worked very hard to give myself a fresh start."

As to Commander Hartenstein, Dönitz said of him: "He was an excellent officer, tough in battle and humane when it was over. Had he lived, I should have appointed him chief of operations in place of my son-in-law, who had done his time on shore."

All the British survivors I have spoken to or heard from are unanimous in praising this man. Their testimonies, published at the end of the book, confirm all the good spoken of him by Dönitz, Hessler and his colleagues in the German Navy. That is why I have dedicated this book to two officers in opposing navies—men who if they had survived would have surely been glad to meet and shake each other by the hand: Hartenstein, the U-boat commander, and Sharp, the captain of the *Laconia*, who died on the bridge of his ship.

There is no doubt that Hartenstein began his rescue operation solely because he heard cries for help in Italian. In his first message to Dönitz he said: "*Laconia* sunk, unfortunately with 1,500 Italian prisoners." But for this he would certainly have withdrawn, as no submarine commander could be blamed for doing. Once he had started on the operation, however, he kept on to the end, even at the risk of losing his own ship.

I cannot close the German chapter without thanking those who have helped me in my investigations: Commander Klug, naval attaché of the German Federal Republic in Paris; Mr. Rudolf Krohne, editor of *Leinen los;* the editor of the magazine *Marine-Offizier-Hilfe* at Krefeld; Mr. E. Scherraus (U-507), who lent me his fine photographs, Messrs. A. Geoge and W. von Kirschbaum, both members of the U-459 crew, who were in fact brought together again by my investigations! I would mention especially Mr. Walter Remmert, once Lead-

ing Wireless Operator on board U-156, who has been very
helpful in supplying documents and photographs; Mr. R.
Rüter (U-506), who gave a vivid picture of his commander;
Mr. Feldmann (U-507) and his translator Mr. Fitchel, who
put his card-index and all his information at my disposal.
Thanks to them I have been able to imagine life on board the
submarines and the figures of submarine commanders now
dead: Hartenstein, Würdemann, Wilamowitz and Schacht.

On the British side the Admiralty regretted that their
records did not contain any relevant information, but
recommended me to approach the Cunard Steamship Company. They put me in touch with Mrs. Rudolph Sharp, widow
of the *Laconia*'s captain, who very kindly let me see some
letters from her husband, and with Mr. Buckingham, the
Laconia's third officer, whose account was of immense help to
me.

I should also like to thank Mrs. Davidson and her
daughter Molly, now Mrs. Lewes; the former sent me her
diary, written in a school copy-book at Casablanca, where
they were interned after the rescue. She apologized for the
unpleasant things she said in it about the French! Mr. Ian
Peel at first refused to answer my inquiries, saying he hated
everything concerned with "those wasted years." However,
my reply to this made him relent, and in the end he sent me
a moving account of those days of terror which he hopes to
forget for ever.

I shall also quote Mrs. Forster, Brigadier H. E. Creedon,
Messrs. Middleton, Batchelor and Large, all of whom told
me about their experiences; and extensively from Miss Doris
Hawkins's book, *Atlantic Torpedo*.[1]

Thanks to Admiral Fioranzo, head of the Historical Department of the Italian Navy, I found a few of the Italian
survivors, who told me of their terrible ordeals. Prisoners of
war are seldom well treated, and when they have to be
transported they are often herded together like animals; it is
natural enough that they should complain vehemently of
their treatment, as these Italians certainly did. Commander

---

[1] Published by Victor Gollancz in 1943. Grateful thanks are due to both the
author and publisher. Miss Hawkins is now Matron of the British Hospital for
Mothers and Babies, in Woolwich.

Marco Revedin let me see an extract from the log-book of the *Cappellini*, the Italian submarine he commanded in 1942, which went to the rescue of the *Laconia* survivors.

I should like to thank the officers of the French Navy who gave me their accounts, especially Lt.-Commander Graziani (of the *Gloire*) and Commander Quémard (of the *Annamite*). These two ships and the *Dumont-d'Urville* were sent to the scene of the sinking in very delicate circumstances, since at that time the French fleet was divided against itself, although officially France was still in a state of armistice with Germany.

I am very grateful to Mr. T. Dobrowoloski for information, received following the publication of the French edition of this book, concerning the Polish guards on board the *Laconia*. This confirms the impression left by other reports that their conduct in the lifeboats and in the German submarines was beyond all praise.

There remain the Americans! An American aircraft, a Liberator, bombed a submarine which was hove to and engaged in rescue operations, even destroying a lifeboat full of survivors from the wreck. There is not the slightest doubt on this subject and all the testimonies agree. Admiral E. M. Eller, head of the Historical Department of the American Navy, wrote to me that a search in Navy Department files and an inquiry into the Department of the Air Force had failed to identify the aircraft; that the British were also flying Liberators, and Freetown was primarily a British base. In answer to a second letter of mine, he said further research had established that if the attacking aircraft was American, it was definitely not a U.S. Navy plane; and he recommended me to inquire direct to the U.S.A.F. Historical Department. I did so, and received a long statement in reply. This acknowledges the possibility that the aircraft in question was a B-24 taking part in the American Air Force's anti-submarine operations based on Ascension Island (see Appendix C).

Possibly the aircraft crew made no report on their action, yet it is quite explicable, even reasonable, in the context of total war: they may have thought the chance of sinking this enemy submarine too good to miss. If so, perhaps they had justification a few days later, when U-156 sank an Allied ship, the *Quebec City*. Whatever their nationality, any aircraft crew might well have done the same in similar circumstances.

Commenting on Admiral Dönitz's memoirs in the *Wash-*

ington Post of September 27th, 1959, the American naval historian Roger Pineau wrote:

> The account of the *Laconia* sinking and its aftermath, which led to the issuance of the "*Laconia* Order" by Dönitz, is told in a straightforward manner. American readers may hope that the service responsible for the unfortunate event following the sinking of this British ship will some day be equally straightforward, and, for the sake of its sister services, clear the air on this subject.

I can only associate myself with this hope, and perhaps my book may bring forward the pilot or a member of the Liberator's crew, or someone at the air-base of Ascension Island, who can give further information.

The unprecedented scale of the rescue operations which followed the *Laconia*'s sinking is reassuring evidence that service to humanity can still function even in the bitterest hours of conflict: over a thousand British and Italian survivors were in the end brought safely to land by French warships. A few days after the sinking Admiral Dönitz gave the order which came to be known as the "*Laconia* Order." This expressly forbade submarine commanders to rescue survivors from torpedoed ships, and it was minutely analysed, discussed and dissected at Nuremberg.

I hope, therefore, that readers will not take *The Laconia Affair* as just another war story. It raises a very important problem which has never been satisfactorily resolved: the rescue of the shipwrecked in time of war.

LÉONCE PEILLARD

THE LACONIA
AFFAIR

Laconia

1

COMMANDER WERNER HARTENSTEIN
AND U-156

9:30 a.m. September 12th, 1942[1]

The tropical sun beat down on a whitish sea without horizon. Heading south, U-156 was 550 miles south of Cape Palma (North-West Africa). She was travelling round the Cape of Good Hope to the Mozambique Channel.

This submarine had been built at Bremen in the Deshimag A. G. Wesser dockyards and launched in October 1941. She was now on her fourth mission, and her crew, all volunteers, had been formed by her commander, Werner Hartenstein, directly she was built. They were young, well-trained, eager for battle and the victory of the Reich. As a ship's company they worked well together, and they had a keen sense of belonging to the "Freikorps Dönitz"—the men who had answered Admiral Dönitz's call for volunteers to man his submarine fleet.

The crew of U-156 loved their ship, in spite of living on top of each other in a cramped space. The bonds of their community were increased by the dangers faced, and they were privileged compared with men in the fleet's big ships. In a submarine the "old man" was not only a chief but also a friend, someone they could talk to direct. In U-156 concern

---

[1]British time (double summer time) will be given for the chapters dealing with the day and night of the sinking. German time was two hours ahead, in this case 11:30 a.m.

For the convenience of ordinary readers, the "civilian" clock will be used throughout the book: e.g. 9:30 a.m. (not 0930) and 8:20 p.m. (not 2020).

1

U-156

for their welfare had even taken the form of a questionnaire on the meals they preferred, so that the officers and petty officers, for instance, often had fried tunny-fish for their midday meal while the ratings might choose sausages and preserves. Almost everyone in the boat had been with her since the last days of her construction at Bremen. They had watched the diesels being mounted, the fitting of the torpedo-tubes. Small wonder if everyone on board was attached to her.

She had been put into service on September 4th, 1941, and directly afterwards training had started at Kiel, then at Stettin. There were calls at Gotenhafen (Gdynia today) and Pillau. Dönitz insisted that exercises should include all contingencies, even the gravest, which might occur in combat. For six days running U-156 dived, surfaced, crash-dived (sixty feet in thirty-three seconds), went nearly four hundred feet below the surface at the risk of being lost—one submarine *was* lost during deep-diving exercises. Everything that might happen during an engagement had been foreseen and put to the test: depth-charges, complete absence of light in the submarine, breakdown of an engine, the pumps, etc. Hartenstein carried instruction to the point of insisting that the men should be able to change jobs: the wireless operator must know how to fire torpedoes or be a sick-berth attendant; the cook a gunner, and so on.

In December 1941 the exercises and final works at Stettin were completed. After commissioning at Kiel, the crew of U-156 left German shores behind them at 10 p.m. on Christmas Eve.

As often happens, the maiden voyage was a disappointment. These young men (the average age was twenty) had dreamed of engagements and of cruisers sunk. It was natural enough at their age. They did not then have either the patience or the stability which the sailor often needs even more than courage.

The submarine met no British ship, but did meet floating mines drifting dangerously on a heavy sea. Going north to keep at a distance from the English coasts, she reached Rockall Banks on the west of Ireland. With the very rough sea Hartenstein had to make several attempts before he could cast two weather-buoys.[1]

---

[1] A weather-buoy is a device looking like a torpedo, about 15 yards long. It floats, held by an anchor; and an antenna, mounted on the spot, automatically gives information by Morse, several times a day, such as the hygrometric state of the air, the temperature, the wind's direction and force, the atmospheric pressure. When the weather came from the west, these floating meterological stations supplied precious information to the Reich's air force and navy.

After fulfilling this useful but not very glamorous mission, U-156 retired from the area unnoticed. An F.T.[2] (wireless telegram or signal) notified Admiral Dönitz, the B.d.U.[3] (Submarine Commander-in-Chief), of the mission's success. On January 8th, 1942, the submarine arrived at Lorient, and two days later they were ready to sail again, this time to the Caribbean Sea. Venezuelan tankers left from these parts for Europe and North America, providing excellent targets for the watchful U-boats.

There was one newcomer, Büsinger, only eighteen years old, replacing a mechanic who had damaged his hand trying to get a torpedo on board. When Büsinger reported for duty, U-156 was ready to sail, lying in the Arsenal at Lorient. Seeing him standing at the foot of the gangplank, which the dockers were already preparing to lift, Hartenstein thought how young and inexperienced he looked, but decided he would soon find his "sea-legs" like the rest. The commander made a mental note, however, that at first the youngster's duties must be shared with the rest of the crew.

Before the submarine sailed, a mass of miscellaneous supplies had been taken on board, and were all over the place: tinned food, drugs, shells, guns in pieces. Hams and loaves were hanging, tied to hammocks and bunks, and there was a crate of potatoes in the middle of the control-room. The issue of tropical kit when Lorient was in the depths of winter caused a lot of jokes and questions. "Where are we going—to the geishas or the black beauties?" At the time Hartenstein himself didn't know their destination. Only out at sea was he to unseal the envelope given him by the B.d.U. at Kernevel and find out.

Stores and equipment rapidly found their proper places, and Heinz Dengler, the cook, quipped: "I've been able to find my potatoes without compass or hydrophone." Directly they were out at sea Hartenstein ordered a practice dive. Then he made comments on the operation, criticizing some people, including officers. Each movement had to be carried out almost to a split second.

The submarine reached the Caribbean without incident, and at first it was almost like a cruise in the South Seas but

---

[2]F.T. = Funk-telegramm.
[3]B.d.U. = Befehlshaber der U-boote.

for the exercises and calls to action stations. During the day the men sun-bathed and fished for sharks. In the evening they gathered under the stars and sang songs, accompanied by Wireless Operators Walter Remmert, playing his accordion, and Hugo Parschau his guitar. The instruments had been presented by the town of Plauen in Saxony, which had adopted the submarine and was her commander's birthplace. Hartenstein himself enjoyed the singing, and the crew soon learnt that one sentimental song, known as "Annemarie," was a particular favourite of his. Among the most ardent singers was the second officer of the watch, Lieutenant von dem Borne, an admiral's son, an exuberant spirit very popular with the crew. He was often to be found in the wireless room chatting to Remmert and Parschau, both of whom were quite fond of a drink.

One evening, seeing the mountains of Curaçao silhouetted against the sky, Hartenstein had "Annemarie" broken off abruptly and replaced by a military march on the loudspeaker. Then the crew heard their commander's voice: "Achtung, Achtung! All the men off watch are to assemble in the control-room." There were about fifty men on the submarine, and about thirty of these crammed themselves round him, pressed against each other so tightly they could hardly move.

Hartenstein spoke to them: "Soon it will be time for action. It is our job to upset as far as possible the course of tankers between Venezuela and the islands of Aruba and Curaçao, *and* to attack the oil refineries—with our guns. Two other submarines are already in the area with my friends Müller and von Rosenstiel. I will give you further details shortly. Till then it is forbidden to fire at ships, except at big armour and aircraft-carriers. Now—I wish you a good night. Dismiss."

A little later U-156 passed a lighted liner at less than one hundred and fifty yards. There was dancing on board, and the sailors, envious for a moment, could see the couples in each other's arms and hear jazz being played... At midnight they were off Aruba, still brilliant with all its lights. What children these Americans were, just asking to be surprised.

Cruising off Aruba for three days, they kept watch on ships' movements, diving by day and observing through the periscope, listening to every screw noise; and by night sailing on the surface at reduced speed. It seemed incredible that they were not noticed. They found the island spectacular: on one side tropical nature, the emerald-green mountain of Holberg between Orangetown and St. Nicholas; on the other the creations of man—hotels, oil reservoirs in shining white aluminium, the refineries with their flashing orange flames.

Hartenstein took bearings carefully, then made his plan and had it communicated to the crew. After this the hours passed all too slowly.

At last, on February 16th, a little before midnight, he ordered the decks to be cleared for action. The big moment had arrived for these men who had never been under fire. When approaching port, U-156 almost ran into a coast-defence ship; they just avoided her, and she disappeared into the night without suspecting that she had been near a German submarine. Then the submarine, slipping between the ships at anchor, got into the roads.

Midnight (1:30 a.m. by Aruba time). Half ahead... starboard 5—Very good, sir—Tubes 1 and 2 ready—starboard 5, sir—Tanker No. 1 coming into line—amidships—amidships, air—stand by!—Tubes 1 and 2: fire!

A slight shock indicated that the torpedoes had left and were shooting towards their target. The water could be heard going into the ballast-tanks to give the submarine her balance. While she was veering to port, the same operation had started again.

Tubes 3 and 4... ready... stand by... Fire.

Luck was with them. Dull detonations shook the submarine. They all looked at each other, understood. A shout of joy, of triumph, a moment of pride... Another detonation, smoke, flames as high as a church tower. A tanker cut in two; her oil was spreading over the sea in a thousand spurts of flame. The flames lit up a swell of great black spirals of smoke, while the torpedoed tankers heeled over and sank.

Then they attacked the refineries with their guns, the 37-mm. and the 105-mm. The 37 fired, but after the first shell the 105 fell silent. Hartenstein couldn't understand it. He was on the bridge, blinded by the heavy black smoke enveloping all the submarine's bow. He leant over to try to find out what had happened below. He heard groans, and in the gleam of a flame saw a bloody shadow leaning against the conning-tower. Obviously an accident. He gave the order to go about, come out of the roads, and retire at full speed. In any case his mission had been successfully accomplished.

Below, Lieutenant von dem Borne lay unconscious, his back against the conning-tower, badly wounded in the knee by a shell fragment, Büsinger, the boy who had come aboard at the last moment, lay near the wreck of the gun, his stomach open and lacerated, his thighs scored. He was taken to the wardroom, where he died three-quarters of an hour later without regaining consciousness. Meanwhile Wireless Operator Remmert, temporary sick-bay attendant, had been dealing with the lieutenant, who had a large open wound with multiple splinters. "Nothing to do but amputate," he decided. Hartenstein arrived, looked at the wound and nodded agreement.

Von dem Borne was now conscious, and watched the preparations. "No, Remmert. Not the morphia, the brandy. Pass me the bottle."

Hartenstein didn't dare forbid this, and as the lieutenant took a long swig, Remmert gave a little envious sigh, then started his hacking. Four men, trying not to see too much, held von dem Borne still. Remmert was leaning over the thigh, which spurted blood from all the arteries. He squeezed the arteries, tied them up, now and then groaning and cursing. The "old man" stood there with his eagle-beak nose and sunken eyes, his teeth clenched.

The leg fell into the pail amidst blood-soaked plugs. Now the dressings and bandages—finished. Remmert looked down at the pail, saw the leg with its shoe and sock which he hadn't had time to remove, and fainted.

They took the surgeon to his hammock and the patient to the ward-room. There he stayed for a long time next to Büsinger's body. No other space was available in the submarine cluttered with ammunition in the post-battle disorder.

Hartenstein ordered: "Stow the ammunition. Everything in its place. Make safe the torpedoes. Jump to it." For a moment he had forgotten the two bodies, one lifeless and one unconscious.

The following evening at nightfall he gave a short address in front of the young sailor's body, which was sewn up in a sleeping-bag and wrapped in the black, white and red flag of the German Navy, adorned in its centre with a big swastika and decorated with an Iron Cross. This happened in the control-room, and apart from the look-outs and a few engine-room men, the whole crew were there, deeply moved. Hartenstein led them in "Our Father...," and even non-believers joined in. Then they sang all together:

> *Ich hatt' einen Kameraden,*
> *Einen bessern find'st du nicht ...*

Very rapidly, as if to get it over, Büsinger's body was carried on to the bridge and dropped overboard, while the crew, officers and men, eyes full of tears, saluted, tight-lipped. The weather was stormy, the sky dark, the sea empty of shipping.

Immediately afterwards Hartenstein carefully examined the breech which had exploded. He made his decision and informed the assembled men of it: the gun could still be used and would be repaired on the spot. It was never established why the shell had exploded on firing inside the gun, but a commander is responsible for accidents that occur in his ship, and Hartenstein fully accepted the responsibility. However, he was never blamed by Dönitz, or Godt, the admiral's Chief of Staff, or anybody else in authority.

Five days later, after asking Dönitz for orders, Hartenstein landed von dem Borne at Fort-de-France, where he was very well looked after by French doctors. Remmert left the submarine in March to go on a training course. The tragic incident helped to mould the inexperienced crew into a tightly knit company—a bond of unity which was to stand them in good stead in many future encounters with the enemy.

In August 1942 they were back once more at Lorient, refitting and preparing for their next mission. On the 17th they put to sea to join four other submarines: U-68 under Lt.-Commander Marten; U-172, under Lt.-Commander Emmermann; U-504, under Lt.-Commander Poske; and U-459, a supplies submarine, a newcomer to Dönitz's submarine fleet, under Lt.-Commander von Wilamowitz-Möllendorf. She was 1,700 tons, and could supply 560 tons of fuel at sea; since she would refuel the other submarines on their return journey from the Indian Ocean, she increased by a good third their radius of action. These five submarines formed the

Eisbär (Polar Bear) group, and they were closely followed by the Blücher group. Their departures from the French Atlantic ports were at different times on August 16th and 17th, and their eventual sailing positions formed a sort of rake, with each tooth cleaning up a fifty-mile sector of the sea.

Friendly rivalry between the U-boat crews was rife, and everyone knew by heart the tonnages sunk each month. Officers and men counted and discussed these tonnages, like the supporters of a football team mulling over the goals scored. An engine-room artificer on U-506 even carved wooden models of the ten ships they had sunk in the Gulf of Mexico, and his commander was so pleased with these that he sent them with his report to Admiral Dönitz in Paris. U-506 was nowhere near the bottom of this wartime "League," having sunk 96,499 tons, not counting two tankers from Aruba— quite a creditable figure. And, of course, everyone was jubilant at the brilliant victories the Reich was winning on all fronts.

The previous month the Canadians' attempt at landing on the French coast near Dieppe had been a dismal failure. In the east, the Germans had planted the swastika on the Elbruz, the highest peak in the Caucasus, while von Manstein was reaching the banks of the Terek. Farther to the north, General Paulus had occupied the outer defences of Stalingrad, and there was fighting in the town itself, which was daily expected to fall. In Egypt, Rommel had Alexandria within the range of his guns. In the Far East, Germany's Japanese allies, after the American naval defeat of Savo Island, were extending their advances to Port Moresby in New Guinea. All these victories were announced triumphantly on the ship's wireless and were posted in brief communiqués in the ward-room; it was characteristic of the German mentality—military fervour combined with a love of music—that the announcements were made following a few bars from Liszt's Preludes. It certainly looked as if before winter the Axis must win decisively.

Commander Werner Hartenstein shared his crew's satisfaction at these victories, and altogether life seemed good to him: he felt confident that under his command the ship, officers and crew, would act as a single unit. Unlike his friend Schacht, commander of U-507—U-156's special rival for tonnages sunk—Hartenstein was unmarried, with no close ties at home. He had come a long way since his youth, for he was a child of the 1914–18 defeat. He was born at Plauen in 1910, and still had traces in his speech of his native Saxon dialect. He could be gay enough, but his laugh often had a sardonic ring, perhaps born of earlier disappointments he had met with in life. While his boyhood companions tried to forget the plight Germany was in after total defeat, young Werner had worked single-mindedly. He carried with him the dream of the Navy, but at that time the Versailles treaty had reduced the German fleet to a few ships. Five or six hundred young men presented themselves every year for the entrance examination to the Naval College—and only about ten were accepted.

Werner tried his luck in 1926 and failed. He then had two years at the university, and in one of the student duels traditional in the old Germany he received a rapier blow on his left cheek, leaving a permanent slight scar. In 1928 he tried again for the Navy, and was accepted, entering as rating and working his way up to midshipman and then officer.

He remembered how frightened he had been that the war would be over too soon for him to fight, and how Admiral Dönitz had said to him at a naval inspection: "Don't be in too much of a hurry, you'll have lots of time to get fed up with it. Don't forget we're fighting against the greatest naval power in the world."

He had indeed seen plenty of action since then. He had commanded the destroyer *Seeadler*, then the *Jaguar*, had become second-in-command of the 6th flotilla of destroyers;

Jaguar

and finally, with this experience of surface ships essential for a submarine commander, had been appointed Lieutenant-Commander in June 1942, at the early age of thirty-two.

And now, on September 12th, 1942, from her position 5° south of the Equator, his submarine could expect more action, more victims. But from this line on she was only to reveal her presence in attack if the quarry was important enough to risk discovery.

At 9:37 a.m. Hartenstein heard a shout from the port after look-out. "Smoke, bearing 230°."

Everyone started focusing binoculars on the bearing. The smoke was difficult to spot drifting on the flat surface of the sea, and the look-out must have had unusually good eyesight.

Hartenstein at once gave orders. He knew they must get as near as possible to this ship, still barely visible on the horizon.

From a cruising speed of 10 knots they increased to 16 knots. The two 9-cylinder diesels each hummed away at their 2,500 horse-power. They could give the boat a maximum speed of 18 knots (just over 20 miles an hour), a speed reached in tests at full power. But here 16 knots were enough to give chase to this ship, which might not even be worth a torpedo.

Hartenstein was correctly turned out, as usual, and wore canvas shoes and white peaked cap. Most of the crew were in shorts and singlets, bare-footed, their heads protected by tropical caps. In spite of the bow wave occasionally washing over the hull, the deck-plates were almost unbearable with the vertical sun right above. But the men could enjoy the extra bit of breeze from the increased speed. The poor blokes in the engine-room were not so lucky, working stripped to the waist, with towels round their necks, in the damp heat of the narrow alley-way separating the diesels. There the air was fouled by the smell of oil, and it was unpleasant to breathe.

Hartenstein watched the smoke through the telescope, which was fixed to the deck and could pivot through 360°. At its base and turning with it, a needle showed the bearing of the target. Was this smoke a target, though? Perhaps. For the moment it looked like one of those low clouds drifting on the horizon.

The handle of the firing-switch was within his reach;

later that day he would be pulling it sharply down to fire the first torpedo. Behind him rose the two periscopes, one for look-out purposes, the other, which he used as seldom as possible, for combat. In this he was following Admiral Dönitz's instructions: "Only dive to ensure the submarine's safety or to attack by day. To dive is to reduce the ship's speed to 7 or 8 knots."[1] And the admiral compared the U-boat attacking submerged to an animal refraining from hunting, patiently watching for its prey to pass. "Acting like that," he summed up, "you can't expect big successes."

So Hartenstein, like the other U-boat commanders, attacked on the surface more often than not.

The off-watch men were disporting themselves on a little elevated platform behind the conning-tower, the surface of which was further reduced by the 20-mm. gun. They called this platform the "winter garden." They were spraying each other with the fire-hose. Hartenstein knew that at the slightest alert—a bomber or an enemy warship—they would all dash towards the conning-tower hatch. You had to be thin and supple to slide into this manhole two feet in diameter. So some, for greater speed, did not hesitate to jump straight down without touching the iron ladder. Below in the control-room they would be promptly pulled away by another man, so that the next man did not fall on to them. The exercise had been repeated time after time. In this way the off-watch men would reach their combat posts: the torpedo men making for the torpedo compartments fore or aft. In the former there were four tubes always ready for firing; in the latter, two. Other torpedoes resting on iron cradles remained ready to replace those which had been fired. There was scarcely any room to move in these compartments cluttered with torpedoes twenty-two feet long. In case of a dive Hartenstein and Mannesmann, the I.W.O.[2] (first officer of the watch), and the two look-outs would go down into the conning-tower. The commander himself closed down the iron hatch, and the submarine, isolated from the outside world, was now ready to submerge.

In the conning-tower were the eye-pieces of the two

---

[1]This was because the batteries, at 8 knots, allowed only for a two-hour dive without being recharged.

[2]I.W.O. = Erster Wachtoffizier.

periscopes. The look-out periscope was a big apparatus as precise and supple in its workings as it was complicated. Sitting on a metal seat which pivoted with the whole of the periscope, Hartenstein would manoeuvre to raise it or bring it down, adapting it skilfully to the continual motion of the waves, so as to leave only the minimum showing. If the enemy approached, he would return the look-out periscope and hoist the combat one, with its tiny eye, almost invisible on the surface of the sea, which only emerged above the surface for a few seconds.

U-156 had one of the German Navy's latest refinements: in the conning-tower, by the side of a second firing-switch, was an electronic board. If fed the appropriate information, it gave the exact direction of the target, straight to the torpedo's gyroscope. But the instrument alone was not enough, for all its precision. An expertise, or rather a sort of sixth sense, was needed. U-156's commander had this in the highest degree.

He had unlimited confidence in his chief engineer, thirty-six-year-old Wilhelm Polchau, who had been with the submarine from the start. Calm and even-tempered—both valuable qualities in a submarine—Polchau had immense technical ability and adroitness. At the moment he was in the control-room, right under the conning-tower in the middle of the submarine—the central point in a dive. At first sight everything here seemed terribly complicated, with nothing to be seen but boards, instruments, levers, tubes and wheels. There were different gauges indicating the depth and the ship's degree of trim. You had to work ballasts, taking account of the submarine's weight almost to a single torpedo. You had to operate screws and fore and aft hydroplanes. Polchau was assisted by the helmsman and two men who worked the hydroplanes. He watched the compass intently. A man was also installed in front of the hydrophone, which detected all screw noises above the submarine and gave their direction.

Leaning over the hatch, Hartenstein thought he could see Polchau's fair hair in the control-room. The alert had not been given, but on his order a man had gone to warn Polchau of the smoke on the horizon.

Polchau came up, blinking, his eyes blinded. He had the blue eyes of a laughing child, slightly veiled with melancholy, a big brow, and wavy hair. Deciding it was a good idea to rest on a submarine when you could, Polchau had been sleeping

on his bunk in the half-darkness. He was still in his pyjamas,
and performed a little mime to ask "Have I got time?" This
was an old ship's joke because one day, surprised by an alert,
he came into the control-room in his pyjamas and was obliged
to remain in this dress till the end of the engagement.

Hartenstein smiled and nodded in answer, as if to say:
"Yes, you've plenty of time to get into more orthodox dress."
He pointed towards the smoke, now becoming more distinct.

So the engineer squeezed his big frame back through the
narrow hatch.

The chase began. It was going to be a long one, for
Hartenstein knew he must not be in a hurry. A hasty and
ill-prepared attack was almost always doomed to failure, not
to mention the risk of being faced by a decoy-ship, within
range of quick-firing guns. So he would have to wait till the
evening in order to approach without too many risks and
strike with certainty.

The black smoke was now more visible. Bad coal, he
thought. The unknown captain must be furious to see his
presence revealed thus on the sea's surface.

Mannesmann too was watching the smoke intently through
the binoculars. "She's following a west-north-west course," he
remarked after a while. "Might be quite a big ship."

Hartenstein scoured the horizon with his Zeiss. "The
British arm their merchant ships. At this distance she can't
see us... It's not her I'm afraid of, but planes. Tell the
look-outs to keep their eyes peeled. Those buzzers are becoming more and more dangerous."

Mannesmann transmitted the order: "Keep a good look-
out for planes." Then he glanced up at the sky, which was
calm and clear, with only the slight haze of those hot regions.
One was dazzled by an invisible sun. And the heat! The
off-watch men, who had just now been freshening up on the
deck, had gone back to their posts.

Hartenstein took off his white cap and mopped his brow.
It was a big brow which set off the aquiline nose and the eyes
sunk into their orbits. With that nose and those eyes, the
hollow cheeks and jutting cheek-bones, the aggressive chin,
the commander had a curious look of Goebbels, some of the
men had noticed. But there all resemblance ended. The "old
man" was tall and had no deformity.

10:20 a.m.

The tactics of the enemy ship, which was now gradually growing larger, were not very complicated: she altered course 40°. She was following the rules of zig-zag navigation, which lengthened the voyage but gave greater security. At least the enemy captain would think that, not suspecting the presence of the submarine with its powerful diesels.

"She's travelling pretty fast," said Mannesmann. "We're hardly gaining on her."

"It's of no importance," Hartenstein answered. "We'll have her in our own time, at nightfall."

Meanwhile, life on board U-156 continued calmly enough. The men, being now experienced, no longer felt excited and impatient—during a chase. Only when the torpedo had been fired, while it was moving towards the target, did the tension mount, second by second, until the explosion which shattered the quiet of the sea.

Hartenstein was a master of the art of keeping contact by remaining far enough away for his prey to be just in view and no more. He would soon go up on deck to take up his position on the bow and be ready to attack at nightfall. The conning-tower was small enough, and little of it was visible on the water's surface. With his binoculars the look-out could observe the enemy ship well before she knew she was being hunted. In a few hours the ship on the horizon, however fast she was now travelling, would be put down among the trophies of the hunt after the small *Lillian* and the cargo-ships *Willimantic* and *Clan MacWhirter*.

11 a.m.

The watches were changed, giving a little bustle of movement to the silent U-boat. The experienced crew no longer bumped into each other in the narrow gangway running the ship's whole length. They slid like monkeys through the hatches connecting the control-room with each of the torpedo compartments—circular openings just over four feet in diameter. Hartenstein was very calm. He didn't drink and smoked little. In fact he was moderation itself except when attacking, and even then the "mad dog," as he was called, kept a watch on himself and controlled his excitement. His eye fell on the 105-mm. gun just forrard of the conning-tower, and he could not help remembering the Aruba incident. Greased and holy-stoned, the gun was now as new, and seemed to be waiting for its hour like the two sailors leaning against the gun carriage trying to find a little shade.

1 p.m.

U-156 was now gaining on the unknown vessel, which was definitely bigger than had been thought at first sight. She was travelling at fifteen knots. With the binoculars Hartenstein could see distinctly her superstructures and high funnel. Not a cargo-ship, an old liner, perhaps turned into an auxiliary cruiser or a troopship. But one must wait for night before attacking, and night fell at 8 p.m. abruptly. Handing over the watch to Mannesmann, he went to get some rest. He slid into the conning-tower, down into the control-room, had a brief chat with Polchau, and took the narrow gangway which ran through the ship, to reach his cabin—if you could call this cubby-hole a cabin, with its narrow bunk, its tiny basin extended to make a shelf-desk, separated from the gangway only by a sliding curtain.

He lay down and tried vainly to sleep. He thought about the unknown ship sailing on the port side. Was she worth a torpedo, the loss of time, the fuel used?

A few hours later he heard somebody singing near him. It was Heinz, the cook, singing as he prepared the evening meal, and the song was "Annemarie," the commander's favourite, as Heinz knew. But today it reminded Hartenstein again of the Aruba incident, and for a moment he had a queer uneasy feeling, as if the song might once again be the forerunner of tragedy.

He went up on to the bridge. When he appeared, Mannesmann gestured with his chin towards the enemy ship, which they had now passed, so that she was on their port quarter. The sun was already quite low in the west.

Mannesmann seemed satisfied with the observations he had made during the commander's absence. "That steamer's travelling at fourteen knots—40° zig-zags either side of course 290°. She has the lines of an old transport ship, about 1905—estimated at 7,000 tons."

"Not bad," Hartenstein answered. "That'll take us over the 100,000 mark."

6 p.m.

The submarine seemed to creep along the water's surface so much that with evening falling she merged with the sea. Hartenstein ordered supper, though the crew had already had dinner, in two shifts, at 3 p.m. and 4 p.m.

The crew was well aware that the order "Supper" came only a little before action. They were calm and cheerful as they swallowed their potato soup.

"They're having dinner too in the yacht over there," remarked Parschau. "In a few minutes they'll be dancing."

U-156 gradually altered course in approaching her. Mannesmann observed with the binoculars: "She's zig-zagging in a north-westerly direction, 310°. She's an old steamer of at least 12,000 tons, converted into an armed merchant cruiser."

"Hm, bigger than we thought," Hartenstein commented. "Is the crew at supper?"

"Yes, sir."

"Let them eat it in peace. And you?"

"I've had a big cup of coffee, that's enough for me!"

7 p.m.

Hartenstein took bearings: 5.0° south, 11.08° west. He was approaching the steamer, which was steering 310°. In the west the sun was touching the horizon, like a big orange balloon resting on the sea. It bit into the surface of the sea, and began setting rapidly.

7:55 p.m.

Night had come. The steamer seemed bigger and bigger. The port-holes were covered, the lights camouflaged, but from a few scattered lights you could guess that the black-out order was not completely carried out. She wasn't a warship, it was obvious from that detail.

On U-156 the crew were at their action stations. The steamer came into view through the periscope.

8:07 p.m.

A long blast on the hooter could be heard through the submarine, and immediately afterwards: "Tubes 1 and 3 ready?"

"Tubes 1 and 3 ready."

In a few seconds the tension had mounted, a sort of fever which gripped the men every time they were about to strike. They knew that the "eels," as they called the torpedoes, would soon be leaving the submarine's bow and gliding invisibly under the water, would strike the hull of the enemy ship and explode, causing a deadly wound.

On the big ship facing them, gradually coming into the spider-lines of the sighting gear, behind thin steel plates there were men and women happy to be returning home, perhaps children sleeping peacefully. Poor wretches, they didn't know . . .

"Stand by! Stand by! Tubes 1 and 3."

Hartenstein looked through the spy-glass one last time, passed the information to the conning-tower: bearing, speed, inclination . . .

"Ready, ready . . ."

"Tube 1: fire!"

Commander Werner Hartenstein, using his body weight, pulled down the lever of the switch. Twenty seconds later he repeated the movement with Tube 3.

"Guten Appetit, meine Herren Engländer," he said sardonically, pushing his cap to the back of his head. "Enjoy your meal."

He could not know that the two torpedoes he had just fired were to be the cause of one of the greatest sea tragedies of the war.

2

ON BOARD THE *LACONIA*

On August 12th, 1942, just a month before, the 19,965-ton *Laconia*, an old liner of the Cunard White Star Line, weighed anchor in the Bay of Suez.

The night before, three thousand officers and men with their equipment and supplies had been disembarked at Port

Tewfik. At that time the zone was frequently being bombed by the Luftwaffe, and the whole operation was carried out in great haste, so that the ship could leave the Canal Zone as quickly as possible.

In the second half of 1942 the battle of the Atlantic had reached its peak in favour of the Axis submarines. The Allies' available tonnage, despite new constructions, had been reduced so badly that every sea-worthy vessel had to be used to the full, both in time and space. Liners armed and converted into troop-carriers were often sent into areas for which they were not suited; ships built to run on the maritime routes of the North Atlantic might be sent to the tropics, while better-ventilated ships would find themselves in convoys to Russia labouring in the icy conditions of the Arctic.

The *Laconia* was twenty years old, having been launched from the C. Swan Hunter and Wigham Richardson dockyards at Newcastle on May 25th, 1922. Her length was 600 feet, her width 74 feet. Equipped with double-gear steam turbines, she had two screws and a maximum speed of 16½ knots. She had one funnel and two masts, and was the first British merchant ship to be equipped with anti-roll devices, though these were nowhere near as effective as the Denny-Brown paddle-board system invented later. She began her career on the Southampton–New York route, and was later transferred to the Liverpool–New York one. Then she was again transferred, this time to the Hamburg–Southampton–New York route. On the outbreak of war she was taken over by the Admiralty, who armed her and converted her into a troop-carrier. She formed part of a convoy of seventeen ships, escorted by the warships *Nelson* and *Renown*, the Dutch cruiser *Heemskirk* and smaller units of the Royal Navy, which sailed round Africa to Suez.

For her return voyage from Suez in August 1942, every available inch of cabin space had been utilized to the full. She was taking on board her usual complement of returning service personnel, and also some officers and men from various regiments, including some badly wounded cases, whom the authorities wanted repatriated as soon as possible. After the last soldier had come aboard, it was the turn of a few dozen civilians destined to travel on her: British officials and their families who had long been resident in Cairo or Middle Eastern bases, trapped by the war and only too

thankful that at long last their turn had come for a berth home. There was a cheerful hum in the gangways, with children running to and fro. Many of these children had been born in Egypt or the Middle East, and it was their first crossing. The passengers cheerfully began settling into their quarters in the old liner's cabins, now doubled and sometimes trebled in bunk capacity. With a good month's journey ahead of them they set about getting to know each other and making the best of the cramped conditions. Everywhere there was the restless bustle of a ship preparing to sail.

Having found their own quarters, several of the passengers went on deck to watch all the activities going on. They showed particular curiosity about a group of approximately two hundred women who were just boarding the ship under soldiers' surveillance. These women seemed to carry only a very small amount of hand luggage, but there was an air of flashy elegance about most of them, and they appeared to be of several nationalities. The passengers soon learned that these women had all been arrested in the towns of the Middle East and were suspected prostitutes, low-grade spies,

H.M.S. Nelson

members of the fifth column. Rumour had it that they were being taken to internment camps in South Africa.

The passengers had another surprise in store. Three hours before anchor was weighed, they saw several army lorries stop on the quayside. Unarmed soldiers got off the lorries, dressed in oddments of green uniform, torn and rotted by the sun. These were Italian prisoners, captured in Libya. Guards with fixed bayonets, bawling and yelling, were trying to put a little order into the motley array.

To the Italians the *Laconia* must have seemed huge and hostile. They had been huddled together on the lighters which took them out to the liner, and as they came aboard they jostled and shoved each other, hurling voluble abuse. They carried strange bundles on their shoulders and clutched some wretched articles of personal belongings, preserved despite the constant transfers into lorries as they were moved from camp to camp. A few carried mandolins and guitars, jealously guarded and cherished.

Slowly the prisoners proceeded along the gangways, went down from one deck to another by vertical iron ladders, to be crammed eventually in the ship's hold. There were eighteen hundred of these wretches, locked in on top of each other. When the battens were closed behind them, they thought they would never see the light of day again.

Watching the prisoners disappear, the British passengers felt a certain uneasiness. The spectacle reminded them of the over-shadowing presence of war, menacing their happiness at going home.

From the Mozambique Channel onwards they must expect attack from the enemy. It was true that the *Laconia* was armed and hoped to defend at all costs her old carcass and the passengers aboard. She had two 4.7-inch naval guns (made in Japan during the first World War), six 3-inch anti-aircraft guns, six 1½-inch anti-aircraft guns, four quick-firing Bofors, two groups of 2-inch rockets, two box kites to be fitted to the mainmast, which could fly at 250 feet with a bomb attached to the wire, and two pairs of anti-mine paravanes.

Captain Rudolph Sharp, C.B.E., R.D., R.N.R., the tall, slightly solemn-looking man who could be seen coming and going on the bridge, was a sailor rich in seafaring experience and tradition. He came from a sea-going family, both his grandfather and his uncle having served with the Cunard Line. One of his sons was already an officer in H.M.S. *Capetown*, and the other, aged seventeen, was also hoping to make the sea his livelihood. Sharp himself was five feet eleven inches tall, rather stout, and looked older than his age. He sometimes showed a certain weariness, which was intensified by any anxieties he had to face.

When first given command of the *Laconia* he had written to his wife: "This ship is not much to my liking, very few of her crew have sailed with me before. But they might be worse and that is all I can tell you."

His misgivings then may have been ill founded, for he was soon on excellent terms with the ship's company. But by August 1942 he had plenty of other worries: in particular, the *Laconia* was badly overloaded with nearly three thousand passengers, and this included seriously wounded men, women, children and prisoners. How were they all to be evacuated if she received a hit! Moreover, she did not have nearly enough lifeboats and rafts (thirty-two lifeboats, forty big rafts and a good many smaller ones).

The captain never intervened in military questions, but had to exercise an impartial jurisdiction over the crew, passengers and prisoners. He was kept informed of everything that happened by his second-in-command, Chief Officer George Steel. A native of Liverpool, aged fifty-two, Steel had long been on the Cunard Line. He was a tireless man, rising very early and never retiring till late at night after dealing with the hundreds of small details which fell within his scope. He was a fine diplomat, settling a great many incidents on board and also points of dispute which might crop up between Captain Sharp and the service officers. He did his utmost to make the passengers enjoy their stay on board.

The senior first officer was J. H. Walker, who had previously served with Sharp on the *Lancastria*. After the *Lancastria*'s sinking Sharp had applied successfully to the Admiralty for Walker to serve under him again.

As the *Laconia* was now primarily a troop-carrier, a high-ranking army officer, Lt.-Colonel Liswell of the Beds. and Herts. Regiment, was permanently attached to her. Assisted by a few of his own officers, he looked after the administration and discipline of the soldiers in transit. The Italian prisoners were under the orders of Lt.-Colonel Baldwin.

As soon as the last prisoner was on board, the ship weighed anchor to go down the Gulf of Suez and into the Red Sea. A great many ventilators were fixed up, ready for the intense heat of the Red Sea, and one of Colonel Baldwin's first orders was to arrange for organized one-hour walks in the fresh air twice a day for his prisoners. They were then allowed to smoke, which was strictly forbidden in the hold. Down there, they slept in rows of hammocks so close that the sides touched each other, while some even slept on the planks or on the tables where they had their scanty meals.

Admittedly the British other ranks were not much better treated, and there were immediate complaints about the food being always the same—hash or stew, and not enough of it. The washing facilities were not built for such large numbers, and there were queues outside the lavatories, which were doorless.

Except for the prisoners and those on duty, everyone on board was allowed on the promenade deck at any hour of the day; and to begin with they might even sleep there, although those who did were pitilessly chased off by the deck-scrubbers

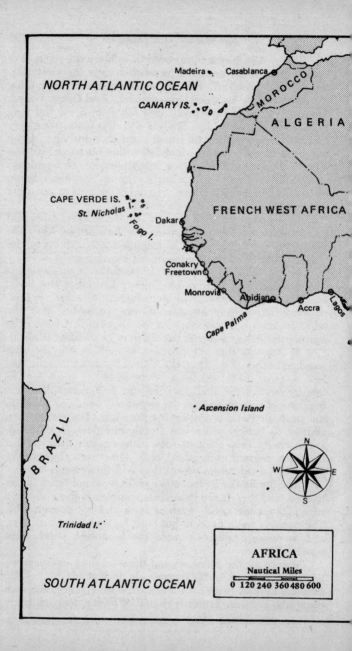

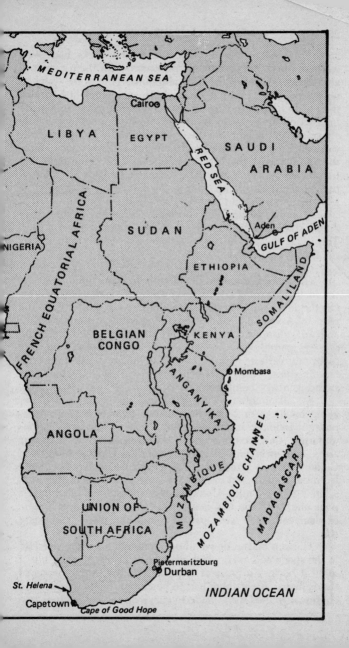

at five or six in the morning. After the decks had been washed down, the first Italian prisoners, with their guards in attendance, came up for their ablutions. They were watched with some pity as they undressed. These scraggy little brown men hadn't much to take off before standing naked under the improvised showers—buckets pierced with holes, hung slightly above a man's height and filled with sea-water by hoses. They were each issued with a small tablet of sea-water soap. After the first few days the British became so used to the sight that they no longer took any notice—except perhaps for some of the women, more compassionate by nature or else thinking of a husband who might one day be like these captives.

At night smoking was absolutely forbidden on the upper decks, since the slightest gleam of light could betray the ship. This was almost the only serious restriction, but it was rigorously enforced.

The first night in the Red Sea there was a full moon. The sea looked like a sheet of silver creased by the ship's wake. On the morning of August 13th the *Laconia* was outside the range of Axis planes, and her passengers began to settle down and form friendships, even start flirtations. Men from the services paired off with the women: officers' wives returning to Britain with or without husbands, nurses, girls from military families. Many came straight from Malta, which was suffering heavy bombardment.

For all members of the crew and service men, whether going on leave or being repatriated, there was compulsory physical training. In the gangways, bare-chested or in various uniforms, they could be seen doing exercises with flailing arms, and springing smartly to attention. Captain Sharp and Colonel Liswell agreed that the men must be kept occupied: lectures, courses and discussions were organized in the small saloons for all ranks. Unfortunately the ship's library was a poor one, with too few books, which were often incomplete or damaged; they were passed round and were in constant use.

The sun blazed down all day, temperatures reached 110° in the shade and over, which made life difficult enough; but at night it became a torment, especially as the ship approached the Equator. Everything had to be closed, lights shaded, and continual rounds were made to check on the completeness of the black-out. The promenade deck was invaded, from 5 p.m. onwards, by passengers settling down to spend the night there, with life-belts for pillows. At dusk panels were opened above the holds to give a few breaths of hot air to the prisoners piled up in the ship's bowels. The officers making their rounds among the prisoners were always greeted with a chorus of moans, lamentations and entreaties. Sometimes they let their hearts be touched, choosing those who looked in the worst shape. A few prisoners were then sent to the ship's infirmary, which was already overcrowded.

The ship put in at Aden. The next port of call was thirteen hundred miles farther on: she refuelled at Mombasa, the big British base on the Indian Ocean. Behind the docks you could imagine a rich industrial and commercial town, flaunting its wealth. Directly the *Laconia* was berthed, a big luxury car was seen stopping at the customs barrier. Two beautiful and smartly dressed girls got out, laughing and joking, their manner provocative in the extreme, and they were encouraged by a male companion making obscene and lecherous gestures. They might have been deliberately putting on an act for the Italians in the upper berths who could see through the port-holes; soon shouts, whistles and cat-calls, a mixture of frenzy and sensual desire, were coming up from the frustrated prisoners.

Meanwhile there was general hubbub and commotion. Impelled by the irresistible need to feel dry land under the feet, passengers and off-duty members of the crew, carrying identity papers and leave passes, presented themselves at the gangways, where they were all warned that shore-leave ended strictly at midnight.

The local police came on board and had the two hundred women prisoners drawn up on a well-guarded corner of the deck. After inspection and two roll-calls, the women disembarked in single file by a special gangplank. On the quay they were pushed into lorries. They could not know that the internment camp which awaited them was saving their lives. A few Italian prisoners, seriously wounded or sick, were taken to hospital. They too did not know their good fortune.

Night came, the town's lights went out one by one, the shadows behind bungalow windows disappeared; and those returning from shore-leave presented their papers to the officer of the watch. A little animation woke the silent *Laconia*.

The following day, August 22nd, revictualling finished, she left Mombasa and slowly sailed down the winding, coral-bordered channel and out into the open sea. Next stop Durban.

In the Mozambique Channel a Japanese ship was signalled, but no enemy ship showed herself. The temperature had cooled down, and while the British found something like their own climate, the Italians in their thin clothes were now shivering. Worse still, the daily shower, which had been so pleasant and refreshing near the Equator, continued to be compulsory, and became an agony.

The Italians dreamed of macaroni, tagliatelle or even a simple minestrone. They were given English food; it couldn't be helped. Their daily rations consisted of two spoonfuls of diluted jam, two cups of weak tea, two thin slices of bread, and a cup of soup with a few scattered vegetables floating in it. A few got a bit more for services rendered—Corporal Setti proved very useful as interpreter, and Sergeant Pocchetino did portraits of the British officers—but such favoured ones were a small minority. And the cold was beginning to make these men hungry, not to mention their desire to smoke, perhaps more acute still. Some rash souls smoked a cigarette in what they called their cage. English tobacco smells delicious, but the smell is persistent. Smoking except on deck and by day was strictly prohibited—the word is much stricter than *vietato*, as the prisoners learnt to their cost. For three days they were all put on bread and water, without even being let off the daily showers.

On August 28th the ship reached Durban. As at Mombasa, crew and passengers were allowed a few hours' shore-leave. Captain Sharp decided that the prisoners too ought to have the chance of stretching their legs on dry land, and gave them permission to walk for a few minutes on the well-guarded quay. The ship stayed three days at Durban, and some sick Italians were again disembarked. On the second day the passengers noticed a contingent of young R.A.F. officers coming on board. They also were coming from Suez, and had arrived at Durban a few days earlier in the *Stratheden*, which was destined for Halifax, Canada. These officers, under Wing-Commander Blackburn, had been put ashore at Durban with a few families and sent to a transit camp while waiting for the *Laconia*. They protested against their transfer; the

Laconia's old-fashioned lines, her stove-pipe funnel high above the water, didn't appeal to them at all. Once aboard, they missed the happy atmosphere of the *Stratheden*, where conditions were much more to their liking.

A certain R. S. Miller, who was among their contingent, although a civilian—he was a specialist in the famous Merlin engine, representing Rolls-Royce in the East—was put into a "single" cabin with three strangers. His berth-neighbour, Sime, was an engineer in the Merchant Navy, who had been embarked at the last port of call, Mombasa. "I've been torpedoed three times," Miller told Sime, "the last time in the Indian Ocean, near the Mozambique Channel. I'll be torpedoed again on this wretched *Laconia*, which will never reach England."

In the contingent embarked at Durban, Ben Coutts, a young Scottish artillery captain, was conspicuous both for his exceptional height and for a horrible wound he had got at Tobruk: a large dressing covered the hole where his nose should have been. After several operations in the Middle East, he was being repatriated for further plastic surgery. He too missed the *Stratheden*, but accepted the situation with good grace, for he was a man of great natural cheerfulness. His infectious laugh could be heard almost as soon as he set foot on board.

Among the other *Stratheden* passengers who came on board the *Laconia* were Major Creedon (nicknamed "Cracker"), Mrs. Davidson, a colonel's wife, and her nineteen-year-old daughter, Molly; Grizel, wife of Lieutenant-Colonel Malcolm Wolfe-Murray, of the Black Watch Regiment, and a nursing Sister, Doris Hawkins, who was returning home with five years as a missionary in Palestine with a baby of fourteen months, Sally Readman, in her care. Sally was the daughter of Colonel "Tim" Readman of the Royal Scots Greys. Both her parents were actively involved in the war in the Middle East, and had asked the Sister to take the baby home to her grandparents. On the *Stratheden* Sister Hawkins and Lady Grizel had become great friends, and they arranged to have cabins opposite each other on the *Laconia*.

One hundred and three Polish soldiers also joined the ship to act as guards for the prisoners. They were a company from a Polish division, formed in April 1942 at Teheran, which had come down from Suez on the *Mauretania*, and had been two months in a staging camp at Pietermaritzburg.

Leaving Durban, the *Laconia* entered the danger zone. Her last port of call was Capetown; and the day after she reached the Cape, the Air Force men saw the lines of a ship they knew well, moving through countless ships at anchor in the roads, to stop alongside the *Laconia*. It was their well-loved *Stratheden*. They learnt by bush telegraph that she had been re-routed and was not making for Canada but for an English port. They at once besieged Wing-Commander Blackburn, pressing him to intervene with the authorities and get them put back on the *Stratheden*. He tried, but was unsuccessful.

Twenty-six R.A.F. sergeants embarked at Capetown. They included four friends who were a regular bridge four—Batchelor, Middleton, Allen and Elliot. Directly they got on board they looked for a corner to start playing.

When she left the Cape on September 1st, the *Laconia* had on board 463 officers and crew, 286 passengers from the Navy, Army and Air Force, 1,800 Italian prisoners of war, 103 Poles, and 80 civilians, including women and children: 2,732 people in all.

Captain Sharp steered south to avoid the mine-fields, then ordered a zig-zagging course by day. The ship's staff conferences were held twice a day. It was decided to break off exercises and lectures. There was a spate of written orders and instructions.

Sharp abandoned his cabin in order to sleep fully dressed in the chart-room. He could thus take personal charge of the ship at any moment. Everyone on board was instructed to keep his life-jacket within reach. The ship's wireless, which received the Admiralty orders by short wave, had to remain silent, so as not to betray the ship's position to an Axis submarine. She was only to give her position in case of attack.

Although now travelling north to the west of Africa, the *Laconia* kept well away from the coasts. An atmosphere of suspense hung over the ship, and the passengers were rather quiet. Despite themselves they kept scanning the horizon, looking for the suspect point in the trough of the waves. The off-duty men no longer strolled on deck; everyone hurried their steps. Nobody now played the well-worn "Yours," sung by Vera Lynn, or any of the other scratched records which had been in more or less constant use on the wretched gramophone in the lounge since the beginning of the voyage. The ship's stores, which only sold soap, toothpaste, sweets, writing-paper and a few oddments, remained without customers. And the rumours began to circulate.

The Polish guards were well armed but had no ammunition. You could imagine the prisoners rushing up on deck in the event of trouble. Once free, they would probably try to get control of the lifeboats by force. There were rumours, too, about the alcohol rations: some heard that the supplies in the life-boats had been drunk to the last drop by certain members of the crew; others, that as soon as an alert was sounded, those in charge of the boats were to proceed to the bar in the lounge to draw sufficient rations for their boat. Would this be possible? It seemed highly improbable.

Gradually the days passed, but they seemed endless. Once a day boat-drill was ordered without warning, and everyone had to get to his boat station, carrying his life-belt, which he must then put on. Some carried out this exercise conscientiously, but others made light of it and were pleased when they could get back to whatever they had been doing.

At the end of the first week in September they came into the trade winds zone, having covered two thousand five hundred miles without incident. To most of the passengers there seemed no reason why this luck should not hold. It was noticed, however, that the captain no longer dined in their midst; he ate his very light meals alone in the chart-room. Knowing the dangers of the area, he was not to be lulled into a false security. But with the sea calm and a return to hot weather, the passengers became used to the state of semi-alert, and resumed their former habits. The R.A.F. officers could be seen disporting themselves beneath jets from the hoses, playing deck games, interminable games of bridge or poker-dice, or collecting round the bar. Laughter was heard again more often on the *Laconia*, and people even began dressing for dinner, to the delight of the ladies, who got out their gayest dresses.

Ben Coutts was much missed; he had to spend a few days in the sick-bay after a minor operation—for a bad ingrowing toenail. Mrs. Davidson and Mrs. Forster, each with a teen-age daughter, soon became friends and spent most of their time together. Mrs. Gibson often joined them.

The *Laconia* had become like a small town with its petty
jealousies, its rumours, its flirtations and clandestine love
affairs. On deck, children played endless games of hide-and-
seek; the leaders of the gang were indisputably two twelve-
year-olds, Geoffrey Baker and Freddy Moore. Freddy's father
had been killed in Malta, and he was returning to England
with his mother. At meal-times the hubbub of the grown-up
voices rising from the tables was lightened by the high voices
of the children enjoying themselves. It was a whole floating
world, complete but transient. In two or three days the ship
should have reached Freetown Harbour.

Shortly before midnight on September 10th, Hall-Clucas,
junior first officer, and Buckingham, senior third officer, were
on watch on the bridge, when a message was received from
the Admiralty. Buckingham went down to the purser's office
to decode it. At 1.15 a.m. the deciphered message was
handed to Captain Sharp. It read: "Alter course, September
11th, two hours after sunset." This was followed by details of
the course to be followed, which would take the *Laconia* into
the middle of the South Atlantic, some way from the coasts of
Africa; the Equator was to be crossed at a point equidistant
from Brazil and West Africa. No reason was given for the
change of course, but Captain Sharp hoped to receive com-
plementary instructions later. It looked as if they might be
going to the United States or Canada, and not London, as
thought. The Italian prisoners' presence on board made such
a supposition very plausible. In any case it was impossible to
know, the Admiralty's purposes being as unpredictable as
those of the Almighty. Whatever the reason might be, the
Laconia's general staff was not unduly perturbed. They were
used to receiving unexpected orders.

Accordingly the ship's course was altered at 10 p.m. on
September 11th. She now had following trade winds from the
south.

The next day began like many others: the fine weather
was continuing. After breakfast the new watch came on, and
everyone went about his occupations as usual. The prisoners
were allowed to come up on deck and stretch their legs. The
watch changed at midday, and again at 4 p.m. At dusk
bearings were taken, and the ship was put back exactly on
course. At 7:20 p.m. Hall-Clucas and Buckingham came
down from the bridge to have dinner in the officers' dining-

saloon, leaving Captain Sharp and the senior first officer, J. H. Walker.

With night approaching the normal precautions were taken: blacking out the lights, and closing all gangways leading to the deck. Chief Officer Steel made a general round of the ship, as affable as ever, smiling at the ladies as they went into the dining-saloon in their evening dresses. The scene might have been any evening during a peacetime cruise on a luxury liner. Steel much preferred this carefree atmosphere to one of anxiety; it was for Captain Sharp, himself and the crew to keep watch and be prepared. He finished his round and went up on the bridge.

The *Laconia* kept on her course. The choppy sea glinted like copper under the setting sun.

3

TORPEDOED

8 p.m. Saturday, September 12th, on board the "Laconia"

The sea was calm and beautiful, like black silk with glints of steely blue. On deck after dinner, Hall-Clucas and Buckingham could just hear the muffled sound of a blues coming up from the lounge.

"Amazing how quickly dusk falls here," Buckingham remarked. "The sun was still going down when we went to dinner. That's less than three-quarters of an hour ago, and now it's night."

Hall-Clucas looked at his watch. "Five past eight. I think I'll turn in and get some sleep before our watch."

Hurst, the purser, came out of the dining-saloon with Jones and Sollace. "Coming for a stroll, you two?" he asked.

"Not me, I'm sleepy," said Hall-Clucas. He turned to Buckingham. "And you promise to drop in at Cabin 17, don't forget. They'll be waiting for you."

He and Buckingham walked off down the starboard gangway in the direction of their cabins. Opposite them was Cabin 17, occupied by an officer in the Fleet Air Arm and his wife, who were being repatriated; he had been seriously ill with Malta fever.

A ray of light shone beneath the door of Cabin 17. "Coming in with me?" Buckingham asked.

"No, I'm sleepy," Hall-Clucas answered. "Don't stay long yourself. Remember we've both got to be on the bridge at midnight." He went into his cabin, leaving Buckingham alone in the gangway.

As Buckingham put out his hand to knock on the door, his mouth half open to say who he was, a sudden crashing explosion from below shook the whole ship. The panelling shivered to pieces, the air was thick with acrid smoke. The lights dimmed and the *Laconia* took a heavy list to starboard. The door in front of Buckingham had gone; there was nothing except fragments of wood at his feet and grey dust. A quivering electric-light bulb left him in a sort of yellowish fog. Through it he dimly saw the couple in the cabin, pressed together, motionless; they might have been turned to stone. For the fraction of a second, which seemed an age, he stayed in the same position, finger crooked ready to knock. The commonplace, automatic gesture was now completely absurd, so were the two stupefied figures. They looked as dazed as if they had been turned into the street in their pyjamas on a cold, foggy night.

Shocked back to reality, Buckingham rapped out: "Life-belts! Get to your boat stations. Leave everything."

He glanced across the gangway for Hall-Clucas. The cabin door was open. Probably already on the bridge, he thought.

The officer and his wife joined Buckingham in the gangway. Together they groped through the debris of wood on the torn and buckled linoleum.

"Get off to A Deck, the lifeboat crews will look after you," Buckingham reassured the other two.

"What about you?"

"I'll be wanted on the bridge."

"Good luck."

Alone now, Buckingham listened. He couldn't hear the engines. Nothing but a vast silence, the silence of three

thousand stunned passengers, and of a ship mortally wounded—
it was more terrifying than the crash of the explosion. He
dashed up to the bridge, where shadows were moving out.
Just as he got into the wheelhouse, the second explosion
came, followed almost at once by the boat-stations alarm. The
sound of the hooters hung dismally in the air.

When the first torpedo hit the *Laconia*'s starboard side,
Dorothy Davidson was sitting in the lounge with Molly, her
nineteen-year-old daughter. A few couples had started dancing. Molly listened absently as her mother criticized the
running of the ship with the authority conferred by her
status, experience and long tours in the colonies. Mrs. Davidson
was wearing a thin silk dress and high-heeled sandals, and
had her bag slung from her shoulder.

There was a sudden thud and a violent jerk. She found
herself across the lounge clinging to a pillar. Less shaken,
Molly helped her mother to recover her balance. Together
they staggered to the door and into the passage, only to fall
over notice-boards which had dropped there. There was a
heavy list to starboard. Like Buckingham, they were struck
by the extraordinary silence. Not a cry, not a shout, nothing.
The thousand noises of this floating town, a ship's whole
medley of sound, even people's breathing for a second or
two, seemed to have stopped dead, suspended in time and
space. As they reached the stairs, they felt a second jerk,
rather less violent than the first, and held on to the stair
rail. A sailor passed them, shouting: "Boat stations . . .
quick!"

The *Laconia* was listing more and more violently.
Thankfully the Davidsons found two friends of theirs in the
crowd, the R.A.F. officers "Joss" and "Dusty," who helped
them fix their life-belts. The throng of passengers making for
the upper decks were impeded by others going down to look
for things in their cabins. There were many collisions, but at
first it was general confusion more than panic. Then the first
Italian prisoners, who had succeeded in getting out of the
hold, were seen trying to break through to the lifeboats. The
Polish guards, with bayonets fixed and guns crossed, struggled to keep them in check and drive them back, but some
managed to get past. In the mêlée passengers were knocked
down and fought with the prisoners.

Mrs. Davidson and Molly held on to each other grimly, and tried to get to their boat stations, but were turned back. At last they managed to push through to the upper decks. There was no moon; it was completely dark. Here and there a drawn face, a badly tied life-belt, a hand groping forwards, were picked out in the faint gleam of torches. Shouts of "Lights out! You'll give away our position!" A few answering shouts, then all was darkness again.

Borne along in the direction of B Deck by the human current, the two women battled on towards their objective. They climbed to the upper deck by an iron ladder, but it was on the port side, and now they were carried into the throng of passengers pulled to starboard by the ship's list. Water poured out of burst pipes and seeped in everywhere, jets of steam hissed. In the shoving, jostling mass, passengers slipped and fell, picked themselves up, got separated from their companions and could be heard shouting each other's names. The Davidsons lurched into Smith, another R.A.F. officer, no friend of Mrs. Davidson's; but at such moments petty disagreements were forgotten, and he pulled them out of the crowd piled against the starboard side. Then Hall, an army officer, noticed Mrs. Davidson in her thin evening dress and called out: "No coat?" "No," she shouted back. He made her put on his coat, helped her fix her life-belt over it, and disappeared. Molly recognized another friend by his great height, and called out "Major Creedon!"

Having finished dinner, the Major had been sitting in a chair in the aft lounge, watching a regular bridge four with the express purpose of listening to their vehement post-mortems after each hand; this was a continual source of amusement to him. They had only just started playing, however, when the first explosion occurred. He quietly went down to his cabin to pick up a few basic things, then joined the throng and made his way up to A Deck, as if it were no more than the usual boat drill. Wearing his sheepskin coat, with a camera slung over his shoulder, he might have been going ashore on some excursion. When Molly called him, he told her in a calm voice; "We'll have to find places for you two in a boat," though inwardly he feared there was now very little chance of this. Disregarding his own position, he set about helping the Davidsons.

Captain Coutts was still in the *Laconia*'s sick-bay, one foot swathed in bandages, chafing at his enforced immobilization, which he found a bit ridiculous: the bandages suggested an amputation, not an ingrowing toe-nail.

When he heard the explosion of the first torpedo, he shook his head, muttering: "Aye, we're in the soup again." He calmly put on his greatcoat over his pyjamas and reached for his haversack, which contained a water-bottle, a bottle of whisky and his precious medical records. Shouldering the haversack, he loaded his revolver and slipped it into his greatcoat pocket.

Luckily his foot was not hurting. As he forced his way through the jostling crowd, he decided they were already on the verge of panic. Near his own cabin, he saw a friend, R. S. Miller, whom he had known on the *Stratheden*. Before Coutts's operation they had often played bridge and deck-games together.

Miller had gone into the lounge after dinner, intending to spend the rest of the evening there. The first explosion made him stagger, but he was unhurt, whereas an officer next to him was hurled against the corner of a table and hurt his head badly.

Miller did not hurry unduly; like the other passengers he felt great confidence in the ship's sailing qualities. Her very size was reassuring, and even if she had been torpedoed she would probably stay afloat for hours or even days, till rescue came.

The lights had failed, but he made his way across the lounge. He didn't come across any of the ship's officers or crew, and found this absence of authority alarming, because it would certainly lead to disorder. But it was also comforting in a way: there couldn't be any real danger if none of the crew were giving the passengers instructions. The ship's list, however, the electricity breakdown and that acrid smell of explosives coming up from the hold, were all ominous enough.

He decided to go down to his cabin to collect some personal belongings. The door of the bar was open as he passed it, and he caught a glimpse of one of the crew filling his pockets with notes from the till. This was a bit of a shock to Miller, and he also noted that no one was taking the rations of alcohol which rumour said were for distribution in case the *Laconia* had to be evacuated.

He found it a laborious business getting down to his cabin. The Italians coming up from the hold were being thrust back by the Poles, but the prisoners, realizing there would not be room for everyone in the boats, were frantically struggling to save their lives. They feared that as prisoners they would be considered last of all. Screaming, calling on God and the Madonna, they tore and fought their way to freedom, slipping past the guns, avoiding the bayonet points. The Poles seemed unable to hold them, hampered as they were by the surging mass of passengers; while the Italians gained confidence, guessing that their guards would soon give up a task as hopeless as it was inhuman.

There was still no one giving orders from the bridge. Pressing on down to his cabin against the stream, Miller wondered what was happening, whether the radio had sent out SOS signals, and a lot of other things. At last he was in his cabin, and then he did something surprising: instead of collecting his personal things, he took down his canvas bag and filled it with lump sugar, dried fruit, raisins and figs, which he had bought at the Cape. It was when he came out of the cabin that he saw Ben Coutts. The Scot was dragging his bad foot and looked a curious sight in his pyjamas, huge greatcoat and haversack. "What a business!" said Miller. "It is that," Coutts agreed phlegmatically. They fixed their life-belts and went up towards A Deck. This took them a quarter of an hour, with Miller trying to protect his friend's bandaged foot.

On A Deck passengers were trying to find the way to their right boat stations. They had learnt the directions more or less carefully at boat drills, but it was a very different matter at night on listing decks encumbered with debris and burst pipes spilling out water. They staggered, slipped, fell down and picked themselves up again, then stumbled on from one boat station to another.

Some of the crew were busy launching the lifeboats. In theory these would be taken from their cradles, let down alongside till level with A Deck, where they would embark their quota of passengers; when filled they would be lowered to the sea. But the list was increasing rapidly, so that in most cases the operation became impossible. Owing to the list, the starboard boats hung too far from the ship's side; and the port boats were immobilized. Moreover, a lot of the boats had been so badly damaged in the explosion that they were unserviceable. Boats 5, 5a and 7a had been completely destroyed.

A few of the Italian prisoners and some of the crew managed to board boats, which were cast off half empty. As the passengers saw these, in which they had hoped to find places, they began venturing on to the rope ladders at the ship's side, clambering down, suspended in space, until they reached the boats. In the darkness the boats filled rapidly without any sort of order.

Amidst the confusion Coutts and Miller were relieved to hear someone showing authority at last, giving clear and definite orders. This was Lieutenant John Tillie, R.N., D.S.C. and bar (Narvik and East Mediterranean campaigns). He was effectively supported by two other Navy men, Leading Seaman Harry Vines and Able Seaman A. V. Large, who had been in the crew's quarters, four decks below, when the first torpedo hit the ship. They at once climbed the ladders, with a speed only possible for practised sailors, and made for their boat stations. Others were now taking Tillie's orders: "Get the women and children on the boats first . . . Cut the hawsers of these rafts . . . Get those floats free . . . Hold your prisoners back," the lieutenant told the Polish guards, as he noticed some of the frenzied Italians trying to board the boats before anybody else. Then he tried to get the port-side boats in operation.

The moon was hidden behind black clouds, so the deck was completely dark. Mrs. Forster, holding her fifteen-year-old daughter Elizabeth by the hand, was another of those wandering from one boat station to another, asking where her boat was, looking for a place, being pushed back everywhere. She was quite desperate when she too picked out Major Creedon, who was with her friend Mrs. Davidson and Molly. Just as she and her daughter were going to join the little group, they were pushed aside and lost sight of it. Then they were caught up among Italian prisoners.

Some people had taken off most of their clothes, putting on their greatcoats and carrying blankets; while others had taken off only their shoes. Everyone tried to regroup with friends or men of the same service. Colonel Liswell helped the young ship's doctor, Geoffrey Purslow, to get a place on a boat for three of his patients. Then the colonel went to rescue women and children, while Purslow got his medical equipment into the lifeboat with his patients. A little further on was William Henderson, the fourth engineer officer, who was making heroic efforts with an axe to free a blocked raft.

An R.A.F. sergeant, who had been in the Narvik and Crete campaigns, was shouting: "R.A.F. over here!"—and the Air Force boys rushed to where their help was needed. Having climbed with some difficulty from F Deck, near the Italians, Sergeant Batchelor pushed through to join his friend Middleton. The two of them had as usual been playing bridge in the warrant officers' mess with Allen and Elliot when the first torpedo hit the ship. They got up from the table as one man. "This is it, then," remarked Elliot, with a slight sigh of regret for the hand he had just put down: his partner would certainly have made three no-trumps.

They at once dashed for their boat station, the same for all four of them. Then Batchelor thought he would have time to collect a greatcoat from the cabin he shared with Elliot. Outside the door of the cabin, he found to his dismay that he had forgotten his life-belt; he had been sitting on it for his game of bridge. He returned to the mess. The little room was deserted and filled with smoke. Ignoring the overturned glasses, the abandoned card-tables, he made straight for his chair: the life-belt was still there. As he collected it, his eye fell on the table. Elliot's beautiful dummy was still spread out, for a hand never to be played; beside it was Elliot's gold wrist-watch, the second-hand moving on with obdurate regularity. Batchelor made a gesture to take it and return it to Elliot. One second, two seconds... for some reason he hesitated. No, time was too precious... three seconds. An obscure sense of the article's uselessness when his life was in danger, the same instinct which had led its owner to abandon it, made Batchelor go off himself, leaving the watch still on the table.

"What about Elliot?" he asked Middleton when they came together on A Deck.

"Haven't seen him," Middleton answered, and immediately he was cut off from Batchelor.

That same evening, hundreds of miles away from the stricken ship, tired after a harassing day, a woman in London went early to bed in one of those small suburban houses

which all look alike, with their little gardens hidden behind a
wooden fence, their embroidered curtains well drawn over
the sash windows. She went to sleep at once, but woke
several times in the night with an appalling nightmare. She
lived through it with such intensity and vividness, down to
the last detail, that the night seemed endless.

Next morning on her way to church, thankful for com-
panionship, she called out to her friend and neighbour.
"Morning, Mrs. Faith, what dreadful weather." "Yes, isn't it,
Mrs. Batchelor." Mrs. Faith hesitated. "But what's the matter? You look as pale as death."

"I'm not surprised." Mrs. Batchelor was thankful to be
able to tell someone about her dream. "Last night I dreamt of
my son Kenneth. He was on a ship and it was sinking.
Kenneth was coming and going in all directions, coming up
from the hold, going on to the deck, going down again, over
and over again, and all the time the ship was sinking. I can
see it all as plainly as if I was there . . . I can't get it out of my
mind. My own son!"

"But isn't your son still in that training camp in South
Africa? I know what these nightmares are, but you really
mustn't worry too much about it."

"But it was so lifelike . . ."

Mrs. Faith could see her friend was near breaking-point.
Taking her arm, she walked with her towards the church as
the bells rang out.

That evening Mrs. Faith took a sheet of paper and noted:
"Kenneth, the son of my friend Mrs. Batchelor, is in great
danger on a ship. London, September 13th, 1942." The sheet
of paper has been preserved, and after all these years Mrs.
Batchelor still remembers distinctly the details of her nightmare.

At the first explosion Ian Peel was making for the lounge
when he was hurled against the wall and hit on the head by a
fragment of blown bulkhead. Half stunned, he staggered to
his feet in the semi-darkness, and began pressing on towards
his boat station. This was difficult because the ship was listing
so heavily. Then the second explosion caused a new rain of
flying matter. Carried forward amidst shouts and oaths—"Bloody
tinfish! Bloody Jerries!"—he found himself on A Deck. Groping ahead, bumping against pieces of wood and other passengers, he could see nothing but vague masses, figures, forms,

going in all directions. Gradually his eyes became accustomed to the darkness. It took him half an hour to reach his boat station, only to discover that the boat he had gone to so regularly at boat drills was now a shapeless jumble of iron and wood. It was at this moment that he felt for the first time a dull ache in his arm. He looked down and saw that the sleeve was torn, his flesh was exposed, and blood flowed where he had been hit by a splinter. He looked for another boat at random in the darkness, but couldn't see any.

He glanced at his watch, which was luminous: nine o'clock. His eyes went to the sea, black and choppy beneath him. He thought he could see overloaded boats with a mass of heads and arms. Someone called him: "Peel! Peel!" Impossible to tell who, in this hubbub. He felt he mustn't stay on the ship any longer; at any moment she might sink abruptly, dragging everything down with her in a terrible swirling suction which no one could resist. He caught a glimpse of two women, one holding a baby clasped to her breast. He was pushed upwards and outwards, he grasped at a rope ladder and was swung over the side willynilly. Hanging between sky and sea, he felt himself slipping between arms, legs, hands, which clutched at anything.

Amidst the contagion of panic, it was perhaps an aid to keeping calm if you were responsible for another's safety, like Doris Hawkins, the nursing sister with a baby in her care. She has described the scene herself in a book called *Atlantic Torpedo*, written when she at last reached home, after an ordeal longer and even more terrible than most survivors had to suffer.

> On the night of the 12th I came up from dinner. As usual I looked at Sally. She was asleep; beside her all was ready in case of emergency. I went into the opposite cabin to talk to Mary (Lady Grizel Wolfe-Murray). We were talking quite calmly about submarines and torpedoes.
>
> Suddenly there was a shattering explosion. The ship shivered, then stood still; the air filled with the smell of explosives. It had happened, the first torpedo had struck.
>
> I fled to Sally. She was still asleep. I wrapped

her in her woollies, picked up her shipwreck bag, and turned. As I did so, the second torpedo struck. The ship rocked; we were flung across the corridor. Sally remained in my arms unhurt.

Just ahead of me was Mary, and together we made our way upstairs, carried on a surging wave of people, some with their emergency outfits, many without. As we went, the lights failed.

All this while the ship was taking an increasingly heavy list, and by now it was very difficult going with my precious burden. I stumbled over fallen doors, broken woodwork and shattered glass to our lifeboat station. Then we waited.

The torpedoes had hit the engine-room, mainmast and wireless transmitter, and some of the lifeboats had been carried away. The list made it very hard to swing out the rest of the boats; moreover it was a very dark night, and a fairly heavy sea was running. The second torpedo had apparently burst among the prisoners, and panic and turmoil were following. They rushed their Polish guards, streamed upstairs, stormed the lifeboats or leaped into the sea.

So we waited for what seemed an age, but was really only about fifteen minutes. Then we were told our lifeboat had been blown away. We wondered what to do. Sally never once cried either then or through the whole experience, despite the noise and confusion around; she remained still in my arms, making only gentle little talking sounds.

There was no one to direct us. Just as Mary and I were considering feeling our way round the deck, Squadron Leader H. R. K. Wells came upon us. Taking Sally from me, he led me from boat station to boat station; but all the boats seemed to have left or be full, or else jammed so that they could not be launched. Nearly forty-five minutes after the torpedoes had struck, we saw below us a lifeboat, already in the water but still alongside the ship. A young Fleet Air Arm officer volunteered to carry Sally. He tucked her down inside the back of his greatcoat, tied a blanket round his waist just under Sally's

foot-level, to prevent her from slipping, and so he
carried her, papoose fashion, down a swinging rope
ladder, and into the crowded lifeboat, heaving and
tossing like a cork. It was well done.

Mary and I followed as quickly as possible. The
lifeboat, filled to capacity with men, women and
children, was leaking badly and rapidly filling with
water; at the same time it was crashing against the
ship's side. Just as Sally was passed over to me, the
boat filled completely and capsized, flinging us all
into the water. I did not hear her cry even then, and
I am sure God took her immediately to Himself
without suffering. I never saw her again.

4

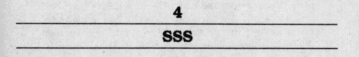

SSS

On board U-156, 8:07 p.m.

It was pure chance that enabled the U-156 to torpedo
the *Laconia*. Either ship might have taken a course a few
miles to the east or the west, or the submarine's look-out
might have let his attention wander for a moment or been
blinded by the sun, so that he didn't see the tell-tale smoke
slightly darkening the horizon. Had the Admiralty not ordered
the *Laconia* to alter her course, she might have reached
the shores of Great Britain unscathed, with her complement
of nearly three thousand.[1]

---

[1] Some have claimed that the German secret service managed to pick up and
decipher a coded signal telling her to alter course and make for Freetown, and that
they informed Admiral Dönitz, who at once advised Hartenstein of the *Laconia's*
position. I asked both Dönitz and Hessler, his Chief of Operations, about this, and
they denied knowledge of any such signal. Had Hartenstein picked up such a
message direct, he would not have been in a position to decode it, for the British
secret codes were changed as often as the German ones. It is true that the Germans
knew the names of almost all the ships travelling to and from Suez via the Cape; in

Everyone on the bridge or deck of the submarine saw the high spurt of water from the first torpedo rise along the ship's side amidships, reach the upper deck and drop to reveal a gaping hole in the hull. It struck Number 4 hold, just behind the gangway. This contained four hundred and fifty Italian prisoners, most of whom were killed. The second torpedo hit the ship at the level of Number 2 hold, also filled with Italians, and to the men watching on the submarine it seemed to have less effect. Both explosions were heard on the microphone in the control-room.

These submariners were beginning to get used to destroying ships and their cargoes. None of them troubled to ask themselves questions or tried to imagine the tragedies they were causing. Does the sailor think of the torpedo gliding under the water towards his ship, of the motionless mine lying in wait bristling with spikes, or the endless hours he might have to face on a raft? No, he does not; if he did he would go mad. Oaths, jokes, laughter, alcohol are necessary, even indispensable, for leading such a life.

"Splice the main-brace." "Let's have a song." "My eels are the smartest afloat." "Two shots, two hits, with us." "Drinks on the house." Such were the cracks and comments to be heard in U-156's forward torpedo compartment after sinking the *Laconia*.

On the bridge Hartenstein was estimating the liner's tonnage: 12,000 tons, perhaps 15,000?

Fifteen thousand tons sent to the bottom; 15,000 to add to the victory scores. That would bring his total well above the 100,000 tons of enemy shipping sunk.

But of course, that wasn't the end of the job. First, he must find out the ship's name, then try to capture her commander and chief engineer. This last was clearly going to be difficult or even impossible at night amidst all the wreckage.

---

fact they had a good knowledge of all naval traffic in the South Atlantic. But they certainly did not know the exact movements of this particular ship, so it is fair to say she was sunk "by chance."

Translator's note: According to Brigadier Creedon, however, one of the British survivors who passed by U-156 in a boat soon after the sinking, asked Hartenstein: "How did you find us?" Hartenstein replied: "Your skipper got a change of course. I knew about this and was waiting for you." He mentioned the names of five ships behind the *Laconia*, four of which were later sunk; only the *Stratheden* survived, having received the *Laconia's* signal.

Warily, very warily, U-156 approached the liner, which was already listing to starboard; she had covered a half-mile, and then come to a stop.

Mannesmann was at Hartenstein's side observing through the binoculars. "The torpedoes took three minutes six seconds to reach their target. She's quite a size, isn't she! Might need a third torpedo—what do you say?"

Hartenstein smiled. "I say you're an extravagant fellow. No, I need my torpedoes for the Cape region and the Mozambique Channel. Let's get nearer—not too near, though. The ship's gunners must be at their guns, ready to fire if they see us. But in the night they won't, except as a cork on the water."

Hartenstein felt like talking this evening. In his racy Saxon accent he went on: "When we were in the Gulf of Mexico, before you joined us, we glided right through convoys at night, sailing between cargo-ships, so that the noise of our screws was mixed up with theirs. This submarine's so low on the water they never saw us. I never felt safer than in the middle of our enemies." He laughed sardonically. "But that's by the way. What do you think this ship can be?"

"A troop-transport in ballast, empty," Mannesmann hazarded.

"I very much doubt that. The British don't usually return empty."

"Then a leave-ship."

"On leave or not, they're soldiers, British bastards, and they're going to get a cold bath. There may be three thousand men there, a regiment. Think of it, Mannesmann, a big liner and a regiment sent to the bottom by a tiny submarine with fifty men on board."

"Not a bad proportion. But I'd like to know the ship's name."

"Patience, Mannesmann. You're always in too much of a hurry. We must have blown up her wireless, otherwise she'd already have given her news. So much the better. After our two bangs on the cymbals, it'll be a funeral without music... How far away are we?"

"Nearly two miles, sir."

"Don't let's get too near—we'll wait. If she starts up again—and it wouldn't be the first time I've had that sort of trick played on me—I'll finish her off with the guns."

In due course he was to note in his log-book:

8:07 p.m.—square 7721. Torpedo tubes 1 and 3 at half angle. Enemy longitude 140. Time taken 3 mins. 6 secs. One shot on target. Second shot heard on target. Steamer must be much larger. She's hove to, put out lifeboats, leaning forward and listing to starboard. We're nearly two miles away, waiting for her to sink.

Through the binoculars the two officers watched the black, tilted mass; now and then, when the moon went behind a cloud, it melted into the night.

"Eight twenty-two. A quarter of an hour since she was hit," Mannesmann murmured. "I'd give a bottle of champagne to know her name."

Just then a sailor dashed up the ladder, holding in his hand a small wooden scoop with a message resting on it. He handed it to the commander, but in his excitement didn't leave him time to read the message. "Sir," he burst out, "she's just given her name and position, 650 yards: SSS . . . SSS . . . 04.34 south . . . 11.25 west *Laconia* . . . torpedoed."

"SSS or SOS?" Hartenstein snapped.

From the top of the ladder the sailor looked up reproachfully at the "old man." "SSS, sir, no doubt at all. She should be repeating her message now."

"The bastard! Jam that message, jam it!" Hartenstein shouted down to the control-room.

He was furious. SOS was three dots, three dashes, three dots. The signal that was being transmitted was three dots three times, which indicated the presence of a submarine.

"I feel like continuing my course south," he said to Mannesmann. "The ship's done for anyhow, and that's the main thing."

As he read the message he heard the voice of one of the wireless operators: "Achtung, Achtung! Control-room to bridge. The vessel sunk is the *Laconia*—White Star Line, 19,695 tons, built in 1922. Has been troop-transport since beginning of war, can take up to 6,000 men, 1,580 passengers in peacetime." And almost immediately afterwards: "Achtung! She's transmitting on 25 metres: SSS—SSS *Laconia* torpedoed . . . We're continuing to jam."

"British bastards!" Hartenstein repeated. "Lucky we're in the middle of the Atlantic. Before anyone comes to her rescue, I suppose we must have a shot at picking up her captain... Slow ahead," he ordered. "Make for the *Laconia* ... port 5°... amidships... steady."

On board the "Laconia," 8:30 p.m.

Returning to the bridge, Buckingham reported to Captain Sharp, and found him very calm, showing no sign of haste or nerves. You would have said it was a mere exercise. But Sharp realized that his *Laconia* was fatally hit, and ordered the evacuation of the ship. He was at the very end of the starboard wing of the bridge; leaning over the rail, he was trying to see the holes which had been made in his ship's side. The sound of an endless roaring came up to him, the noise of the sea surging through these holes at the rate of several tons a minute. Turning round, he saw Buckingham.

"Shall I throw the codes and log-books overboard?" asked Buckingham.

"Yes, immediately."

Leaving the bridge to carry out this important duty, Buckingham heard the captain ask Walker, his first officer, if the water-tight doors and bulkheads were closed.

"Everything holding."

"Good, go to the boat-deck and get as many boats as possible launched."

Then Buckingham passed Rose, the second officer, who shouted to him: "All the telephone communications are cut. They can't be repaired. The captain has given orders to abandon ship."

To reach the safe in the chart-room, Buckingham went through the officers' mess, which a few hours before had been noisy with conversations and animated with the movement of stewards carrying dishes. The tables had been left in the disorder of the unfinished meal. There was soup growing cold in some of the plates, while others had been knocked over. A napkin ring had fallen on to the parquet flooring and rolled stupidly. The indefinable smell of ships—cooking, soap, tar, strong cigarettes—was now mixed with the pungency of explosives.

When he got to the chart-room, Buckingham went straight

to the safe and opened it. Arranged on the shelves, the secret documents, log-books and codes were ready to be dropped overboard in canvas bags pierced with holes, a kentledge at the bottom of each bag to make it sink. But in the time available Buckingham couldn't possibly carry all the contents of the safe to the bridge by himself. He saw a sailor and called him to help. They made several journeys. The lights were all out in this part of the ship, and they shone torches. It was very exhausting work carting the heavy bags, and their strength was beginning to give out when they tipped the last one over the rail.

Unfortunately a few of the bags fell in the middle of the first survivors trying to swim away from the ship, and some of them were knocked out by the kentledges.

The harassing work took Buckingham a good quarter of an hour. "Finished," he reported to the captain. "Order carried out, sir. All the bags are in the sea."

"Good. The transmissions are cut. Go to the wireless room and report to me the messages sent."

The wireless room was behind the funnel, and to get to it Buckingham had to go down to A Deck and then come up again to the boat-deck. He at once ran into the flood of passengers, who tried to question him, but he hadn't time to stop and answer. Preoccupied with his mission, he elbowed his way through, and eventually reached the wireless room. The door was closed. He went in.

8:36 p.m.

He found the third wireless officer, H. C. Cooper, and two senior operators sitting in front of their switchboards. The two senior operators calmly worked the plugs, attentive to the slightest message which might reach their ear-phones, sending out their distress signals on 25 and 600 metres. After the SSS these gave the Laconia's position and the time of the attack. The two men seemed as if they did not hear the thousand noises of the ship sinking beneath them. Here in the wireless room they must ignore everything and remain at their posts until they received the order to evacuate—if that order ever reached them.

Cooper swung round his tubular steel chair when he saw Buckingham come in, and his face brightened in a half-smile, a look of silent relief, as if to say: so the bridge hasn't forgotten us?

Buckingham didn't answer this mute question. For the moment there was no question of evacuation for them. They must remain at their post up to the last moment.

"Communications on board are cut. The captain asks you if you have transmitted the SSS messages and given bearings."

"Yes, several times on 25 and 600 metres. But we've had a lot of trouble with the aerial. The power is failing—soon we shan't be able to send any more."

"Are you receiving?"

"Yes, but it's weak and indistinct."

Buckingham dashed off to report this to the captain. In his haste he didn't notice, nor had Cooper told him, that one of the two operators had blood streaming from his shoulder, a wound from the first explosion. Admittedly the man gave no sign of the pain he was suffering, but sat at his post, impassive.

Buckingham decided he would get to the bridge quicker by going farther below, using the ladders, and then through the narrow passages in the bowels of the ship. Also he would be able to see what was happening there, or at least get some idea of it.

On B Deck he found a group of passengers sitting huddled tightly against each other, reluctant to abandon the false security given by the ship's warmth, the lights, however faint, and these travelling companions to whom they had attached themselves. Buckingham talked to some of them, insisting on the urgent need to go up on deck and evacuate the ship. His words seemed to make little impact on them, so he left them and went below. There his steps resounded on the metallic grating, and he felt horribly alone in the narrow gangways between walls lined with piping in various colours; some of the pipes were burst and emitted scalding jets of steam. As he ran all the way along these gangways, he was gripped by a claustrophobia bordering on panic. The lamps with their trembling yellowish light might fail abruptly, go out and stay out. The passages criss-crossed and were linked by vertical emergency ladders. If the lights did go out, he would be lost, he would have no earthly chance of escaping from the labyrinth and getting back into the air.

He began to feel very tired. It was about forty minutes since the first explosion, when he had left the Fleet Air Arm officer and his wife. Where were they now, and had they managed to find a place in a boat?

He came up from E Deck to D Deck, and heard the cries of the Italians. They seemed to have lost all self-control. The calmer ones were praying out loud, invoking the Holy Virgin, holding prayer-books above their heads, trying to save this most precious possession. He hurried over to a group of these wretches and showed them the way. What followed was a dash for Heaven.

He was forced back himself. He turned and went along deserted gangways, climbed ladders, went down them again, heard the water rising, the water-tight bulkheads being blown. He went up again for the last time, re-crossed the officers' mess. When he reached the bridge, Captain Sharp was in the chartroom, leaning over a map he had put on the ledge and examining it intently, shining a torch on the paper studded with pinholes and scored with lines.

"All the rescue messages have been sent, sir. Faintly, I'm afraid, it was all they could do."

The captain raised his head. He seemed weary and sad. "Thank you, Buckingham. You will now go to your own lifeboat. Go on, Steel, you too. And you, Walker." He turned towards a boy of eighteen, the second wireless officer, who had not moved. "You too." There was resignation in his voice and also unshakeable resolution. He was fulfilling his last duties towards his well-loved ship, well aware that his authority, all-powerful till now over that ship's smallest recesses, was deserting him.

"Go on. Hurry up, all of you. I'm giving you an order. Save yourselves."

Buckingham left the bridge. Yes, he knew he must think of himself now. He thought of Dorothy, his young wife. Yes, he must abandon the old *Laconia*, and try to save his own life.

Indescribable disorder reigned on A Deck when he got there. He came out in front of a staved-in boat with buckled davits. At the end of them hung ropes with frayed ends, swinging in the night like the ropes of men who have been hung. In the darkness the wretched passengers were bumping into each other, some trying to go below so as to be nearer the sea when they jumped into it, while others wanted to climb higher to get away from it. The officers and crew did what they could, but they were swamped, and their appeals and instructions went unheard. Walker went from one boat to another, vainly giving orders. Figures could be seen in frantic motion, then disappearing, merging into each other.

Aft, on the heeling deck, two men behind a 4.7-inch gun scoured the blackness of the sea. They couldn't see anything to fire at. Leading Seamen Vines and Petty Officer Lester raged that they couldn't place a single shell on the enemy. Beside them the sailors were piling up shells never to be used.

Buckingham went over the whole stern of the huge deck: there were still two or three boats which could be put to sea, a few rafts which could be slid over the side and would float when the *Laconia* was no more. The end was approaching.

5

SAVE YOURSELVES

The ship was heeling to starboard and sinking by the bows. Her hull was burst and torn amidships and aft, with the sea roaring through holes several yards wide. The last passengers still on board wondered how much longer she would stay afloat. Like frightened animals they wandered from deck to deck, stumbling against greatcoats, packs, a rifle with its bayonet, and all manner of abandoned goods. Many of them poured back towards the stern which was pointing skywards, or tried to get near the bridge, still bearing the futile notice "Forbidden to Passengers." Strong swimmers knew they could keep going for several hours, but what of the others? Would the life-belts fulfil their function when everything else on the ship failed, or would they only weigh their bearers down?

Buckingham thought of all this as he watched one lot of people and then another. How many of them would still be alive when day came? Near him they were almost fighting to get on to a boat crammed with people standing up to take less space. The boat was being lowered, and then something terrible happened. Whether it was a block giving way or a badly tied rope, the boat came loose in front and abruptly emptied out its contents. With a horrible cry a hundred or so people were hurled into the sea like discarded puppets.

The Air Force men had disappeared, John Tillie's team also. A high-ranking army officer was still giving a few orders: "Lower the Jacob's ladders. Quick!"

"Take this raft, put it to sea and save yourselves," another army officer told Riley, the man at one of the Bofors. Riley and his men did not want to leave their gun except on the captain's orders, but now he realized they must abandon the ship. Having pushed the raft overboard, he slid down a rope, followed by his gunners. The night was black above the sea, which they could guess was now near, getting nearer and nearer.

Buckingham saw Dorothy Davidson and her daughter, with Major Creedon urging them to go down a rope ladder. "There—hurry!"

Mrs. Davidson still hesitated. It was a hard thing to go down into the darkness, on a rope ladder hanging in the air, fifty feet above a boat which mightn't be there any more when she got to the bottom.

"You first, Molly."

"No, you, Mummy."

"You see . . ."

Then the girl decided. "Follow me."

Behind them other passengers were waiting.

Molly put a foot on the first rung of the ladder, and held on as hard as she could with both hands. Below her was space and night; above her, night and two hesitant feet. Horrified, she realized they were not her mother's. Molly went down. The sea was there, black, lacquered, heaving and subsiding like a monstrous breath. At last she put her foot on something soft—a shoulder, an arm. A hand seized her and she let herself go. At the same moment she felt a violent blow on the head. An oar, the boat's rowlock, a boat-hook? Stunned, she fell amidst the bodies. She thought vaguely about her mother— did she follow me, did she manage to get on another boat?

The boat Molly was in was crammed with people. Pulled by a few oars badly handled, it drew away from the dying *Laconia* in the pitch-black night.

Major Creedon was still trying to get Mrs. Davidson on to the ladder. "Quick . . . quick . . . hurry up." Someone behind them shouted: "Jump!"

A cord of her life-belt had come loose, and the life-belt fell off. The major gave her another and put it on for her. Meanwhile other passengers had got over the rail and gone down the ladder. "Hurry, I must hurry," she muttered, and put a foot on the ladder. She was beginning to go down it when the new life-belt got crossed, impeding her, choking her. With one hand she put it back in place, with the other she clung to the ladder. The rungs were slippery. She must go on: above her others were following. She could hear their cries, she shared in their terror. The climb seemed endless. At last she saw a black, sticky swell frothing on the Laconia's side. Beneath her feet there was only the sea. Then, with a scream, she let go. Her first impression was of warm water. She saw the shadow of lone swimmers, the outline of boats, in which a few lights came on, then went out again at once; she caught glimpses of dark masses floating, wreckage or people. Suddenly a boat emerged, nearly hitting her with its stem. With a strange calm she caught on to a painter; clinging to it, she made a supreme effort to haul herself up. She was about to let go when two men in the boat helped her to get out of the water. Exhausted, she rolled to the bottom of the boat and closed her eyes; she was saved . . . Then Dorothy Davidson sat up again abruptly: what about Molly? She struggled to control herself, and without knowing why, she felt certain her daughter was in one of those boats whose outlines she could see. A little way away the Laconia was sinking. Mrs. Davidson felt as if she were watching some horror film, a nightmare that had become real.

Around her Italians were swimming, and shouting for help: "Aiuto! Aiuto!" These three syllables were to ring out on the sea a very long time, right till dawn. In the boat a stranger called out: "You must row." People were rowing, or trying to, and slowly the boat drew away from the Laconia. Some of the other boats sank by the bow. One had women and children in it, and there were screams and calls for help, quickly drowned by the sea. This was the boat in which Sister Hawkins had been.

Sally had gone, and the Sister found herself among numbers of Italians screaming and struggling in the water.

One, in his terror, grasped me, both arms round my neck, and dragged me down, down under the water. Thoughts came to me in that moment with amazing clarity, and I heard, as though she were beside me, the voice of Sally's young mother as she bade me farewell. "Never forget," she had said, "that if anything happens and Sally has to go, you must do all you can to save yourself—we cannot replace you and you have work to do." Her courageous words came as a clear message to me. I saw, too, my parents eagerly awaiting my return... I struggled, and I came to the surface.

My hand touched a piece of wood and I clung on. Another Italian began to drag at me, but I shook free. Finally I came to a raft which I managed to hold. Already four Italians were hanging on to the sides, but they were quiet; they helped me up to the top. I lay there, and we drifted away from the ship.

Major Creedon, on the deck of the *Laconia*, after getting the Davidsons down the ladder, had sought in vain the boat he was supposed to occupy. It was much too late, of course; all the serviceable boats had long been put to sea. But he saw a crew lowering Boat 13a, and slid along to it by a hawser. When it was put to sea, those who were in it found to their horror that the water was rising fast in the bottom. It seemed intact, and they looked for the cause. An A.B found it: the bung was missing. With cloths and tow he and the major managed to block the hole, and then took turns to bale out the water.

The eighty-four survivors in this boat were saved miraculously, five days later, drifting in mid-ocean, when a look-out on the French cruiser *Gloire* happened to spot the momentary flare of the last match they had left.

Ben Coutts was handicapped by his nailless toe, which was hurting and also impeding his movements. He saw Sister Hawkins and Lady Grizel Wolfe-Murray go down the ladder behind the lieutenant carrying Sally. The ladder was still there, within his reach; but leaning over, he saw no boat, no shadow of a craft floating beneath it. There was nothing but a hundred or so men floundering in the black sea.

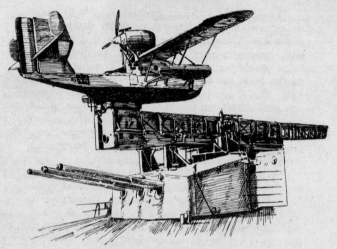

Gloire: Catapult atop rear 6″ turret

He went to the port side, which had a rope ladder
running along it. This side of the ship was gradually tipping
over towards the horizontal. He even found it rather funny to
be walking on the tilted hull as on a house roof, and to put his
feet by the side of the port-holes, to see the receding lines of
their closed eyes turned towards the sky. He crossed the long
red trail of the water-line, letting himself slide on the rusty,
gnarled hull. The sea was now a few yards away, near the
keel. He jumped for it.

His greatcoat impeded his movements. A wave came on
to him, lifted and then took him under. The water went into
the gaping hole where his nose had been. This was unexpected. He swallowed a good mouthful of salt water, and at once
spat it out; the water came out by the hole of his nose, by the
eyes. He nearly sank, but a raft passed within reach, and he
was able to catch on to it and so get his breath back. After
this he took care to keep his head above the water. Near him
was his friend Miller, who had gone the same way and
jumped into the sea soon after him. Miller could still hear
Lieutenant Tillie shouting to him: "She hasn't much longer,
quick, jump overboard." He slid along a rope which was
hanging: there were several of them, and this was Tillie's

work. The moment he touched the water, the rope came away, hitting the water with a loud smack, and Miller found himself in the sea near Coutts, between two rafts. Beside them the *Laconia* rested on the sea like a huge shark mortally wounded. Was John Tillie still on board trying to save a few more unlucky souls?

Hanging on to a raft, Miller and Coutts tried to push it away from the ship. They knew that in her death-throes she might make unexpected movements: might swing round abruptly, crushing them with her immense mass, or sink by the bows in one go, making a seething crater of the sea.

They tried to push the raft in front of them, but it didn't move an inch: it was still moored to the ship! Miller, a good swimmer, had taken off his shoes and coat. In his trousers pocket he found a small knife, and at once set to work cutting the rope. It was a good thick rope, quite new, and in the darkness, despite the rise and fall of the swell, he cut and sawed away, strand after strand. At last the raft was free, and the two men could push it away in all haste. The *Laconia* was still threatening them, standing against a blackish sky. Pushing frantically, they would sometimes glance at the ship to see how they were getting on. They made very slow progress: after ten minutes of intense effort they were barely sixty yards away. The ship seemed to have stopped her movement towards the sea. She was almost horizontal now, lying on her side. They could see her stern in the air, the screws out of the water, motionless, useless. Still hanging to ropes, clinging to emergency ladders, the last passengers were trying to escape. Who were they? British troops? Women, children, Polish guards, Italian prisoners? They were all equal in disaster.

It fact there must have been more people left on the *Laconia* than Coutts and Miller thought. There were the hesitant ones and the casualties lost in the darkness below with the sea roaring in, blinded and scalded by the jets and spirals of smoke from burst pipes and waterlogged boilers. Some were still wandering in the bowels of the lightless ship, as the sea took possession of her. None of these survived.

Ian Peel and Gladys Forster were among the last to leave. It was almost an hour since the ship had been hit, and they were still clinging to a rope ladder a few yards above the water. They heard cries of despair which were barely human.

Below Peel the heaving mass of heads and arms was like a picture of the Inferno. He thought he could still hear some-one calling him: "Peel... Peel..." There were such hun-dreds of noises: screams, spluttering, whistles of steam, the hull's creaking and groaning, the hollow noise of a ladder dropping abruptly on the surface of the sea, the bark of some unknown sea-creatures.

Peel let himself slip into the black waters. For the first time a cry rang out in three languages: "Sharks!... *Pescecani!* ...*Rekiny!*..."

In fact it was barracuda that were there, each about five feet long, gliding amidst the shipwrecked, taking off a piece of buttock, slicing an ankle, with one bite of their sharp teeth. For a brief moment the sea was dyed with blood, though this was not seen. But the horrible screams reached the ears of those who could still hear them. More formidable than two or three big sharks, which would have killed a few people in one bite, the barracuda attacked in complete shoals, stripping bodies of flesh piece by piece.

Peel saw a boat passing near. In a few strokes he was within reach of its hull, and could see by the mass weighing it down, by the water-line, that it was full to sinking. He was allowed into it, even so. It filled with water from the bottom and he had not been there ten minutes—ten minutes of respite—when it abruptly capsized, and everyone was back in the sea. An Italian who couldn't swim hung on to him. Peel lost his breath in a brief struggle to make the man let go, then found a piece of wood floating in the darkness. Clinging to it desperately, he began to get his breath back, when another prisoner tried to grab him. Rallying his last reserves of strength, he pushed the frantic Italian away.

At last he saw a raft and hung on to that. There was only one person on it, a woman, lying on her back, inert. From the water, four men, Italians, were clawing on to the sides with their nails. Peel was able to haul himself up and find a place on it by the woman—who proved to be Sister Hawkins. Of its own accord, as if pushed by the current, the raft moved away from the *Laconia*, while Peel gradually regained his strength. For a moment he closed his eyes, no longer caring what happened.

Mrs. Forster was certainly the last woman to leave the *Laconia*. She had lost her daughter Elizabeth in the jostling and the darkness, and wasted time looking for her. She searched the deck vainly for where her own boat should have been. Shoved and hustled, she hesitated a long time, till the deck was almost empty, looking at once desolate and distorted in the havoc of wreckage. At last a sailor told her: "Go aft, the captain's boat is going to be put to sea. Hurry."

This boat was the last to come off the ship. As soon as it touched the water, some Italian prisoners saw it was almost empty and began swimming towards it. Just then the ship's boilers exploded with a tremendous crash, and the explosion reverberated on the water and through the air. Everyone in the motor boat was shot into emptiness, then sucked towards the bottom of the sea. A curious detail: Mrs. Forster felt her shoes being pulled off her feet. When she came up to the surface again, the sea was still shaken by a thousand swirls and eddies. The *Laconia* was gone.

Gladys Forster began swimming, and managed to get on to a raft which already carried over a hundred people. All of them, and all those still struggling to save their lives, whether they were in the water, clinging to a piece of wreckage or a raft, or squeezed up in one of the lifeboats, had seen the old *Laconia* disappear. She had reared half out of the water, stayed motionless for a moment as if taking a final breath. Then abruptly, like a great monster, hissing and roaring, she sank. It was 9:25 p.m.

According to tradition, Rudolph Sharp, a British sailor, the son and father of sailors, had remained on the old ship's tilted bridge; but he was not alone. As he leaned over the rail one last time, assessing the disaster, he heard a voice behind him. It was George Steel, his second-in-command. "I'm staying with you, sir."

Those who raised their heads towards the *Laconia*'s bridge could see the brilliance of a shirt front, wide gold stripes and two hands gripping the rail, strong, almost luminous, standing out against the sky.

6

"AIUTO! AIUTO!"

8:15 p.m. on board U-156

Wilhelm Polchau's blond head appeared out of the conning-tower, to look inquiringly at Hartenstein and Mannesmann on the bridge.

"She's a goner," said Hartenstein. "Unfortunately she's given her position, and it won't do us any good to stay around."

"What about collecting her captain, though?"

Hartenstein made a gesture with his chin towards the sea, covered with wreckage, men swimming, and corpses. "Difficult to find him in that."

It was not the first time Hartenstein had sunk an enemy ship, but till now they had only been tankers and cargo-ships. He had seen their crews going down into the lifeboats, trying to save themselves. Some had been killed by the explosions and others drowned, but they were sailors, men used to risking their lives on the sea—it was part of their job. Here, he felt the case was different. There must be thousands of people on this ship. Most of them would not be sailors, there might be civilians, women, even children; now they were all shot into the sea by his act. "Still, that's war," he muttered to himself.

"30° starboard . . . 200 revolutions," Mannesmann ordered.

"Don't go too near," Hartenstein warned.

The *Laconia* was a mile ahead to starboard. The submarine was entering the zone in which there were more and more pieces of wreckage. She had to manoeuvre all the time so as not to hit a plank or a raft. It was nightmarish. The two officers and the helmsman could see men clinging to the flotsam, others swimming aimlessly. U-156 moved at a reduced speed, only three or four knots, towards death and destruction. Hartenstein was considered tough and unsentimental, and certainly it was hard now to read the thoughts behind that lean, impassive face with its aquiline nose, jutting chin and prominent cheek-bones silhouetted against the darkness.

The survivors could be seen distinctly, in their overcrowded boats, very low in the water. There was a necklace of grey balls, like fenders, round each boat. There were the bobbing heads still in the sea, people swimming or clinging to the ropes which festooned the boats' sides.

Silence reigned on U-156. Then the men on the bridge thought they heard cries of *"Aiuto! Aiuto!"* The two officers looked at each other in surprise, but the submarine went on, leaving the calls behind. The *Laconia* was in front of them, hissing, letting off jets of steam, her one funnel topped by a high column of black smoke, her deck still streaming with puppet-like figures.

Hartenstein had a clear view of her stern, lifted high out of the water, and on it a gun and gun-crew. No shot was fired, so apparently no one on the torpedoed ship had discovered the U-boat's presence. When she passed another boat, there was a movement of recoil among those in it, a squeezing together of heads and chests. Hartenstein fancied he could see women in the boat. They imagine I'm going to machine-gun them, he thought. Propaganda!

He wanted to watch the end of this ship.. Then he would send the C.-in-C. a signal, "Have sunk *Laconia*, 20,000 tons, British . . ." and continue his course southwards in search of new quarries, leaving the shipwrecked to their fate: after all, they had lifeboats and rafts. Besides, the *Laconia* had sent out an SSS, giving her position and warning the Admiralty of an enemy submarine's presence. It would be best to leave this dangerous area as quickly as possible. Also, he decided, it would be bad for his crew's morale to watch these people floundering in the water.

They saw another raft, went alongside it. There was one woman on it, half naked, and men still in the sea hung to its sides. Further cries of distress were heard in the darkness.

"*Aiuto! Aiuto!*" This time the calls for help were quite distinct. They came from two men clinging to a crate surrounded by scattered oranges floating on the surface.

"That's Italian," said Mannesmann.

"Yes, what do you make of it? Better have some of them fished out."

A few minutes later the two men grabbed a line thrown to them and were pulled aboard, haggard men with streaming clothes which stuck to their thin chests and flabby legs. They were brought before the commander, who was standing on the bridge, leaning against the top of the conning-tower.

"*Italiener?*"

"*Si, Italiani.*"

They began giving wordy explanations to Hartenstein, who did not speak Italian. He realized, even so, that something unexpected and serious had happened. Pointing to the men swimming round the U-boat, he repeated the question: '*Italiener?*" One of the two rescued men nodded and gave a figure, adding: "*prigionieri.*" From his slight knowledge of French Hartenstein guessed there were over a thousand, and that they were prisoners of war. He was aghast. The second man was still trembling with fear and anxiety, but a little reassured by the presence of an Axis submarine; surely this meant he was free again. He had a wound in the arm, a wide gash from which blood was flowing.

"*Una baionetta,*" he explained. "*Da un Polacco.*" Then he swore.

Hartenstein understood the word "Polacco." After Italians, Poles. How did *they* come into it?

"Take these men to the crew quarters and see they get something to revive them. Tell the cook to keep lots of soup on the go all the time. Coffee, too. Have the rum reserves brought out, only go easy on the distribution."

Meanwhile, the crew had hauled out other survivors, all Italians. Perhaps they had been the only people on her, except for her crew and a few women. They were all in a pitiful condition. Some were wounded, but these cuts on the heels and ankles and buttocks were fresh. They looked like cuts from a sharp knife, and did not come from bayonets. At last a corporal who spoke a little German, was uninjured and seemed less exhausted than the others, was brought before Hartenstein.

"How many of you Italians were there on the *Laconia*?"

"I don't know exactly, at least fifteen hundred."

"Fifteen hundred!" Hartenstein gave a start.

"We've been through hell on that British tub. Treated worse than animals we were. In the mornings they made us go on deck in the terrible cold, and then have icy water sprinkled over us. Those who objected to this torture were pushed under the icy water at bayonet point by the Poles."

"By the Poles? Why?"

"The British don't like being jailers."

A sailor brought a big bowl of milky coffee to the Italian corporal, who swallowed it in two huge gulps, wiped his lips with the back of his hand and continued:

"We all knew there were Axis submarines in the area. Oh, everyone's afraid of death, of course, but to die like that, shut up in the hold, unable to see the sun, the sky, the stars, without a chance to breathe the fresh air for the last time, to die suffocated behind bars—horrible!"

Imagining the death which might have been his, he crossed himself, and tears came to his eyes. But they did not flow: the pupils were damaged by the salt from the sea, the oil, all the floating dirt and cinders from the *Laconia*. Hartenstein made a sign to say: "That's enough, go and rest," but once launched the Italian could not be stopped: "When the torpedo hit the ship, I was alone in a corner, not doing anything. Friends had just called me to play cards. I got up... the explosion... the ship was lifted up... Packs, tables, ladders, lamps, all came to pieces. The smell of explosives got into our throats..."

Hartenstein put up his hand. "Ein Moment!"

Half a mile away the *Laconia* was sinking. Her stern was out of the water and silhouetted against the sky. There was a breathless pause. Then, with a roar, the ship slid to the bottom of the sea. The water shook and seethed, as if a volcano were suddenly going to erupt from the depths and spit out the ship, destroying everything still floating, including this tiny craft which was the cause of her death. Human beings, rafts, planks, hundreds of broken and bent pieces of wreckage, came to the surface again. Everyone on the submarine was silent; there was no sound but the hum of the diesels. The moon touched with silver the moving crests of

the waves. The pieces of wreckage drifted slowly with their
cargo of survivors.

Hartenstein turned to the Italian. "Go on," he said,
anxious now to break the silence.

"I ran to my life-belt, and put it on. I wanted to save
myself... Yes, I wanted to save myself. I took a friend in my
arms, and we silently embraced, while terror reigned around
us. They were crazy. One swore and shook his fists, another
was on his knees praying, another ran about and banged his
head, fell down, picked himself up, yelled. Another was
tearing his hair and weeping. Others, dumb with fear, frantic
or mad, were going in all directions, one of them grinding his
teeth like a wild animal. Then the second explosion came..."

As he spoke these words, the air and sea were shaken by
a dull explosion, followed by others, like mines that have
been set off. Their violence knocked over the men on the
bridge. Two sailors pulling out survivors on the bow fell
overboard. Hartenstein himself was hurled against the conning-
tower, but saw them go. "Get those men back, quick," he
shouted, and watched intently till the two men were back on
board. Then he glanced up at the sky. No plane in view, and
if there had been they'd have heard the whirr of its engines.
A ship? Apart from the boats sinking on the water, there was
no sign of any other craft.

"Perhaps the *Laconia* was carrying depth charges,"
Mannesmann suggested, "and they went off at a certain
depth. Lucky we weren't closer."

"I doubt it," said Hartenstein. "I don't think they'd have
gone off without being primed."

"More likely the boilers exploding," the Italian put in.

"Go below," Hartenstein told him. "We'll want to hear
more from you later. At the moment we've got other things to
do."

For a long while he stayed silent, reflecting. He had a
big decision to make, one affecting the life of his submarine
and crew.

The situation was clear enough: he had torpedoed a big
British ship—fine. But the ship contained nearly two thousand Axis soldiers, and that was catastrophic. True, these men
were prisoners, and therefore no use for continuing the war;
but although he didn't bother with high politics, he had a fair
suspicion that things weren't too good between the Axis

partners. They would not be improved by this torpedoing. Moreover, he remembered the ship off Aruba where there was dancing; he had let her pass without torpedoing her, admittedly so as not to betray his own presence. But here he had seen that raft drifting, with one woman lying on its planks, half naked and unconscious. She would not be the only woman who'd been on the *Laconia*. It went against the grain to let all these people drown.

Yet to decide this meant risking his submarine. The enemy had given her position on two wave-lengths. He'd tried to jam the messages, but too late; they would almost certainly have been heard. Enemy planes and ships could be expected at any moment, and they might well not respect a submarine busy picking up survivors. Rather than save a few lives they might prefer to send her to the bottom and stop her sinking more precious tonnage; a submarine with a trained crew wasn't easily replaceable. Yes, it was certainly reasonable for him to retire at once; and yet, and yet...

He went up on to the bridge again. Mannesmann, as if following his commander's train of thought, said, "By saving these Italians, we risk being attacked ourselves. Shall I ask the C.-in-C. for orders?"

"No, we haven't time. I'm deciding for myself. We go on with the rescue operation."

Just then the first British survivors were brought before him.

He hadn't said whether a distinction should be made between British and Italians, but everyone realized that all those in the sea must be rescued. For one thing, there was no choice; you could hardly throw a man back in the sea if he turned out to be British. In fact, the submarine was in an area where most of the survivors were Italians. Many were in as pitiful a state as the first two, with bayonet injuries as well as those caused by falls and shark-bites.

Soon the two torpedo compartments were filled with survivors. With so many people around, it was very hard to get through the ship's gangway. Only the control-room and the tower remained clear, on the commander's orders. He put the number of survivors on board at about ninety. Standing squeezed against each other, they joyfully swallowed the hot coffee they were handed, or avidly devoured a plate of soup.

As U-156 went alongside boats, women's and children's cries came up from them. The rescue operation was nearly beyond the submarine's powers, and yet they had to go on with it.

Polchau came up on to the bridge. He gave assurances that despite the exceptional overloading everything was working well.

Hartenstein took the counterfoil-book he always kept with him, wrote a signal and handed it to Mannesmann. "Get that transmitted."

"Aye, aye, sir." Mannesmann read the signal, which gave their position and went on:

Sunk British *Laconia*—unfortunately with 1,500[1] Italian prisoners. 90 rescued so far.

Five minutes later the signal was sent off in code.

7

NIGHT ON THE SEA

Buckingham floated to the surface. The sea was calm and peaceful. A warm, soft swell gently rocked his motionless body. There was no boat near him, no voice, no sign of life. Even the sea's murmurings seemed muffled, remote. The sky above him was a pale green, almost phosphorescent. He stayed lulled for some time in this strange tranquillity. Then he made a movement, and a stab of pain brought him back to harsh realities. His hand touched an object in his pocket, a cigarette case. Quite useless now. The stupid cigarettes reminded him of something, his wife's photograph. He felt under his shirt, but there was no photograph. He tried to remember, and had a picture of a cabin, looking as though a cyclone had

---

[1]This figure, based on the estimate of the first Italians rescued was repeated even in the Nuremberg Trials. In fact there were 1,800 Italians on board.

passed through it. At an angle of 45°, everything askew, the hanging calendar, the clock—he saw the hands at 9:10—the deck strewn with papers, the desk with all its drawers open.

Now it came back to him. At the last moment he had gone back to the cabin to get Dorothy's photograph, as if it might somehow protect him. Why hadn't he got it now, and why had he taken the cigarette case? Ah yes, he remembered: he had just shone a torch on the photograph and picked it up, when there was a dull explosion coming from below. He had realized the ship would not last much longer, and had dashed out of the cabin again, leaving the photograph in his haste.

He remembered crossing the hull of the heeling ship, following the line of the port-holes. Then he had taken off jacket and shoes, and found a place to dive from. When he had come to the surface again, he found the water seething and swirling, wide columns of spray shooting to the sky with a tremendous roar.

He drew a deep breath. It was good to be alive, however precariously. He was drifting back into a blissful somnolence when he was again pulled out of it, this time by a cry, a call for help. He swam a few strokes towards where it seemed to have come from, and found nothing. But he saw a tiny gleam of white, a pin-point in the vast expanse of the sea. It was a sign of life, and he swam vigorously in its direction. Now he could see nothing, not a glimmer. The night's silence enveloped him. He stopped swimming, then started again. After a while he found an overturned boat, so low in the water that its keel barely came above the surface. Two men were clinging to it; one was the *Laconia*'s second officer, Stokes.

"It's you, Buckingham! I've broken my leg." He was obviously in great pain, his face distorted.

Buckingham called to the other man for help. "Give us a hand. He's broken a leg. Let's haul him astride the keel."

After great efforts the two of them managed to pull Stokes out of the water and straddle him on the keel of the overturned boat. His right leg, fractured and disjointed, hung uselessly beneath the knee, forming an angle with the thigh. "Lie down, Stokes," Buckingham advised, "and hold on to the painter. Don't move, we'll stay with you."

Could this upturned boat hold firm all night with three men trying to hold on to it? Buckingham was trying to estimate the chances when a wave stronger than the rest submerged them, sweeping Stokes from his precarious support. But he managed to hang on to the boat, which hadn't sunk.

"Three are too many," said Buckingham. "Hold fast, Stokes. I'm going to try to find a boat that is still afloat. I'll come back and fetch you." He swam off into the night; he never saw Stokes again.

After his swim without a life-jacket, and the exhausting efforts to hoist Stokes on to the boat's keel, Buckingham thought it would be best to stop for a bit and keep afloat, conserving his strength as much as possible. The breeze had freshened, and the sea kept breaking in little waves on his face, sometimes covering him, making it hard for him to stay above the water without effort. Yet he would have to do just this all night. By turns, he floated, swam a few strokes, floated again. The cold was numbing his limbs, so he massaged them with one hand before going on swimming. The time passed very slowly. He wondered vaguely what time of night it was. He kept hoping to find something to hang on to, a plank or a crate, if not a raft or boat. But there was nothing, absolutely nothing. He stopped again, weariness crushing his limbs; for the first time he thought he mightn't survive, that he would drop off to sleep, and his defeated body would give up the struggle. He closed his eyes, and left it to the sea, the sea he knew so well, to keep him afloat a few moments more.

But suddenly, in a last desperate surge of energy, he began swimming again, vigorously this time, not sparing his forces. He swam for perhaps five minutes and stopped to listen. Nothing. He started again in another direction, stopped once more. He heard only the endless murmur of a sea utterly deserted. He decided it would be easier if he took off his vest and socks, but this brief undressing in the water exhausted him.

The night and the sea seemed infinite, merciless. He wondered why he had swum like this, why he had swum away from the area where the ship was sunk. Wouldn't it have been better to stay amidst the other survivors, the pieces of wreckage?

Till then, apart from a brief moment of depression, he had kept calm enough to weigh up his physical forces and more or less balance the resting periods with the swimming. But he felt that couldn't last much longer. As he let himself

relax on his back, his head met a solid object which was
floating. In his surprise he made a movement, and the object
dived so that he could feel it pass beneath him, could ride on
it. Then it sank, to reappear a few seconds later before his
horrified eyes: it was a body. It carried a life-belt. This was
the first thing he noticed. Was there still a breath of life in
the body? He looked at the face. It was the face of a man with
hair cut short, almost cropped, and he was dead. The body
seemed intact. "Why didn't he survive when the life-belt was
in good condition?" Buckingham asked himself, hanging on to
the drowned man's back. He told himself, too, that this
strange companion brought him unhoped-for help, that he
mustn't be parted from it. An hour passed like this, perhaps
two. The night seemed to be going on for ever, holding back
its minutes. The two bodies rose and fell with each wave,
thousands of times, with a monotonous regularity. At last he
saw the first faint gleam of dawn.

To all the survivors that night of September 12th–13th
seemed endless. Most of the people huddled in the boats
were at first utterly exhausted and had no clear thoughts.
Everything round them and on them was soaking wet. They
hadn't even the strength left to lift their feet out of the water.
After the great heat of the day, the night felt icy. Some braver
spirits took turns to row. The masters of the boats, or those
who had taken charge of them, tried in the darkness to make
an inventory of their contents, which in most cases were few
or nil. The less fortunate clung to rafts, or lay on them,
avoiding movements which might make them overturn.
Swimmers could be seen going from one plank to another,
from crates to rafts, in a desperate search for surer means of
survival—or, like Middleton the R.A.F. sergeant, trying to
join up with men of the same service. Above all they wanted
to be among their own kind. There were struggles with fists
or nails, to keep above the surface for a few moments more.

In the boats, after the initial stupor, people looked at
each other, counted their numbers, asked each other questions. "Did you see my mother go down into a boat? She was
behind me, and I'm afraid she may have fallen into the sea."
Nobody answered Molly Davidson.

In fact, her mother was in a boat astern of them, leaning
against the knees of the boat's master. She had found people

she knew: "Smithy," the handsome, smiling Air Force officer, and a Black Watch officer's wife, Mrs. Walker, who had lost her child. Smithy, trying to comfort her, was saying the child was sure to be in another boat.

About one o'clock in the morning they saw the shadow of a German submarine, doubtless the one which had sunk their ship. They thought it might well machine-gun them, and they were worried about having Italian prisoners in the boats with their excitability and lack of control.

While those in Mrs. Davidson's boat saw the U-boat gliding over the sea, others like Miller and Coutts heard the noise of her diesels. They called to her, but the noise was drowned in the spray. The two men were then in an empty boat, for which they had abandoned their raft. The water came up to its benches, but because of its buoyancy tanks it didn't sink. During the night the two men picked up three other survivors. Huddled against each other, they waited for the day.

Doris Hawkins was about a hundred and twenty yards away from the *Laconia* when the great ship sank, hissing and roaring.

An awe-inspiring sight. I thought of the men who had built her, of the money spent on her, the work she had done in peacetime and in war, the cargoes she had taken safely back and forth, our men whom she had carried to and from the theatres of war. Her epitaph would be: "The Admiralty regrets to announce that a ship of 20,000 tons has been sunk in the Atlantic. The next of kin have been informed." In sharp contrast I pictured homes where the shadow of anxiety and grief would lie, of men and women and little children, whose loved ones would never return: "Lost at sea by enemy action, September 1942."

I recalled my thoughts to hear the voices of Squadron Leader Wells and Lieutenant L. J. Tillie, R.N., D.S.C. and bar, calling to find if there were any more English people about. I answered the call, and Squadron Leader Wells swam towards me.

At that moment there was a loud explosion. It

was the bursting of the ship's submerged boilers, and sounded terrific through the water. I felt a sickening pain in my back, and Wells, facing the explosion, seemed to curl up just as we reached his and Tillie's raft. His condition improved as the night wore on, but he never lost his abdominal pain. My own back was injured, as was shown by an X-ray weeks later.

I was helped on top of the raft. There were nine or ten Italians clinging to it. Later we put them on to another raft, to which some more of their compatriots were clinging. Then all we who remained were British. One of them was Lieutenant Ian Peel, who had apparently joined me on the earlier raft after the ship sank.

In the water we had swallowed a good deal of thick oil from the wreck as well as sea-water, and in turn we were all violently sick. Our hair and faces were thickly covered with oil.

We were cheerful and even optimistic. I remember Wells saying: "This is a lie, it can't have happened to us"—and so it seemed, unreal, fantastic. We felt detached from it all.

Tillie seemed in splendid form; he cheered us with assurances of rescue on the morrow, led us in community singing and made us confident, at times almost merry. He decided each man should take it in turns to sit beside me on top of the raft, and they changed places every ten minutes. After a while he produced from his life-jacket a small flask of brandy, passed it round from time to time; and when the contents were getting low, someone let the salt water in. All he said was: "Salt! What a pity! Never mind."

Suddenly he became quiet, and I felt suspicious. He changed places with the man beside me, and leaned heavily against me. I felt his pulse and found it very weak, and I became very anxious. He spoke slowly and a little thickly in answer to my questions, though he declared he was all right. It was only then I noticed that his right shirt-sleeve was soaked in blood. We had nothing out there on a small raft with which to stop the haemorrhage. He refused to stay more than the allotted ten minutes out of the water. Wells supported him with one arm as he became exhausted. After some time he lost consciousness, and about midnight he died.

He had rallied the small naval draft he was in charge of, told them to help get the women and children away. He only clambered over the side when he saw the last boat go. As the ship was about to sink, he jumped, and injured his arm on the way down.

I took his watch and promised that if I ever reached safety I would somehow get it to his mother. It is in her keeping now; his name is engraved on the back.

Throughout the long night the men continued to sit beside me in turn. They were terribly cold in the water, and I out of it. My thin wet clothes clung to me, and I shivered and longed for dawn. We saw lights in the distance from time to time, showing the positions of other rafts, but we didn't contact any lifeboats. All through the night the mournful cry for help rose, and wailing from the Italians wherever they were. We occasionally met other rafts, carrying men and women; we passed doors, orange-boxes, oars, pieces of wood, large and small, with men clinging on desperately and crying for help. Sometimes our raft overturned and we were all flung off into the water; each time it was harder to get back, for our limbs were stiff and our fingers cold from clinging on so tightly. When at last dawn came, there was a fairly high sea; only occasionally did we glimpse any other raft or lifeboat as we rose on a crest . . .

In the stern of her boat Dorothy Davidson watched the sea growing pink. Near the boat one of the corpses floated with arms dangling, swollen like a goatskin bottle, kept on the surface by a life-belt, his face turned towards the sea. A wave lifted the body up, for a moment she caught a glimpse of the face and gave a cry of horror. It was John Tillie.

With a sudden luminous violence the sun rose. Day was

breaking on Sunday, September 13th, comforting the forlorn and frozen survivors with warmth and light.

8

RESCUE UNDER WAY

11:25 p.m., September 12th, Paris

All was quiet at the German U-boat Command, which was quartered in a large building on the Boulevard Suchet; there were sentries at the gates, while the Gestapo took care of the surroundings. Before the war this building had contained a large block of luxury flats, with wide bay windows looking out on to the Bois de Boulogne.

One of the flats had been maintained, and was now occupied by Vice-Admiral Karl Dönitz; it consisted of a bedroom, dining-room and office. Dönitz did not look his fifty years. He was slim, and everything about his features was somehow pointed: his nose, his large ears, his mouth carved like a sabre cut, his determined chin; his steely-blue eyes seemed to bore into the person he was talking to.

Since the outbreak of hostilities he had been in charge of the submarine arm, with the responsibility for all U-boat operations, the training of their crews, the maintenance of their morale, and the construction of new submarines—which was not going fast enough for his liking.

He was asleep after a harassing day, spent preparing for a conference in Berlin which Grand Admiral Raeder had fixed for the end of the month. On the maps of the North Atlantic Dönitz had had traced the "free space" in which his submarines could sail in complete safety, outside the range of attacks from enemy aircraft. This space was being reduced daily, and immediate plans had to be made to deal with the increasing threat. He had therefore written a report on the new British detection apparatus of Radar, whereby in May 1941, despite fog, the *Norfolk* and the *Suffolk* had been able to follow at a distance the powerful *Bismarck;* they had alerted the Home Fleet which assembled, tracked and finally sank her, though not before she had sent the *Hood* to the bottom in five minutes of combat.

At that time German naval headquarters knew nothing of Radar, and they had been taken entirely by surprise. Since then, although they did not have complete details and couldn't build a Radar apparatus themselves, the German services did have considerable knowledge of the Radar technique. The Gestapo had actually arrested a British expert with the secrets of Radar in his possession. One day he was brought into Dönitz's office, and the Admiral tried to get him to talk by using a friendly, man-to-man approach. He was unsuccessful. The Gestapo pushed the prisoner into another room, and questioned him again. They came to Dönitz more than once, asking him to authorize the use of "inhuman methods," but each time they were refused.[1]

In his report Dönitz set out the measures he proposed, which were to be submitted to Hitler: submarines to be equipped with new apparatus which would tell them if they had been located; priority for perfecting the Walter submarine with hydrogen peroxide turbine, that is to say, single propulsion both submerged and on the surface, and giving special speed when submerged. Finally—and here was the delicate point, in view of his difficult relations with Goering— the Admiral pressed for the Navy to be given sea-planes which could range up to 140 miles over the open sea, that is, the region of the convoys.

Dönitz slept. His uniform was near him on the back of a chair. Suddenly the telephone rang. It was Hessler's voice. "An important signal from Hartenstein has just arrived, sir."

"Good. Come to my office, I'll be waiting for you." He quickly put on his uniform, and soon afterwards Hessler was there. Tall and slim, with a mop of fair hair brushed back, with very clear blue eyes, Hessler was thirty-four and looked a little like the future Duke of Edinburgh. He and Dönitz did their best to forget, and see that others forgot, that he was

---

[1] I am quoting from the account of ex-Commander Hessler, who made the point that Dönitz refused to allow third-degree methods, although realizing that the lives of several thousands of Germans were involved, perhaps even the outcome of the war.

the Vice-Admiral's son-in-law. Dönitz, an officer in the 1914–18 war, served Germany through Hitler, with whom he had only service relations, though he admired the Führer's military successes; but Hessler, with the fervour and decided opinions of his age, was more deeply involved in the new Nazi Germany. Generally he had an easy, urbane manner, but if an argument arose on service matters, his eyes hardened, and you could guess that he was finding it hard to control a quick temper.

He handed Dönitz the first message from Commander Hartenstein to be decoded at the Paris headquarters. The Admiral took it and read it out loud, a habit he had. Then, after a long silence, he put it down on his desk, and said: "Good. Leave me."

All the curtains were drawn, and the room was in darkness but for a lamp on the desk, which illumined the sheet of paper like the beams of a projector on a target. The Admiral picked up the sheet and re-read it. The thing which struck him most was the figure of fifteen hundred Italians. In a world war so many Axis prisoners were a drop in the ocean, but these were *Italians,* and one of his submarines was responsible for what had happened. Occupied as he was with his U-boats and crews, he did not follow politics closely, but he was well aware that friction existed between his Führer and the Duce, that important decisions were taken on both sides without the slightest consultation. He knew above all that any new incident between the Axis partners must be avoided. In the first World War Marshal von der Goltz had impressed on him that you could not always find in another country's soldiers or sailors the qualities you expected yours to have; he had given orders for his German sailors based at Bordeaux to behave tactfully and without any trace of arrogance towards Admiral Parona's Italians, also based there. He imagined the political complications which might occur from this unfortunate torpedoing: that was one facet of the problem before him.

Another was equally important. He knew that from now on Hartenstein and U-156 might meet with disaster; they had taken risks which could lead to their destruction. He approved of Hartenstein and thought him a sound, if sometimes rebellious, officer—but then Dönitz liked men of character.

After all, he was himself one of the men who dared say "no" to the Führer on occasion.

He thought of Hartenstein, who had come to see him after the Aruba affair, troubled about the accident on board the submarine. He had congratulated the commander on the refineries set on fire, the tonnage sunk, and the repair of the gun. All he said about Lieutenant von dem Borne was: "He's at Fort-de-France, and I have good news of him." He was in fact intending shortly to make Hartenstein his Chief of Operations at headquarters, replacing Hessler, who had done his time on shore; he didn't want to be accused of favouring his son-in-law, and was stricter towards Hessler than towards any other officer.

For a moment the Admiral thought of giving the order to throw everyone into the sea and continue the mission. From a military point of view he would be right to do so. A U-boat is built to fight and not to rescue the shipwrecked. Moreover, the crew's fighting spirit might well be affected by the sight of these wretches being pulled out of the water, by the wreckage and corpses. On the other hand it was hard to imagine Hartenstein and his men pushing back into the sea the people they had pulled out a few hours before—even without the screams and curses they would have to face. It was then that the crew's morale would be most seriously affected, and their high morale was one of his chief preoccupations. At this very moment Hartenstein was saving these survivors from almost certain death; should he, the Admiral, give the order to hurl them into the sea? Impossible!

He must help Hartenstein, give him his support. U-156 mustn't stay alone amidst these thousands of survivors in the sea. The submarine had taken ninety of them on board; would she be able to dive in case of attack? Probably, for she was sturdy and manoeuvrable, and Polchau, her chief engineer, was a skilful and experienced officer. But the Admiral still felt he must warn them, give them an order: "Stand by to dive at any time."

For the first time he thought of possible help: what about engaging other U-boats, ordering them to converge on the area where Hartenstein was? That was one solution—only it might cause the loss of not only U-156 but the vessels going to her aid. All these thoughts seethed in Dönitz's mind. What should he do?

He went to the window overlooking the Bois. Paris was calm, asleep. Most people were in bed; a few working, fleeing or hiding. Far away from here, in mid-ocean, U-156 was rescuing shipwrecked people, the survivors of a ship she herself had sunk.

It was about half past three when the Admiral walked briskly over to the desk, his decision taken. He sat down, took a sheet of paper and wrote: "Schacht, Würdemann, Wilamowitz, head for Hartenstein at full speed. Square 7721..."[1]

A few minutes later the message had been coded and was transmitted to the wireless station at Melun, which told the three U-boats that they were to go to Hartenstein's aid.

Admiral Dönitz returned to his room. He knew by experience and instinct that he would have to stay at his post a long time. He tried to sleep, but in vain. He saw himself as a young man again, commander of a submarine.

On board U-507

U-507 was commanded by Lt.-Commander Harro Schacht, aged thirty-three. Married, with two young daughters, he came from a well-to-do family, was always correctly turned out, had a calm voice and manner, and the modest air of a sailor doing his duty as a matter of course. Entering the Navy in 1926, he passed out first from the Naval College. He had little regard for the Nazis, and in this respect almost all U-507's crew shared his opinions. The chief engineer, Peter Ahlfeldt, aged twenty-seven, came from a prosperous Hamburg family, and was even known as an Anglophil. So was Ekkard Scherraus, then second warrant-officer, also from Hamburg and four years Ahlfeldt's junior. He had a beard and long wavy hair; ashore, his turn-out was as impeccable as a pre-war English yachtsman's. He and Ahlfeldt set the tone in the ward-room, and Schacht regarded them with amused tolerance.

Börner, the first warrant-officer, aged twenty-four, had been a Hitler Youth leader and was a rabid Nazi; he could not be expected to approve of his fellow-officers' outlook. Apart from his criticism, sometimes forcibly expressed, the atmo-

---

[1]Messages from headquarters gave the submarine commander's name, or even Christian name, rather than the vessel's number, which was sometimes changed.

sphere aboard was excellent, nor was discipline impaired by the element of light-heartedness. In the evenings the sailors would often gather round a loudspeaker, to listen to English records from Scherraus's collection. Amongst these officers the enemy was respected, admired and sometimes imitated.

U-507 had sailed into the Gulf of Mexico, gliding boldly into the midst of convoys and sinking her fair share of cargo-ships and tankers. Later she was ordered along the coasts of Guinea, then down the coast of Brazil. In the evenings Scherraus and Ahlfeldt enjoyed seeing the gaily-lit villas, the car headlights suddenly revealing lovers locked in each other's arms. One day they watched a game of tennis through their binoculars, and would have given anything to go ashore and play a set with these young, attractive girls.

Among U-507's torpedoed ships were five Brazilian ones. In sinking them she unwittingly made history, for this was the cause of Brazil's declaring war on Germany three weeks later (August 22nd, 1942), claiming that the ships were sunk within her territorial waters. Germany insisted they were outside those waters.

On the night of September 11th, the submarine sailed from the American coasts for Freetown. By 8:15 p.m. on the 12th she had covered two-thirds of the distance. Scherraus was on the bridge, much struck by the beauty of the night, when a wireless operator brought him a message. It was Hartenstein's announcement that he had torpedoed the *Laconia*, and that there had been fifteen hundred Italian prisoners on board. Schacht was informed at once, and came up on the bridge to discuss it. "If Hartenstein's picking up survivors," he commented, "it must mean the *Laconia* was travelling alone, without escort."

"It's amazing," said Scherraus. "With those numbers on board, you'd have thought there'd be some ship near to come to her aid."

"Oh, all their shipping is well tied up, you can bet. Still, it's odd she wasn't in a convoy."

News travels fast in a submarine. Everyone was talking about it in the control-room, and soon in the crew space from hammock to hammock. "Hartenstein will be needing a hand," was the general opinion, and Schacht thought so too. He ordered a slight increase in speed. The submarine continued on her course.

At 1:55 a.m. on the 13th Admiral Dönitz's order arrived. Schacht noted that his name came first in the order, probably because he was nearest to Hartenstein's area. He went down into the conning-tower, studied the compass and determined his own position on the map, then sent off a return message:

Am making for point of torpedoing 750 miles distant at 15 knots. Can be there in two days. Schacht.

He returned to the bridge and told Scherraus the plan, adding, half to himself: "Forty-eight hours is a long time, much too long."

On board U-506

U-506, under Lt.-Commander Würdemann; was U-507's sister submarine. They had been commissioned at the same time, and had done their tests together. They had both carried out their mission in the Gulf of Mexico and been in action together; but then they were sent in different directions. While Schacht's U-507 was operating on the north coast of South America, U-506 moved up towards New York. There she sank an American auxiliary cruiser armed with twenty-six guns of all calibres. There was the usual rivalry between the two submarines over tonnage sunk, and Würdemann could claim nine ships in the Gulf of Mexico besides the cruiser.

He commanded U-506 from the time she was commissioned, in September 1941, till she was sunk in July 1943 in the Bay of Biscay; he went down with her. He too was from Hamburg, and had nothing of the typical German officer about him. He even looked rather Latin, with black curly hair, fine regular features, brown eyes and very thick eyebrows. He was unmarried, and was the eldest of the submarine commanders, though he looked much younger than his forty years. He was a popular commander, very much of the old school in his general attitude of "Discipline and hard work when you're at sea; do what you like on shore but avoid scandal."

At noon on September 11th, U-506 crossed the Equator, and the traditional "crossing the line" celebrations took place, with Chief Engineer Glasow officiating, and another officer acting Neptune.

The heat was terrific that night, and again on the 12th. At eight o'clock nobody felt like sleep, even those who would be going on watch at midnight. If Würdemann had allowed it, the whole crew would have slept in the open, in the "winter garden," or on the deck behind the bridge. A smell of oil and fuel came up from below, and everyone put off the moment of going down and slinging their hammocks. Finally the commander shouted from the bridge: "Everybody off watch go below," and the men reluctantly left the relative cool of the "winter garden." The submarine was enveloped in a stifling fog of heat.

Suddenly Würdemann thought he saw the shadow of a huge ship pass. The vision had been so swift and brief that he wondered for a moment if it hadn't been a hallucination due to weariness and this hazy atmosphere. But Schneewind, the first warrant-officer, standing beside him, had seen it too. What on earth could she be, this ship which had appeared to them so colossal—perhaps because of the fog and because the submarine was so low on the water? But hard as they looked and listened, they saw and heard nothing more. For ten minutes Würdemann kept up fourteen knots, then he decided to waste no more fuel chasing after a phantom vessel. Since chance had brought her near him once, he hoped it would do so again. He returned to a more economical speed.

At a quarter past eight Rüter, one of the wireless operators, recorded Hartenstein's announcement. The first warrant-officer decoded it, and two minutes later Würdemann, having come down into the conning-tower, was given the message. "Nearly twenty-thousand tons—m'm. Pity, I might have sunk her. Still, good for Hartenstein. Except for those fifteen hundred prisoners in the sea." When he thought about that, Würdemann didn't like it at all. "Ninety extra men on board, that's a bitch for him. He'll need help. Full speed ahead." U-506 resumed her fourteen knots, heading for the scene of the sinking.

At five minutes to two Rüter received another message, the order from Admiral Dönitz to head for Hartenstein. Advised at once, the commander gave new orders: "See the ward-room is emptied, and hammocks are slung there. We're going to take a lot of people on board. Prepare the surgical dressing-cases."

He went below to the control-room, and slid through the

round panel separating it from the forward torpedo compartment. The men were clearing a space between the torpedoes and slinging four hammocks there. Satisfied, Würdemann returned to the control-room and went aft to his tiny cabin. He wouldn't be sleeping there tonight, but no matter: he was used to long, wakeful nights.

Two yards farther on, the cook was already leaning over a boiler, with an assistant squatting at his feet, peeling potatoes. The "old man" went on to the engine-room for a word or two with Glasow, and finished his inspection in the stern, where the men were arranging hammocks. Then he went back on his tracks, to climb to the bridge again. The fog had vanished, and a few stars could be seen. It was a magnificent night.

On board U-459

U-459, of the 7th Flotilla from St. Nazaire, was not a submarine like the others. Her tonnage was much bigger—nearly 1,700 tons to their 740—and she had no torpedo tubes. Her only defence was a 37-mm. anti-aircraft gun forward, and two heavy machine-guns. Having 700 tons of fuel on board, she was the group's "milch-cow," capable of giving the others from 400 to 600 tons, according to how much her own engines used. Thanks to her, Dönitz hoped to have 90 tons supplied to each of the submarines of the Polar Bear Group in the area off Capetown, which would enable them to get to the Mozambique Channel. They were to signal their fuel stocks on short wave between 5° north and the Equator, and the rendezvous with the fuelling submarine was fixed for September 20th.

Her commander, von Wilamowitz-Möllendorf, known to his crew as "Wild Moritz," was an old submariner of the first World War.[1]

Leaving St. Nazaire on August 19th at 3 a.m., U-459 took her place on the far starboard tooth of the rake. Being heavy and not very handy, she did her best to avoid Allied aircraft by first sailing westwards, submerged to two hundred

---

[1] It will be noticed that all the U-boat commanders involved entered the Navy before the Nazi regime, or at least were not trained in Nazi naval schools. From 1943 on, these commanders having disappeared, U-boats were commanded by younger men, often less competent, and with a different outlook.

and sixty feet by day, and remaining on the surface at night, when her batteries were recharged. Even so, she was attacked twice by planes, at midnight and at two in the morning, and had to dive quickly and surface again a quarter of an hour afterwards. Unfortunately a breakdown occurred in her new sounding apparatus, the Metox. A hundred miles west of Ferrol, she came out of the danger zone, and sailing on the surface headed south at a speed of seven knots.

On September 2nd, St. Nicholas, one of the Cape Verde Islands, was in view. The following morning in very fine weather they passed the island of Fogo. The next afternoon, they had some excitement: a boat under sail, in mid-ocean. Wilamowitz gave orders to approach it. As he thought, it was a lifeboat, and it contained four white men and twelve mulattos. Their ship had been sunk off Trinidad, and the boat had been driven by winds and current into mid-Atlantic. They were given food and cigarettes, and the helmsman was shown on a map the boat's position in relation to the Cape Verde Islands. Waving good luck, the submarine left them and sailed on.

It became hotter and hotter below, and Wilamowitz had a new device set in motion, which had been fitted before they left for tropical regions. The temperature in the crew space fell quickly from 105° to 70°. On September 12th U-459 crossed the Equator.

On hearing Hartenstein's announcement that he had sunk the Laconia, Wilamowitz considered changing course, but decided against it. His submarine was too far away to be able to give the slightest help.

When he received Admiral Dönitz's order at 1:55 a.m., he worked it out again on the map and reached the same conclusion. Schacht and Würdemann were both nearer Hartenstein than he was, and would head towards U-156 at full speed. He was definitely too far away, he would get there after the others when everything was finished, having wasted the fuel so essential if the Polar Bear Group was to continue its expedition. He would, of course, be disobeying his Admiral's order, but a commander worthy of the name must be able to take such responsibilities.

Five minutes later he gave his orders: "Normal speed eight knots—direction south-east."

With good reason "Wild Moritz" left the task of rescuing the *Laconia*'s shipwrecked to the two other submarines nearer the scene.

9

THE LONG SUNDAY

On Sunday, the 13th, the torments of the day proved almost worse than those of the night for any survivors still unrescued. Doris Hawkins's account goes on:

> The sun came up and warmed us; it rose higher and scorched us. By midday an Equatorial sun was blistering our arms, legs, faces and every exposed surface. An Army captain shared his emergency chocolate ration with us. An orange floated by— someone grabbed it—we divided it and chewed the peel for hours.
>
> During the morning I saw a vessel on the horizon. I told the men, who could see nothing and thought it was a product of my imagination. After a time I could see it was light in colour and hoped it was a hospital ship. Soon we could all see quite clearly that something was coming towards us. We made out that it was a U-boat travelling on the surface, and it passed within two hundred yards of us. Our hearts pounded. We had heard so many "atrocity stories"—we feared showers of machine-gun bullets. The U-boat passed on and stopped about half a mile away. We drifted very slowly in the same direction, and after some time came up to a raft on which there were two R.A.F. officers and one Italian. We joined their raft to ours with a rope.
>
> We were now nine on two rafts. One or two, too exhausted to hold on any longer, had dropped

off into the sea. Around us in every direction there were now corpses and wreckage, from time to time other survivors on rafts and pieces of wood.

The submarine moved from place to place, and once we saw people being pulled on board by means of a life-line. Wells decided to try to make for the submarine. Normally he was a magnificent swimmer. Summoning all his strength, he tied a tow-rope around his body and struck out, towing two rafts and nine people. Lieutenant Peel followed him at once, helping him. When we were within a few hundred yards of the submarine, it set off in another direction. Wells and Peel were exhausted and very disappointed, and for the rest of the day we just drifted around.

At one time I felt a sudden sharp pain in my right hand, which was hanging in the water. A purple jelly-fish, said to be deadly poisonous, had stung me; its sting, a long violet-coloured tentacle, was wound round my hand, completely detached from the jelly-fish itself. I shook my hand, and the sting fell off, but unfortunately it hit one of the men and wound round his hand, stinging him in turn. Our hands and arms swelled violently. With a stick another man beat the jelly-fish against the side of the raft and killed it. Some time later a third man grasped the end of the stick, on which some of the poison must have remained. At once he felt a stinging pain in the palm of his hand, and his hand and arm swelled too. The pain was intense, but we each held our affected limbs in the sea for hours and nothing worse occurred. They took some days to subside.

The day wore on, and I pictured my family in church. I knew that they and my friends, both in Palestine and at home, would be praying that I might reach home safely. In that moment I felt a conviction that somehow we should be saved.

The sun was low when a second submarine appeared. The sun set; we began to dread a second night. Suddenly the first submarine turned and

came straight towards us. German sailors threw us a
life-line, and we were all taken aboard...[1]

Whereas they had at least been together, Buckingham
had spent most of the night with the corpse he had found.
Indeed he had kept on the surface by leaning on the man's
floating back, and had sometimes even forgotten that this
stranger was dead. At dawn the bluish-green glints of the
sea faintly lit up the face, and he could see that it was
a man of about forty; by the clothes he recognized it as
one of the *Laconia*'s crew. The body bore no trace of
struggle, and only the shoes were missing, probably taken off
before the man jumped into the water. He felt a bond had
somehow been forged between them by the hours they had
spent together, and that he would lose something indispensable
if the body disappeared. He could not bring himself to strip
it of its life-belt, and merely caught hold of the strings
which hung from the belt.

His strength and courage returned, and he was sustained
by a great hope. His watch still read 9:20, the time at which
he had jumped into the sea the evening before. The stars
grew dim and disappeared, wiped out by a pale pink sun
which rose majestically. The day would be burning hot, and
with the vast expanses of water in front of him he knew he
would stay dry-throated, without saliva. With the clarity of
day the drowned man's face appeared to him in its horrible
details: popping, glassy eyes, lips cyanosed and swollen. Now
he was aghast at this corpse, and had only one idea, to get
away from it, to find a living being like himself, to be able to
talk and hear words.

But the corpse was still useful as support, to inspect the
horizon, come out of the water a little, hoist himself up as
high as possible. A dozen times he would seize its shoulders
and lean on them to get his head well above the surface and
look in all directions in turn. Each time the corpse went
down an inch or two. Exhausted, he was going to give up,
when he saw a sort of protuberance in the sea, far away to the

---

[1]*Translator's note:* Miss Hawkins remains quite certain that there was in fact a
second submarine. Her identity is still a mystery, however, since of course none of
the rescuing submarines had arrived in the area by then.

south: the heads and shoulders of two men. He realized at once that as they were not swimming they must be keeping up without moving on something which floated; but he couldn't see what it was.

An oar perhaps. Yes, it was certainly an oar that one of them was clasping in his arms. The sight of these two living people, far off as they were, seemed to him like a blessing from Heaven. He was overcome with joy, which in retrospect he found excessive. Giving a last glance at the corpse, he abandoned it and began swimming in the direction of the two men.

It must be about nine o'clock, he thought. The sea was a bit rougher, and he went up and down with each wave. He stopped quite often to get his breath back and rest. For an hour he swam in a southerly direction. Sometimes the two men and their oar vanished dishearteningly. Suddenly, quite near, he saw a boat come out of the waves. Its gunwale could be made out distinctly, with a compact mass of men on it. It moved away. He was completely confident that he would reach it and be saved. It had gone farther away now, but he swam stubbornly in that direction.

An hour later he was within fifty yards of it. The free-board was less than a foot above the water, and it was crammed to overflowing with people squashed against each other. It couldn't have held another person. Apart from a line of men sitting on the gunwale, hands and arms locked so that no one should fall into the sea, they were all standing. The boat was surrounded by a wreath of heads, shoulders, arms, to a radius of ten yards: survivors buffeted and broken by each movement of the waves, but clinging desperately to the fenders, the stern, each other, anything to keep them afloat.

In the stern Buckingham could distinguish the young ship's doctor, Geoffrey Purslow, standing a good head above the others. On the point of calling to him, he thought better of it, because Purslow seemed to have his attention elsewhere. As he reached the outer ring of the swimmers, one of them held out a hand to him, and Buckingham seized it silently. He stayed half an hour amidst the people bobbing up and down in the water, till he was able to get near the stern and call: "Purslow!"

Purslow looked down and recognized him.

"Any other boats round here?" Buckingham asked.

"Yes, one, to the east—but a good way away. It doesn't seem to have many people in it."

"What about the *Laconia*'s officers?"

"I saw Ellis round this boat at dawn, but since the middle of the morning he's disappeared. Hope he's found another boat. I'm afraid there are sharks about."

Buckingham's face must have shown dismay, for Purslow went on: "They're keeping at a distance and have only attacked people on their own. Stay near us."

But as there was no room for him in the boat and he still had enough strength, Buckingham decided to look for the half-empty boat. He swam away with a vigour which surprised himself. Sometimes he stopped to look round him and beneath him. He thought of the sharks. If one of them attacked him, he probably wouldn't even see it coming. He set off strongly again. About half an hour after leaving Purslow, he saw the other boat. It was still a good way off, about fifty minutes' swimming. Haunted by the thought of the sharks, he kept up his speed despite extreme weariness. Slowly, all too slowly, he saw the boat grow larger, and sometimes wondered if he would ever reach it. But at last he was near enough to shout "Ahoy!"

The men saw him, he was handed an oar and seized it by the blade. Two yards less to swim—thank heavens. Breathless and dead-beat after a night and morning in the water—with no other support but the corpse—he flopped into the bottom of the boat, which was like a sea-water bath. His arms and legs ached, and a glance at his hands showed them swollen, white and shapeless. Indistinct, unfamiliar voices reached him, muffled and booming.

After a while, feeling his strength returning, he made an effort to sit up. Someone helped him, and it seemed to him that the men round him were Italians. But there was one R.A.F. man, in a surprisingly complete uniform.

"How's this—are you the only Englishman?"

"The boat left the *Laconia* with these Itis. During the night they pulled me out of the water. There are fourteen of them."

So they were two British in mid-Atlantic, in a boat with prisoners who could now consider themselves liberated. True, the Italians had so far been friendly and helpful, but partly for safety's sake Buckingham thought it would be best to

contact Purslow's boat; also he could then take a few from
that overcrowded boat into this one. Almost all the oars were
in place, and on his order the Italians began rowing. Meanwhile, he made an inventory of what his present boat contained. All the fittings were intact, the sails in their cover, the
mast and rigging complete. There was even a compass which
could be used for taking bearings later on. The boat moved
slowly, for the rowers were both inexperienced and exhausted;
moreover, although an Italian was baling out the water, he
was not very successful and the boat became heavier. Everything was done in silence, no word was spoken, only the signs
and gestures between Buckingham and the Italians served as
means of expression. At any rate the prisoners seemed very
co-operative, or perhaps they were so dejected that they
obeyed blindly. Holy pictures fallen from a missal were
floating in the bottom of the boat.

The sea had got up, and he decided it would be dangerous to get nearer than fifteen yards to Purslow's boat. He
counted at least twenty-four people in it, and there looked a
good hundred swimming round it. Soon he was near enough
to shout: "Purslow!"

Purslow looked round.

"Tell these men to swim towards me. I can't come any
nearer."

But only one man left the rest and swam a few strokes
towards Buckingham's boat, then returned to his companions
in distress. Either he was too tired to swim the few yards in a
rough sea; or else he preferred to stay in the circle of men he
had been with all night; their solidarity was cemented by fear,
the fear of sharks and of being left on their own.

As an officer of the *Laconia*, Buckingham felt responsible
for these people. He made sure there were no sharks in
sight, then dived into the clear water and swam nearer the
heads and shoulders and arms. "My boat is almost empty...
Follow me..."

A dozen Italians broke away from the mass. When they
got near Buckingham's boat, their compatriots helped them
to haul themselves on to the gunwale. Buckingham made
several journeys, and now Purslow was encouraging the other
swimmers to make for the second boat. Seventy-three men
were thus pulled out of the water, among them a British
signalman.

"I can see two half-empty boats coming towards us," Purslow shouted, as Buckingham swam towards the doctor's boat for the last time. When Buckingham got back to his, the two men continued their conversation from one boat to another.

"We should be able to get everyone left in the sea into boats."

"Have you got food and water?"

"Very little, not enough for everyone. How many days are we from land, Buckingham?"

"Thirty days by sail, perhaps more."

"Do you think anyone can come to our rescue?"

"Yes. Our wireless has given bearings several times. I know that, I was at the operator's side."

Buckingham was well aware that the *Laconia* had taken a course outside the convoy routes. British convoys sailing round Africa kept close to the coasts, where they had air protection from Freetown, and the French didn't go down beyond French Equatorial Africa. He also knew that all these people could not survive on a voyage of over five hundred miles with only a few biscuits, a few Horlicks tablets, and so little fresh water. But his answer to Purslow was designed to reassure those who heard and could understand it; and he concluded, again for their benefit: "We'd better stay here a few more hours."

One of the Italians on board knew a few words of English. Through his interpreting, the others learnt that Buckingham intended to hoist sail on the next morning, and was going to organize the distribution of food and fresh water between the eighty-six Italians and three British. During the hours which followed, Buckingham instructed his two compatriots how to set sail. Two other boats having come up, plans were made for the night: all the boats were to keep close together; each boat to have a hurricane lamp ready, but to light it only in case of bad weather, if they were driven a long way from the others. Only Buckingham's boat would keep a lamp burning at the masthead all night, as a guide mark.

When night came, everybody left in the sea had been taken into one of the boats, and the inventory had been made. The boats kept at a fair distance so as not to risk fouling each other, but near enough for the look-outs not to lose sight of the beacon on Buckingham's mast. No one in the boats would be able to lie down, space was too precious. Watches had been fixed, also shifts for baling out water. Those on the periphery could sit on the gunwale; but they were so dead tired that they were in danger of dropping off to sleep and falling into the sea when the boat swung in the swell.

One of the three Britons had to be on watch all the time, so as to see signals the other boats might give, and also, it must be said, to keep the Italians under British control— these enemies who had become temporary allies in the common struggle against death.

"I'll take the next turn," Buckingham said to the R.A.F. man at midnight. "Lend me your watch, will you? Then I can hand over at four without having to wake you."

Slowly the hours passed. Buckingham looked up at the stars, some bright, some in a sort of halo, in small clusters. The hurricane lamp at the mast-head raked the sky in an incessant, monotonous, regular movement. Other boats appeared for brief moments on a phosphorescent sea.

One of them, commanded by Walker, the *Laconia's* first officer, contained forty-eight people, including three women and two children. About thirty Italians had to stay all night in the water hanging on to the boat's painters. He could do nothing for them except speak periodical words of encouragement, though in the morning he was to take a few of them into the boat, making sixty-four occupants in all.

A mile or so away Mrs. Davidson was lying back against the knees of the man at the tiller. It was still the same man, for he had practically no work to do, and there was no point in taking turns. She was wrapped in a blanket someone had passed to her, but she could not sleep for worry. Where's Molly? she kept asking herself. Perhaps she's in one of those boats I saw going past us. But the people in them were squeezed so tight you couldn't recognize anybody.

She couldn't get out of her head the sight of Lieutenant Tillie's body, held up by his life-belt. Then her thoughts went to Smith, the Air Force officer, who for some obscure reason had threatened to kill one of the Italians; to Mrs. Walker, the Black Watch officer's wife, still desperate at having lost her child. Mrs. Davidson, on the other hand, still felt sure she would see her daughter again.

At last she dropped off to sleep for an hour. Then she

woke with a start, and looked at the sea, this sea with shoals of sharks around. She wondered how many survivors were still alive in the water; there couldn't be many. All through the day swimmers had been pulled out, but many of them hadn't been able to get into the boat. So they stayed hanging on to the sides, and finally let go. Sometimes she fancied she could hear their calls for help, growing fainter and then dying away altogether.

At one o'clock in the morning, she thought she could hear a noise of engines, probably those of the submarine which had passed near them the afternoon before. She could still picture the submarine commander, with his bird-of-prey head, hear his voice saying in guttural English: "Are there any wounded among the Italians? I am taking them on board." So that damned German is only concerned with Italians, she had thought.

About twenty of them had gone on to the submarine. Then the German commander had continued with a ring of sincerity in his voice: "I am sorry for you, but your ship was armed as an auxiliary cruiser. You will surely be rescued, since wireless messages were sent. I shall not attack rescue ships."

The sound of engines was an illusion. Mrs. Davidson could hear nothing but the confused noises of the sea: the lapping of a wave as it came out of the sea, swelling with a roar, then dying in distant murmurs. She was terribly thirsty, and opened her mouth to catch a little of the night's moisture. In the afternoon she had received a biscuit and a bar of chocolate, but she hadn't been able to drink more than a mouthful of water from Smithy's bottle, and the boat's tank was empty. Now, as day broke, she could see the lines of a boat quite near, but it was not yet light enough to make out the people in it. Perhaps Molly was there... The sun appeared and talk started in the boat. She joined in, so as to stop herself thinking.

On the Sunday morning, when the numbers in Miller's boat were counted, there proved to be nine British and six Italians. Among the former was Rose, the *Laconia's* senior second officer. Being the eldest and the most experienced, he naturally took charge. The bottom of the boat was staved in, and it was leaking badly. The fifteen men had taken turns all night baling out the water with a bucket. They had also taken a bundle of gear from a locker and put that over the main hole.

Rose saw a group of four boats some way off, and decided to make for them. When his boat was near enough, he and his men called, but nobody seemed to pay any attention to the calls, so they gradually moved away. In the afternoon they saw other boats towards the north, and a submarine which seemed to be making a tour of the boats. They wondered if it was the one which had sunk them.

At the end of the day they saw her heading for them again, and this time she hove to close by. Three men were on the bridge, and sailors forward and aft were giving soup to the rescued, mostly Italians. The hatchet-faced man with his white cap pushed back was certainly the commander. He shouted to them in English: "Any wounded on board?"

"No," said Rose.

"Do you need help?"

A moment's reflection, then again: "No."

"Right. You will soon be rescued from Ascension, and perhaps from Dakar. I have done the necessary."

"Is there any room on other boats?" Rose asked. "We're leaking badly."

"I will see what I can do."

The submarine moved off.

Rose then had the mast and sail rigged. He knew the sail was useless, because the weight of the water made any tacking impossible, and as there was no compass they couldn't follow a fixed course anyhow; but the activity would occupy their minds for a while. Suddenly Miller saw a big raft drifting. They recovered it and tied it to the boat's stern; in case of disaster, it could always be used.

Ben Coutts, his spirits as good as ever, cheered everyone up, even the Italians. They didn't understand what this giant was telling them, but he inspired confidence. "Och, we'll be rescued in a few hours," he kept repeating.

But alas, the boat was drifting, and rapidly moved away from the other boats collected to await rescue. For the first time Rose distributed food: biscuits, pemmican, Horlicks tablets and even a little to drink, very little. Now the other boats were only visible as dots when one rose on the crest of a wave. Everyone was worried by the growing isolation.

In this boat, as in the others, there was no protection against the sun, and skins began to grow red with burns. The only shade was a little corner by the sail. Coutts maintained his optimism, although his foot was hurting, and he even got a little fun out of his turn-out. "A Scotsman caught in his pyjamas, it's no' the thing."

The water was still rising in the boat, reaching ankle height. Everyone knew it would never keep afloat till the next day. Seven o'clock; night would be falling abruptly. Rose consulted Coutts and Miller, then took a decision: the Italians must go over on to the raft. But how to make them understand the need to lighten the boat for the common good, perhaps for their own salvation? Coutts used smiles and expressive gestures, Rose gave them some food. Without much pressing five of them went on to the raft. Only one lost his head, cried "Mamma mia!" several times, then toppled into the sea, where he drifted for a moment before disappearing.

After the tropical heat of the day they found the night icy. They had water up to their ankles, and felt that it was rising all the time. They could see shadows on the raft, some stretched out, some sitting up with feet in the sea. No glimmer came from the other boats, there was no sound of any submarine engines.

When the sun rose, the nine Britons saw a deserted sea, an infinity of water—not a boat in sight. On the raft still tied to their stern only one Italian was left.

10

ORDERS AND COUNTER-ORDERS

Sunday, September 13th, 4 a.m.

Sitting at his little desk, Hartenstein started writing up the log. Having given the submarine's position, he went on:

Visibility moderate. Sea calm. Sky very cloudy...
According to the Italians' information, the British,
after being torpedoed, closed the holds where the
prisoners were. They used arms in driving back
those who tried to get to the lifeboats.

He put down his pen for a moment. Was it really true?
He knew the British well, and could not believe them
capable of such monstrous behaviour. Yet he had questioned
two or three of the Italians through an interpreter, and even
allowing for their Latin volubility and tendency to exaggerate,
the basic details of all their versions were identical. One
human skeleton, dressed in rags, whose name was Dino
Monti, poured out the following description of the scene:

"In the hold, exits closed, shots rang out. Blood began to
flow in the cages. The Polish guards had opened fire, and
were driving back at bayonet point those of our men who
were nearest the bars; but immediately, while dead and
wounded fell, others took their place. The bars bent under
our pressure and gave way. People were laughing hysterically,
yelling, shouting, cursing. I stood against the bulkhead,
trying not to see or hear. Many tried to kill themselves by
beating their heads against the partitions. Unconsciously I
said a prayer, and this calmed me. I told myself the guards
would see that the ship was heeling over, that she might sink
at any moment, and they would be forced to abandon their
posts. Then I should be able to get out, to escape. Our crazed
terror gave us extra strength, and at last the bars were broken
down, we were through them. Trampling over those who had
fallen, my companions and I dashed to the ladders. There
was complete darkness. We bumped against closed hatches,
doors blocked or so badly warped by the explosion it was
impossible to open them.

"Some ladders fell to the deck with their load of broken
and bleeding bodies. Some were so appallingly hungry that
they stayed looking for food instead of trying to save themselves. I was carried along by the frenzied mob, but at last
managed to shake free, and came out on the deck with the
boats where I could see the sky again.

"Most of us dashed towards the boats, but were thrust
back with gun butts by the soldiers and sailors. One of these
boats, full of civilians, women and children, was badly han-

dled, so that it remained attached by one side only and tipped everybody into the sea. Having gone to a higher deck, I took off my shoes and threw myself into the water. Afterwards I had to struggle with someone who was trying to seize my life-belt."

The Italian talked on and on, then suddenly fainted at the foot of the tower. Hartenstein had him carried to the crew quarters, where he was now asleep in a hammock.

Hartenstein felt like a sorcerer's apprentice. He had set in motion a drama of the sea which had got completely out of his control. How and when would the C.-in-C. react to his report? He wished he could simply have added to his score the tonnage sunk, and then resumed his course. But he had only to look up to see the men standing squeezed against each other in the narrow gangway, trying to find a little sleep and forget the horrors they had witnessed and experienced.

He closed his log, and returned to the bridge. At 1:55 a.m. a sailor brought him a copy of Dönitz's order to Schacht and the others: "... head for Hartenstein at full speed..."

For the moment at least this was more a moral satisfaction than effective help. These three submarines were seven hundred miles away, and would take at least two days to reach him. For forty-eight hours he would be alone amid the crates, beams, masts, oars, drifting overloaded boats, and floating bodies fought over by the sharks.

Before disappearing through the conning-tower hatch, the sailor added: "The wireless operator can hear messages in code quite distinctly. The transmitting ship must be near."

This news both reassured and worried Hartenstein. If a British ship was near, he could just decamp and leave her the task of saving her nationals and the Italians. If she was a warship, he must keep his eyes open.

"How many shipwrecked on board?" he asked.

"A hundred and ninety-three," said Mannesmann. "Twenty-one of them British."

So there were over two hundred and fifty people on this submarine designed to hold sixty at most. In case of attack he would not be able to defend himself. He was pretty safe tonight, of course, so far from the coasts; but what about tomorrow? In twelve hours, after the *Laconia*'s SSS, British and Americans would have time to make their plans and attack him. He called up Polchau from the control-room, to hold a little council of war with the engineer and Mannesmann. He looked at the sea not many feet below him, and saw intermittent glimmers of light, nothing more. "We have one hundred and ninety-three shipwrecked on board," he told Polchau. "Can we dive?"

Polchau had already studied the question. "Yes," he answered at once.

"Good. We'll do a practice dive."

But just then another message from the Admiral was received:

F.T. 0200/13. Inform me immediately if ship sent appeals for help. Are shipwrecked in lifeboats? More details about area of wreck?

Hartenstein made a gesture of irritation at these stupid questions from Paris. They could not imagine the sight of the sea covered with wreckage and corpses, of sharks tearing arms and legs from the survivors. They hadn't got before their eyes that drowned woman whose belly had been split open by a shark-bite, exposing the intestines. They didn't know... For the first time Hartenstein was acutely aware of pity. It was not his function to kill men, women and children. Yes, he had seen children in the boats.

Eventually he took his pad, and wrote:

F.T. 0237/13. Ship telegraphed exact spot. Have 193 men on board, 21 British among them. Hundreds of ship-wrecked are afloat with life-jackets.

Then, after a moment's hesitation, he added:

Suggest diplomatic neutralization of area of sinking. According to wireless receiver unknown ship was quite near area. Hartenstein.

This signal was transmitted on American waves, arrived at the Paris headquarters, was decoded, registered, and then at once presented to Dönitz.

He was in the operations room with Godt, Hessler and the duty officers round him. On the huge map on the wall they were all looking intently at the points in the South

Atlantic where Hartenstein, Schacht, Würdemann and Wilamowitz were. The three submarines alerted couldn't reach U-156's square, so small on the map, in under thirty-six hours: before that, Hartenstein might well be attacked and sunk. With these thoughts in mind Dönitz had sent for further details. Now he had his answer.

The others stared at him as he read the message, his face impassive. Between the lines he could guess at Hartenstein's irritation. It was not the first time a submarine commander had made the Admiral feel the difference of mentality between U-boat Command at Paris and the men at sea. This was why, in fact, he always wanted to take into his entourage officers with many months of sea experience behind them.

"'Ship signalled exact place. Have on board one hundred and ninety-three men...'" he read out. "'...Suggest diplomatic neutralization...' What do you think of that suggestion?" he asked.

"The enemy will never accept it," said Godt.

"I agree," said the Admiral. "Still, it's for them to save their shipwrecked—British women and children."

Hessler controlled himself with difficulty. "I'm with Godt," he declared harshly. "Such a suggestion would never be accepted, and we mustn't make it."

"Diplomatically it would put the Allies in a difficult position. By refusing to carry out an act of humanity, they'd be doing the very thing they accuse *us* of so often."

"All that's a waste of time."

"You may be right," said Dönitz. "Well, we won't make any such approach, then. Especially as Hartenstein informs us of an unknown ship quite near the scene of the wreck. She can only be British or American, there aren't many neutrals in the area. She'll rescue the survivors."

Hessler had an idea of his own, but had not ventured to express it till now. "As Chief of Submarine Operations I propose we resume Operation Polar Bear. There's a great movement of ships round the Cape, and we must have all submarines available to strike. Let Hartenstein, Schacht, Würdemann and Wilamowitz return to their normal course of operations. Leave this unknown ship to pick up the *Laconia*'s survivors."

The Admiral brushed this aside with his hand. "No. I've made my decision. Hartenstein can't throw all these people into the sea. Both for his own sake and for his crew's, who started the rescuing. Don't forget, either, that it's mostly Italians they're rescuing. I'm going to inform the General Staff of what's happened, and also Admiral Parona at Bordeaux. There are some Italian submarines near Freetown."

"Yes, the *Cappellini*," said Hessler.

"Right. They'll send the *Cappellini*, then, to rescue the survivors along with our submarines. Godt, please do what's required in this matter. Meanwhile I'll be getting on to Berlin."

He could imagine the Führer's rage on learning that four submarines were not only not fighting but risked being sunk while rescuing survivors. The more Dönitz thought about it, the more this aspect of the problem preoccupied him: by the order he was giving, he risked the loss of four submarines and two hundred and forty young, experienced and brave men, trained in submarine warfare. But what else could he do?

It was then that an idea occurred to him: looking at the map of the South Atlantic just now, his attention had been attracted by the name of a port—the great port of Dakar, where most of the Vichy French fleet lay. In September 1940 the British had attacked Dakar, and the ships had taken refuge there: the *Georges-Leygues*, the *Gloire*, the powerful but immobilized *Richelieu* with her big guns. The French Navy were not enamoured of the British Navy, but this, Dönitz knew, would not make them want to join Axis ships in fighting against it. On the other hand, French sailors would be ready to go to the rescue of the shipwrecked. Yes, this was the solution.

During the next half-hour the wires buzzed. Hessler reported to Naval Headquarters the orders issued to the submarines, and the suspension of Operation Polar Bear for those involved. He also asked for the Italian government to be informed, and for a request to go to the Vichy government, through the Armistice Commission in permanent session at Wiesbaden, that French ships should be sent to the area without delay.

After this there was nothing Dönitz could do but await the Führer's reactions.

3:23 a.m.

U-156 surfaced.

"Stop," ordered Hartenstein.

The submarine stopped. The conning-tower hatch was open, and a little fresh air penetrated to the control-room. Hartenstein climbed quickly on to the bridge, which was still streaming with sea-water. Round him the night seemed blacker than before the dive. His eyes were not yet used to it.

The half-hour dive, such a delicate operation with the very heavy load, had been carried out successfully. Polchau had shown the same mastery of his submarine as ever. There was not even any panic among the passengers, though they were bewildered and dismayed at first when Polchau in the control-room gave the order: "Stop diesels. Electric motors half ahead 300 revolutions. After planes 20°... fore planes 10°..." Some of them heard the ringing, the hooters, the quieter note of the electric engines after the diesels' hum, the

Georges-Leygues

water going into the ballast tanks. Anxiety could be read on some faces, but no one had moved.

The submarine had operated well.

200 feet... 250... 300... 450 feet.

Hartenstein had the speed increased.

400 revolutions...

When the submarine's tests had been made in the Baltic, no one would ever have thought she could dive with so many people on board. It was wonderful, and Hartenstein was delighted. He felt with such a ship—and with Polchau—he could undertake anything.

During the half-hour submerged, however, he had assessed the full extent of the disaster and was appalled. He knew that not all the lifeboats could have been put to sea,[1] that hundreds of survivors must be still in the sea, some clinging to a raft, some with only a life-jacket. He knew there were sharks around; he had seen the terrible wounds from shark-bites as his sailors dressed them. On surfacing again, he stared into the night, and it was as he had imagined. The sea seemed to reveal the agonies of men making their last desperate strokes before going down. He felt the contrast with himself, safe on his bridge, several feet above the surface. His hands gripped the side more tightly. What should he do? How could he rescue these people? Schacht and the others wouldn't arrive for another forty-eight hours, and before then... And what was this unknown ship, sending messages during the night?

He went down into the conning-tower, took a sheet of paper and wrote in English:

> If any ship will assist the wrecked *Laconia* crew, I will not attack her, provided I am not attacked by ship or aircraft. I have picked up 193 men, 4° 52′ south, 11° 22′ west. German submarine.

Leaning through the hatch, he saw Polchau still standing, checking the submarine's balance. "I want this signal sent out at once. Read it, Polchau."

Reading it, the engineer looked at his commander in surprise, but made no comment.

[1] It is impossible to say for certain how many *were* put to sea. Hartenstein counted twenty-two, some survivors say there were only eighteen; Creedon saw sixteen.

"It's three-fifty. I want it sent out en clair, in English, on 25 metres and 600 metres."

It was transmitted at 4 a.m. on 600 metres and at 4:10 a.m. on 25 metres. After this there was nothing to be done but wait for the day.

On the deck sailors in shorts, bare-chested, caps over ears, were circulating among the *Laconia* survivors, who preferred the sea air to the fouled atmosphere below. Many had beards, rough-grown on their drawn faces. In the galley, about one yard square, the cook and his mate had been making soup continuously. Below some of the survivors were dozing or asking for a little water to wash. Large bowls of coffee were distributed.

The British were grouped in the bow. "Hope there won't be any trouble between the British and Italians," said Mannesmann.

"There won't be. But I'll warn them, anyhow." Hartenstein went to the microphone, and spoke in English.

"Attention, attention. The submarine commander speaking. You are here all shipwrecked without distinction of nationality and we shall treat you all alike. I shall not tolerate any dispute between you, and if any should occur you will be punished with great severity and without distinction."

These words were followed by a long silence. In fact, no one in U-156 felt like quarrelling with his neighbour. The British were too pleased to be still alive, and preferred to be looked after and fed on board an enemy submarine, rather than freeze on a raft or in a boat. As to the Italian prisoners, so strangely liberated, they were already thinking of going home to Italy. After all, their luck might be in.

5:20 a.m.

The day revealed a vast expanse of water with hundreds of dots on it, each representing a man. A signal arrived. Hartenstein was nervous. Would this be a rocket from the Admiral for sending a message en clair in English, or would it be an answer from some British ship to say she was coming at all speed? He read:

Hartenstein, remain on the spot but ready to submerge. Other boats to take on board only as many as they can without interfering with their ability to submerge. Neutralization follows.

So U-boat Command was following his suggestion for neutralization. Then everything would work out. But meanwhile he must try to rescue these people.

For instance, there was a raft in sight. "Slow ahead," he ordered.

The raft was within reach. Survivors were stretched out on the planks, watching, motionless. A line was thrown to them. Two of the U-156 crew pulled the raft in. It tossed against the submarine's hull as she rose and fell in the swell, letting out cascades of water each time through her orifices, like some sea monster breathing.

5 a.m.

Dönitz and his staff were amazed at Hartenstein's signal in English en clair. It was quite unprecedented for a submarine commander, having sunk an enemy ship, to ask the enemy to come and rescue their shipwrecked. Of course, if the British refused, and if they rejected the request for the area to be neutralized, they would surely be showing themselves as lacking in humanity as they always accused the Germans of being. But even so, Dönitz could not help feeling the idea was hopeless, and both Hessler and Godt were indignant at the very suggestion.

"The Allies will never accept," Hessler exclaimed with his usual vehemence. "They'll be sure the appeal's a trap—that when ships get there, they'll find a pack of submarines waiting to send them to the bottom."[1]

"Of course they'll never accept." Godt left the conference table and began pacing angrily up and down. "We must continue operations and leave all the shipwrecked to their fate. Our submarines will be running a terrible risk. After all, the enemy knows their position from all the signals. He'll know the number of submarines involved, their type, everything. Hartenstein must be mad..."

Just then the telephone rang: Berlin at last. Would the Führer be on the line himself? What would his orders be?

---

[1] The Admiralty was indeed afraid of this.

Everything was silent as Dönitz walked briskly over to the phone a sailor was holding out to him, and listened.

It was Admiral Fricke speaking, on behalf of Grand Admiral Raeder. "The Führer has been informed of the *Laconia* affair. He is displeased, and asks you urgently, if you continue the rescue operations, not to take any risks with the U-boats...no risks at all...We have urged the French Armistice Commission to send French ships to the area at once."

"Good. Thank you very much. As to the submarines, they have orders which I shall confirm: to be ready to submerge at any time." The Admiral wondered whether to mention Hartenstein's message in English, but decided against it. After a few more words he broke off the conversation and returned to the conference table. They all looked at him. "Right," he said.

As a German patriot he obeyed the Führer, but did not always agree with him. Faced with orders contrary to his judgment and conscience as a sailor, he had often told Hitler: "As Submarine Commander-in-Chief it is impossible for me to do this."[1] He had thus been able to obtain special rules for the Navy, the only service where Nazi officials had no influence on the Command. And Hitler was all the more prepared to respect this Admiral who dared oppose his ideas, because he himself knew absolutely nothing about the sea.

"Right," said Dönitz. "But to go back to Hartenstein's message: I agree neutralization may be dangerous, but we can't blame him, surrounded as he is by all the shipwrecked. The phone call from Berlin can be summed up like this: to run no risks at all with the submarines. Well, a submarine which rescues the shipwrecked is bound to run risks, since to do so part of the crew is obliged to stay on deck quite a way from the hatch. A well-trained submarine needs two or three minutes to dive deep enough to be safe, and a plane appearing on the horizon needs about the same time to arrive above its target.

---

[1]For instance, in May 1942, at a conversation between Hitler and the Japanese ambassador in the presence of Dönitz and Godt, Hitler had proposed to give an order that "if foreign seamen could not be taken in as prisoners, which in most cases is not possible on the U-boats at sea, they were to surface after torpedoing and shoot up the lifeboats." Dönitz and Godt had opposed this order, which accordingly was never given. See the extract from the Nuremberg trials (Appendix D).

"Therefore, we must give up the rescue of the *Laconia's* survivors, or else risk the submarines. Now, I realize that according to the age-old naval rule in wartime the submarine's safety is more important than rescues, and that developments in air warfare must be taken into account..."

"Then let's break off rescue operations," Hessler interrupted.

The Admiral ignored this. "But there are other factors, and I have decided that even neutralization is a possibility. We must see how the situation develops, and be prepared for all eventualities. Here's the signal to be sent: 'Hartenstein, remain on the spot but ready to submerge...'"

Soon afterwards a message came in from the Italians saying that the submarine *Cappellini* had been sent to join the rescue operations. "Inform Hartenstein, Schacht and Würdemann," Dönitz ordered. At a quarter to six the signal was sent:

Polar Bear Group, Schacht, Würdemann. *Cappellini* arriving in *Laconia* area, by signal 10.

This was the first of a series of signals between U-boat Command and the U-boats in mid-Atlantic.[1] The U-boats were told to go to the wreck area, were asked the numbers of survivors on board, their fuel reserves, and above all they were warned to be ready to submerge at any time.

At 6 a.m. U-boat Command learnt that Hartenstein had transferred thirty-one British and Italians into the lifeboats to lighten his own load; at 7:30, that he was preparing to spend the whole day pulling out survivors and putting them into less crowded boats. Then there was a long silence till 4 p.m., when he reported having pulled out one hundred survivors and placed them in boats; the rescue operation was continuing.

At 9 p.m. he gave his position and hove to.

The Admiral and his staff were still in the map-room. The orders to be given to the U-boats and a minimum of other business brought them a little distraction; but their thoughts were concentrated at the square on the map where

---

[1] It still seems surprising that so many messages were sent, in view of the risk of their interception.

three submarines, perhaps four, would soon be collected, rescuing survivors, exposed to the enemy's blows. Hartenstein had been informed that the idea of neutralization was now abandoned as too dangerous.

Dönitz and his officers were to stay there another two days and two nights, finding, in their suspense, little difference between day and night.

11

ITALIANS AND FRENCH CALLED IN

On August 13th the Italian submarine *Cappellini*, under Lieutenant Commander Marco Revedin, scion of an old family of Venetian sailors, had sailed from the Italian base at Bordeaux (known to the Italians as Betasom), to carry out a mission in a vast area a little above the Equator. Revedin had a first-class crew serving under him and officers as keen and experienced as himself. The *Cappellini* had orders to operate alone, or, according to circumstances, with the *Barbarigo* or the *Archimede*.

On September 13th, at 8:10 a.m., Revedin received the following telegram:

> Betasom to the *Cappellini*. Make urgently for sub-square 0971.[1] Other allied units heading same zone.

He soon found the sub-square indicated. It was in the zone going from 4° to 5° south and 11° to 12° west, lying north-east of Ascension Island. Why so far south? he wondered: oh well, I'll soon know. Orders of this kind were as frequent

---

[1] With the aim of keeping operational secrets, the Italians divided the map of the Atlantic into numbered *quadratini* (sub-squares), and these into *sotto-quadratini* (little sub-squares): one figure marked the vertical columns and another the horizontal. The numbering changed often, three or four times a month. Each sub-square was sixty miles in latitude and sixty in longitude.

in the navy as in the army, often followed closely by counter-orders. One must simply obey and await further details. So the submarine headed south towards sub-square 0971.

That afternoon Revedin received another message, with very grim news for Italian ears: Betasom informed him that a British ship with fifteen hundred Italians on board had been sunk, and that several U-boats had received orders to make for the rescue area. The *Cappellini* was to head there at a speed of twelve knots. She was still a long way from the area, and Revedin at once had the speed increased to twelve knots, as ordered.

During the night the weather changed. She came into the south-east trade wind zone and was badly shaken. Higher on the water and less stable than the U-boats, she strained, and rode the sea unevenly. But Revedin kept up the twelve knots. He wondered anxiously how, even with the aid of a few German submarines, he could save fifteen hundred fellow-Italians, probably mixed with as many British. A hospital ship was what was needed.

A little after midnight he received further information. The U-boat he was to meet carried the number 506, she was in the little sub-square 53 of the sub-square 0971; she was to give some of her shipwrecked on board to the *Cappellini*, and some to another U-boat, U-507. Eventually all the submarines were to hand over their shipwrecked to French warships. At 2 a.m. he entered another message giving the recognition signals to be exchanged with both German and French ships.

The day of September 14th passed without any incident of note, except for a change in the meeting-point: it was now the sub-square 0971, indicated as being the area of the wreck.

At 8:47 p.m. Revedin noted for the first time the name of the ship sunk, the *Laconia*, and those of the French ships he was to meet: a cruiser, the *Gloire*, on the evening of the 15th, and the sloops *Dumont-d'Urville* and *Annamite* on the evening of the 17th. The French ships would carry a big national flag at their mastheads. They had orders to arrive only by day, and were to transmit a signal on 600 metres.

At midnight on the 14th the *Cappellini* crossed the Equator, but nobody on board thought of celebrating the crossing of the line. Those not on watch were asleep. Revedin on the bridge saw a deserted sea without any sign of a ship or gleam of light. Ten minutes after midnight he went to his cabin and lay down fully dressed, his first officer, di Siervo, having replaced him on the bridge. He knew that on the coming day he would need all his strength and experience to rescue the *Laconia*'s survivors. It was best to sleep while he could.

Dakar, 12:30 p.m., September 13th

A torrid heat weighed down on Dakar, and the atmosphere was so heavy and clammy that men, animals and vegetation seemed immobilized, petrified. Yet the look-outs in the fortified posts on the coast, and on the ships at anchor in the outer roads, kept their eyes fixed on the sea or scanning the cloudless sky, a sky so intensely luminous that you could not look at it for too long. The cruiser *Georges-Leygues*, commanded by Admiral Longaud, leader of the squadron, was moored next to the cruiser *Gloire*, under Lt.-Commander Graziani.

At the Dakar Admiralty, the naval Commander-in-Chief, Admiral Collinet, was alone in his office. It was Sunday, and he was getting ready to go out to lunch in town after a full morning's work: reading and criticizing reports on the period of exercises in progress for the fourth light squadron, commanded by his friend Longaud. Sometimes his eyes went to the big map on the wall representing the quays, roads, and anchoring berths of the cruisers *Georges-Leygues*, *Montcalm* and *Gloire*, which were some way away, off the beach of Tiaroye; the destroyers *Fantasque*, *Terrible* and *Malin;* and the powerful *Richelieu*, immobilized but still formidable with her 380-mm. guns ever turned towards the open sea ready to fire.

None of the admirals or the officers on board these ships trusted the somnolent quiet hanging over this part of Africa, this sea which looked so calm. Since Mers-el-Kébir and the attack on Dakar in July 1940, they knew that an incident was always possible and could have very serious consequences for French policy. They all cursed the artificiality of the situation: armistice with the Germans, who watched these ships with the eyes of a cat for a live mouse on the other side of the river; peace with France's former allies the British, who—for

Fantasque

fear that the French ships went over to the enemy—thought
only of sinking them. So these sailors were prepared to
defend themselves against any attack, from whatever side it
came.

The clock was striking one when the duty officer brought
the Admiral a message from Vichy. Admiral Collinet read it:
he was ordered to make all arrangements for picking up the
survivors of the British ship *Laconia*, at the limit of territorial
waters, on a line with Abidjan. Axis submarines were to take
them to this rendezvous.

Which was the ship nearest to Abidjan? He had no need
to look at the operations map or consult his files to know it
was the sloop *Dumont-d'Urville*, which at this moment
should be at Cotonou. Yes, Madelin should have reached
there at the end of the morning with his convoy. The Admiral
at once wrote a telegram and had it coded:

> *Dumont-d'Urville*, sail immediately to cruise 20
> miles south-east Port-Bouet. Meet German subma-
> rines, who will give you survivors *Laconia*.

Admiral Collinet had heard of the *Laconia* the morning
before. He had even been told of a wireless appeal in English
sent by a German submarine requesting help for the ship's
survivors. A surprising message, perhaps a stratagem. But at
that time it was not his business. Now, however, he had to
send the *Dumont-d'Urville*. He didn't care for this sort of
mission. A French ship meeting a U-boat at sea could get him
accused of collaboration. Besides, at this precise moment, he

feared the intervention of a British warship which, not being warned or refusing to listen to a signal, would engage with French ships. The political situation between Vichy and the Allies was quite complicated enough without adding new troubles to it.

On the other hand, the commander of an Axis submarine, tired and on edge, having had insufficient or no warning, might also torpedo a French ship. There was therefore everything to lose except honour in this affair. Still, from mere humanity, there could be no question of not going to the rescue of the shipwrecked; and if the Vichy Admiralty gave him the order, the circumstances must be serious, exceptional . . .

At about this time Commander François Madelin was bringing his sloop, the *Dumont-d'Urville*, to anchor outside Cotonou.[1] It was so hot on board you couldn't touch the deck-plates, and despite her well-ventilated gangways there wasn't a breath of wind. Except for the roar of the surf, all was quiet.

At 7:30 p.m. a signalman brought Madelin a coded message, no doubt from Dakar H.Q. He bent over it a long time, but could not decipher it; the atmospheric conditions had evidently garbled it beyond recovery, for his second-in-command was equally unsuccessful when shown the message. Madelin had the wireless room warned to listen carefully for a repetition or for further messages. Darkness had now fallen on Cotonou, and the surf's roar blended with other background noises of the tropical night, the chirping of crickets and the croaking of frogs.

Back at Dakar, 1,250 miles away, Admiral Collinet was not to know that his first message had been so badly distorted that Madelin could not decipher it. But he had realized that the little *Dumont-d'Urville* would not be able to collect all the *Laconia*'s survivors. At 3 p.m. he had himself been informed by the German Armistice Commission of a change in the rendezvous point with the submarines: it was now 1°57′ south by 11°22′ west, two hundred miles north of the

[1] 1,969 tons, with engines giving a speed of 15 to 16 knots, she had a ship's company of 14 officers and 121 crew. She was armed with three 138-mm. heavy guns, a large number of anti-aircraft guns and about forty mines.

wreck. This was the content of a second message to Madelin, which arrived as garbled as the first.

He was not unduly worried when Madelin did not acknowledge either message, for wireless silence was prescribed by orders; but he thought it best to arrange at once for a second ship to be sent. He thought of the *Annamite*, at present escorting the cargo-ship *Carimaré* to Conakry. For a moment he imagined the telephone calls, instructions, orders, being exchanged between Admiral Dönitz's headquarters in Paris and the Armistice Commissions at Wiesbaden, Turin and Vichy. The effects of all these interacting pressures would of course be felt in this office, leaving him with big decisions to make in very tricky circumstances.

On September 14th the *Dumont-d'Urville* was still at anchor outside Cotonou, and Madelin was worried. He guessed that something unusual was happening at sea, but what? The cargo-ships of his little convoy, at anchor in the outer roads, were about to begin loading bananas and coffee for unoccupied France. At 8 a.m. a message arrived from the naval commander at Cotonou, the retransmission of the orders which the ship's wireless couldn't grasp the previous day. This time Madelin knew where he stood. He would have liked to sail at once, but had to wait till he had got in his stores of food, fresh water and fuel. He would also have to disembark the sailors who were patients in the sick-bay, and all that took time.

It was, in fact, 5 p.m. when the *Dumont-d'Urville* left Cotonou, heading for the rendezvous nearly a thousand miles away. Madelin calculated that, travelling at fourteen knots, he would not reach it before the evening of the 16th, perhaps even the morning of the 17th. Land was still in sight when the ship's wireless received, clearly this time, a new message again changing the rendezvous: he must now head for the actual area of the wreck, 4°52′ south by 11°22′ west. Madelin wished he were not commanding such a slow-moving ship.

The *Annamite* was a sloop of 647 tons, capable of up to 20 knots, armed with a 100-mm. gun and four 13-mm. machine-guns. She was under Lt.-Commander Quémard, who, like Madelin, was always at sea, convoying small cargo-ships in difficult conditions and with few facilities. He was strolling on the bridge of his small ship, which was moving slowly to keep near the *Carimaré* like a sheep-dog with only a single sheep to look after. He inspected the sea through his binoculars: it was deserted; and no disturbing noise of engines came from the sky. In the bow the men were taking down the washing spread out in the night. He could see sailors going round with mess-tins full of black coffee and round loaves under their arms. Good, thought Quémard, the voyage will pass without incident. He really preferred this calm, although he possessed all the courage and spirit of his Breton origins. (One day, escorting a solitary skiff in the Gulf of Benin, he had passed a British squadron of battleships, cruisers and destroyers. The British admiral had scornfully sent the *Annamite*'s commander the signal: "Have no fear, we shall not attack you." "Nor I you," Quémard had replied.)

Suddenly the officer of the watch came up to him with a wireless message. "We're to go to the rescue of a wrecked British ship, sir."

He handed the message to Quémard, who read it carefully: he was to escort the *Carimaré* to the limit of French territorial waters, tranship eight military passengers he had on board, and then make for a rendezvous fixed with the U-boats to take the *Laconia*'s survivors: 4°52' south by 11°22' west.

Quémard gave the order: "12 knots." He couldn't go faster without losing the slow-coach he was escorting. He signalled to her: "Full ahead."

It was not the first time Quémard would be rescuing the shipwrecked. He had often met them on his course, in small boats without food or water, on the brink of madness and death. He wasn't too fond of the British, for he had been in the engagement at Mers-el-Kébir, and had also had trouble with them when convoying cargo-ships. For instance, he had once seen a small cruiser, flying the Union Jack, mingle with the ships he was convoying and order one of his cargo-ships to follow her, hoping thus for a cheap addition to the units of her own convoy. Quémard simply aimed one of his heavy guns at the cruiser's water-line, following her very closely. She had understood and moved off: it was one example among several. So he knew what he was risking by putting his ship's nose into this international mix-up.

The *Annamite* was faster than the *Dumont-d'Urville*, and also nearer the submarines; but she had first to look after her

cargo-ship's safety. He worked out that he would be able to leave the *Carimaré* in the vicinity of the Loos Isles that night.

While the orders were going out from Dakar to the two French ships, the Italian government, alerted the day before, realized the extent of the disaster: fifteen hundred Italian soldiers lost, drowned. The first feelings were stupor and fury against this U-boat commander who was sending Italians to the bottom of the sea. But when it was learnt that the Germans were dispatching several submarines to the survivors' rescue, everyone realized that only the fortunes of war—or misfortunes—could fairly be blamed. The Armistice Commission at Turin had also been asked to extend the rescue forces. Telegrams and telephone messages crossed. The French delegation at Turin pressed for "as generous consideration as possible to be given to the German request relative to the saving of the Italian prisoners." The French Admiralty therefore decided to send a cruiser to the scene of the wreck, the *Gloire*.[1]

Admiral Longaud, commander of the *Georges-Leygues* and leader of the squadron, was a frequent visitor to the Admiralty at Dakar. He was there on the 13th, and had been told about the torpedoing of the *Laconia* and the dispatch of the *Dumont-d'Urville* and the *Annamite:* so he was not surprised to receive a phone call from his friend Admiral Collinet giving orders and instructions for the dispatch of the *Gloire* as well. He was not too pleased, though, to be detaching this large cruiser from his squadron and sending her into mid-ocean to meet Axis submarines. He had the same anxieties as Collinet. Even if the survivors were trans-shipped to the *Gloire* without the slightest incident, if the British learnt of it, they might not accept the presence of ex-Italian prisoners sailing under the French flag. When the *Gloire* was returning, they might try to recapture those prisoners, not to mention the British soldiers and sailors they would recover at the same time. There was also the question of fuel oil, which was in very short supply. Who would replace it, once used? The ships might afterwards be immobilized as a result.

Longaud sent a message asking Graziani, commander of the *Gloire*, to come on board his ship, and at 4 p.m. on the

[1]7,600 tons, 585 feet long and 57 feet wide, she had a crew of 540 men and 17 heavy guns, 40 anti-aircraft, and torpedo tubes.

14th Graziani arrived. Longaud and his chief of staff, Bosvieux, met him on the gang-plank, he was piped aboard, and they went at once to Longaud's office.

"I have a delicate mission for you, cher ami," said the Admiral. "How soon can the *Gloire* sail?"

"In four hours, sir."

"Many men ashore?"

"No, sir, only two landing parties."

"Have all your men recalled for immediate sailing. The *Gloire* is to make for 4°52' south by 11°22' west, where she will meet the *Annamite* and the *Dumont-d'Urville* with hundreds of survivors from the *Laconia* on them, or at least I hope so. The *Laconia* is an old British steamer which has been torpedoed and sunk by an Axis submarine near Ascension Island. Besides British nationals she had fifteen hundred Italian prisoners on board, perhaps more. The sloops will arrive before you, and will give you the survivors they have picked up. You will no doubt meet Axis submarines as well. Your mission is solely—I repeat, solely—to collect the largest number of survivors without distinction of nationality. There may be women and children."

"Right, sir. I will make my plans for taking them on board. But I must draw your attention to the fuel oil position. We're practically greasing our engines with peanut butter!"

"I know, and will deal with the matter. I'll ask the Germans to replace what you use.[1] Your mission is strictly a rescue operation, nothing else. You will not open fire unless attacked. To avoid all uncertainty as to our ships' nationality, they are only to reach the area of the torpedoing by day. I repeat: only by day—this is very important. You will transmit special reconnaissance signals by rockets or searchlights according to the instructions here, and you will keep a big French flag at your masthead. At twenty knots you should get there in forty-eight hours. Here are the silhouettes of the Axis submarines you'll find there."

Graziani glanced at the sketches of the U-boats and the *Cappellini*, and noted the reconnaissance signals. "That's all?" he asked.

"That's all. You now know as much as I do. Try and manage as best you can."

---

[1] The Germans did in fact replace the fuel used during this operation.

"Aye, aye, sir." Graziani smiled, and they shook hands.

The bathing parties had gone off to the beach at Tiaroye under Sub-Lieutenant Vivier, who watched them enviously as they undressed and plunged into the sea, splashing and shouting. It was so hot, and the march there had been tiring; he would have loved to go too, but knew he must remain in uniform. Beyond the bar he could see the *Gloire*, her fine lines standing out on the horizon. Suddenly he saw swirls of black smoke rising from her funnels. What on earth might that mean? You didn't waste fuel like that without good reason. Then the flag went up at the yard-arm, meaning: "Immediate recall of all boat crews." It meant they were sailing immediately.

Vivier gave orders, and the sailors returned to the shore, grousing a bit. Ten minutes later the two bathing parties got back into the launches and were approaching the *Gloire*, while other boats coming from the land brought the cruiser extra food stores. There was great activity on board, hauling up the boats, getting the fans going and the awnings taken in. The bugles blared. Lieutenant Prache was inspecting the gun-turrets, Signals Officer Demon checked his equipment. Commander Graziani was on the bridge with Arden, his second-in-command.

"Slow ahead."

At exactly 9 p.m. on September 14th the *Gloire* got under way, heading south. Soon she had reached a speed of twenty-one knots. The sea was rough, and she rolled during the night. As usual Graziani and Arden shared the watch. The first night was without incident.

About 9 a.m. the next morning a look-out signalled an

Sunderland

Allied plane. Did it know where the *Gloire* was going? At a height of about five thousand feet it was approaching rapidly. What would it do—bomb the ship, try to sink her? The gunners were at their guns, standing by to fire on an order from the bridge. The rang-finders showed 6,000 yards, 5,500. The plane was a Sunderland, and it was getting near the range at which Graziani had orders to fire. 4,500—wait for it—4,000—the guns wheeled menacingly. The order should have been given at 4,500, but the commander still waited, impassive. Suddenly the Sunderland turned and went off eastwards, to fly over a P. and O. steamer heading north. Graziani had calmly stuck to his orders: he was to collect survivors of a shipwreck, and not to engage except as a very last resort.

At 3 p.m. the same day there was a second alert. Another Sunderland showed up and maintained close contact with the *Gloire* for three hours, keeping at a respectful distance, ten to twenty miles astern of her. Then it disappeared.

At twenty-one knots, according to Graziani's calculations, the *Gloire* should reach the area of the wreck on the morning of the 17th: two more days' sailing.

12

SAVED OR ADRIFT

Doris Hawkins, Wells, Peel and the other six on the two rafts were picked up by U-156 on the Sunday evening, just as they were resigning themselves to another night in the sea. Sister Hawkins wrote:

> We could scarcely stand, our legs were swollen and stiff from the sun and salt water, and we were helped along the deck and down the conning-tower by the commander and his men. I was taken to the officers' ward-room, where, to my joy, I found Mary [Lady Grizel Wolfe-Murray], who had been picked up five minutes before. We heard that about two

hundred survivors altogether had been picked up during the day, from rafts, floating wood and such-like, and put into our own lifeboats. When these were full, the remainder of the survivors, another two hundred in all, had been taken aboard the submarine before nightfall. They included about one hundred and fifty Italians.

The German officers took charge of our women (four altogether). Our clothes were taken from us and dried, and we were given hot tea and coffee, black bread and butter, rusks and jam. We found it difficult to eat, but we drank everything we were offered. Four of our officers, who were in the worst condition, and we four women remained in this cabin-ward-room; at present it served both as sleeping quarters for the German officers and dining-saloon for the whole crew. The officers gave up their bunks to us, and many of the crew gave up their hammocks to our men and to the Italians. They themselves sat up all that night and Monday night, and snatched only a brief rest for themselves during the day.

The Germans treated us with great kindness and respect the whole time; they were really sorry for our plight. One brought us eau-de-Cologne, another cold cream for our sunburn, which was really bad; others gave us lemons from their own lockers, arti-cles of clothing and tinned fruit. The commander was particularly charming and helpful; he could scarcely have done more had he been entertaining us in peacetime. I did not hear "Heil Hitler" once; I saw no swastikas, and only one photograph of Hitler, in a small recess.

Cigarettes were given to our men, who were allowed to smoke on deck at any time, as the submarine had to stay on the surface because of the large numbers of people on board. We were given food and drink three times daily, but some of us could only manage the fluids.

It was interesting to see the kinds of food which the Germans ate. For breakfast they had large plates of porridge, black bread from sealed tins, plenty of

Norwegian butter, also strong coffee with tinned milk made in the South of France, and French or German preserves. For lunch they had tinned macaroni with tomato, or meat and vegetables in a thick gravy, also from a tin; fresh potatoes, more black bread, tinned fruit, and tea or coffee, or a fruit drink made from a tinned syrup, a German product. Their evening meal consisted of a variety of things. On the table were savouries such as sardines, cheese, and bacon eaten uncooked on slices of bread and butter, and small sausages with bright red skins, preserves, plenty of butter, bread as usual, and rusks.

They wasted no time over their meals; seven or eight men would sit down and eat their food quite quickly with very little conversation. As they finished, their wooden plates and cutlery were exchanged for clean ones by a boy, and their places were immediately taken by others, until the whole company had been fed, officers and crew having the same food.

The water was distilled from the sea at the rate of several gallons per hour, and tasted very good. They told us they used to catch and cook fish for a change, to give them some fresh food, and they always carried lemons and tomato juice. Frequently they chewed energy tablets during the day, which they assured us helped to keep them fit and muscular. They gave us a number of these for ourselves; the tablets seemed to consist of compressed glucose and fruit juice. We saw no spirits or intoxicants at all, and the officers and crew all appeared to be remarkably fit.

One of the survivors was an Italian doctor; he was allowed to treat the sick and wounded irrespective of race and he did so to the best of his ability, the Germans providing bandages, ointment and other necessities, also tablets of opium. Our senior officer was Squadron Leader Wells, who was consulted on all points. Although he had severe abdominal pain, and was badly sunburnt, he organized everything and never complained. His uniform had disappeared when he handed it over to be dried, and so, with only my silk dress tied round him, he moved from bridge to ward-room, and round the crowded decks, giving and receiving orders.

There was little room to move about... and much of the time I was in my bunk, as I was very stiff and every muscle ached from sitting upright on the raft for twenty-two hours. My legs became more swollen each day from having hung down in the salt water for so long, and my face and arms were raw. Added to this, I was badly bruised, and had strained my left knee. It was fearfully hot in the submarine, and we longed for a vessel to come and take us off even if it did mean our being interned.

On the Tuesday (15th) the captain told Squadron Leader Wells that he wished to bring on board the women out of the boats he had contacted that day, as well as any men found to be in bad condition... volunteers from the strongest of those already in the submarine must go into the boats in their stead. Wells called for volunteers, saying he would himself go among the first. A dozen men soon responded, and they went up on deck. The captain would not allow Wells to go, as he was obviously a sick man and had not adequate clothing; and so he remained.

Several women came on board, and a number of men, among them an army chaplain who had lost one eye since I had seen him on board, and whose other eye was practically sightless. He was always cheerful, and quietly grateful for everything that was done for him. During the night, when one of our number died, he unflinchingly conducted a short burial service for him, and committed us all into God's hands, whether in life or in death.

Hartenstein kept watching the sea anxiously, inspecting the sky, showing his nervousness when he was brought a new wireless message; especially as he knew it was a risky business exchanging all these messages with H.Q. At two on the Monday morning he had sent another telegram reporting four hundred survivors provisionally rescued, two hundred distributed between twenty-two lifeboats and rafts, all completely

filled; the rest still in the submarine. There was no further
signal from the unknown ship which had been in the area.
During the day there were several calls from H.Q., asking for
the numbers on board and in the boats, and insisting for all
the U-boats involved that they must take only as many people
on board as would leave them able to submerge; finally the
map square was given where the submarines were to meet
and hand over their passengers to the French warships.

Various rumours had spread on board: a big U-boat was
to come up and land the survivors in France, where the
Italians would be released and the British interned; there was
also talk of an Italian ship. Finally Hartenstein himself informed the survivors that French ships would soon be arriving.

Monday was an even more terrible day for those not yet
given help by U-156. Under a grilling sun, the vast expanses
of water burnt their eyes with glints, flashes, reflections; the
sea seemed to be on fire. Squashed together, they received a
little pemmican, a Horlicks tablet, two biscuits and some
drops of water from the man who had taken command. They
were upset at having to fulfil natural functions in public. They
tried to protect themselves from the merciless sun with a rag
dipped in seawater, a knotted handkerchief over their heads.
The men's beards grew, the women's faces hollowed, and
their dishevelled hair was sticky with salt from the sea. Mrs.
Davidson thought she heard a plane. She saw a submarine
firing rockets, hoisting a flag. She couldn't be sure what was
real and what imagined. Her senses were numbed by drows-
iness, confused by the hours spent on the water, by the sight
of the floating corpses, by hunger and above all a scorching,
unbearable thirst.

There were also those whose boats had drifted so that
they found themselves completely isolated. They missed
hearing other human voices, except those of their companions with whom they had to live in close confinement. When
the boat was lifted on the crest of a wave, they would stand
up and look in all directions, to be disappointed again and
again when there was nothing at all in sight.

Such was the case with the boat commanded by Rose,
with Coutts, Miller and four other British in it. There was
also the one Italian, whom they had brought back from the
raft after the other Italians had disappeared during the night.

He died a day later, and so did one of the British; their bodies were lowered overboard.

The sea was heavy, and the boat was still making water badly despite the improvised plug made from a bundle of rope. The days passed very slowly, the nights were interminable. The six survivors didn't bother with the sail; it was futile, except to give them some slight protection from the sun.

At last dawn came on the fourth day after the sinking. They all thought they were the victims of a mirage; around them were five, six boats filled with survivors. They heard the men's voices, mostly Italians. During the night the currents had miraculously pushed the boats towards this collecting area. The nearest to Rose's was a small motor boat, but immobilized for lack of fuel. A Briton surrounded by Italians seemed to be in charge of it. "Many Italians?" Rose asked him.

"Too many," came the answer. "Far too many for the boat."

"Turn some of them on to ours. We've got provisions we'll leave with them. Then we'll go with you."

"All right—if they agree."

They succeeded in persuading a few Italians, who seemed too listless to care. The boats came side by side. The first Italians were just going to go over into Rose's boat when they all saw a submarine approach and heave to. On her deck there were a lot of half-naked survivors, with knotted handkerchiefs over their heads. They were moving about amidst German sailors recognizable by their caps and their perfect physical condition. The submarine commander shouted in English from the bridge: "Your position is known. You will receive help." Then he withdrew, no doubt thinking that other survivors had more need of him than these men busy changing boats.

The boat Rose and his five men now occupied was in a better condition than the one they had left, which was moving away with its load of Italians. Besides the motor it had a small wireless set and a sail. It was very small, however, and now contained fifty-two people, packed like sardines, instead of the twenty-four it was built for. The wind and currents took it away from the other boats towards the north-east. The boat's occupants knew that the nearest coast was in this direction, but as it was some six hundred miles away, this was not encouraging.

Coutts lay down on the benches for a while to protect himself from the sun. He was in great pain from his toe, but, as usual maintained his cheerfulness.

Soon the other boats were lost to sight, and by dusk on September 15th their boat was alone.

Some miles away four boats were under sail and also heading north-east towards the coast of North Africa. They sailed on, following the leading boat, while there was any visibility at all, but soon the dark had isolated them. They then followed the instructions Buckingham had previously given them for navigation by night. His energy and competence had made him the obvious leader of the four boats.

That morning Buckingham had assessed their chances of being rescued, and found them very small. To the west the distance to Brazil was about a thousand miles. Even with the help of the equatorial current and the trade winds, he could scarcely hope to do more than a hundred miles in twenty-four hours. So if all went well, he would take at least ten days to reach South America. It was better to head north-east where convoys passed. The wreck of the *Laconia* had been signalled by the ship's wireless, as he knew, and planes would be flying over the area before long. The problem of fresh water was becoming more and more acute, and he came to long for a good storm with torrential rain. The lamp which had served as a beacon to the other boats had long since gone out for lack of oil, and was stowed in the stores locker.

At nine in the morning he had informed the other boats that he was intending to hoist sail and move north-eastwards. Each of the three boats was to align itself on him, and to follow him well spaced out from each other and keeping visibility, if possible, for three miles on each side. By these dispositions Buckingham hoped to intercept a convoy whose look-outs would spot at least one boat. He started to make a common inventory of stores for the four boats, and to redistribute them for a voyage of thirty days; but he gave it up. There was not nearly enough to distribute, and he found that the reserves of fresh water were almost gone in all four boats.

He was so furious at this that he even accused the R.A.F. man of having used up the water in his and Buckingham's boat. The man was equally annoyed and swore he hadn't touched the water while he had been alone with his sixteen Italians. Buckingham was sure the boat hadn't left the *Laconia* without its water reserve, so this must have been drunk the first night. In fact he was trying to defend his ship, on the assumption that everything on the *Laconia* must have been correct; deep down he could not feel quite so sure.

The argument created a tension between the three British and eighty-six Italians squeezed into the boat. Ugly looks were exchanged, the Italians began muttering to each other, and Buckingham suspected that his and his two compatriots' lives were in danger. The only weapon he possessed was a clasp-knife in his pocket. He quickly hid it under the planks in the stern. Then he and the British signalman, going forward bench by bench, ordered each man to turn out his pockets. More than a dozen knives were found and at once thrown overboard. Buckingham kept his, but this was because it might be extremely useful to him in the coming days—as a kitchen knife!

All these precautions delayed them, and it was past ten when the head of the little Armada hoisted sail and moved away from the other boats, after giving the other three boat-captains precise instructions so that they shouldn't lose sight of each other, and above all that the look-outs should keep their eyes open for a possible rescue ship. Unfortunately Buckingham's boat was so heavily loaded, so low on the water, that despite a good breeze it only managed to do two miles in the first hour. After an hour and a half's sailing he noted that the sea was deserted behind him; apparently no boat had followed him. He was preparing to go about, to give new instructions, when the first sail appeared on the horizon. At three in the afternoon the boats were sailing in single file, and all seemed to be in order. At five he had some rations distributed: biscuits, milk tablets, and about a wine-glass of water.

None of those on board could sleep properly, for the sea was rough, and to alter course it needed several to move the rudder. Shoulder to shoulder, back to back, legs entangled, the people in the boat were so tightly packed that if one of them dozed he did not fall. At least the water had stopped coming in, so no further baling was needed.

A little before midnight, judging that they were on the

right course and all was well, Buckingham made the rudder
fast. He looked astern, and it seemed to him that the
phosphorescent wake was disappearing very slowly. Space
was made for him on a bench, and there, between two
Italians, he dozed for an hour, perhaps two.

13

THE SUBMARINES MEET

The night of the 14th–15th passed more quietly on board
U-156 than the previous one. British, Italians and Poles were
grouped by nationality, and some got a few hours' sleep.
Hartenstein dozed on the bridge. He had some coffee at
hand, and occasionally smoked a cigar. At 3:40 a.m. a sailor
brought him a message from H.Q. He shook himself, went
down into the tower and read:

> For the *Laconia* group. Sloops *Dumont-d'Urville*
> and *Annamite* will probably arrive morning 17.9.
> Cruiser *Gloire* coming high speed from Dakar . . .

This was followed by instructions for contact, and the
warning that the meeting must take place only during the
day.

Thank heavens, thought Hartenstein, feeling he could at
last see light at the end of the tunnel, though it was still a
long way off. It would be forty-eight hours before he could
put all the rescued on to a big ship, though before then he
should have handed over some of them to Schacht and
Würdemann. He went back on the bridge, and looked at the
sky with a quieter mind: fleecy white clouds were slowly
moving across it in the luminous night.

Sometimes he thought he could hear a noise of engines—
British or American planes? Suppose they bombed him while
the submarine stood out on the still water, with these rafts
and lifeboats round him? He began to regret his message en
clair and in English asking for help. As a naval officer without

political experience, he ought to have asked permission before transmitting it. It had produced no reactions, so presumably the C.-in-C. was disowning the appeal and the Allies had rejected it. But even if it was a rash action to have taken, he still felt he had done his duty by his men—and by these survivors.

When day came, he could see a dozen or so boats grouped within a few miles. There were no swimmers left. Those who hadn't been able to get into a boat, on to a raft or some wreckage, were dead. Corpses floated here and there, partly eaten by sharks.

He had coffee, tea and soup distributed, and then called the senior British officer to ask for volunteers to go into the boats so that women, and men in bad condition, could come on to the submarine. The transfer took place satisfactorily.

At 11:32 a.m. a look-out shouted: "Ship in sight, port 263°."

Hartenstein focused his Zeiss on the point: a ship was indeed heading for U-156. Suppose she was an enemy destroyer? But his anxiety was only for a moment. He was too familiar with ships' lines and behaviour not to recognize almost at once that this was a U-boat. Everyone was looking at her. Who would it be, Schacht or Würdemann? Probably Würdemann, he had been nearer to them before.

Würdemann it was, and soon U-506 had come alongside. Hartenstein could see her commander's friendly smile, the thick black eyebrows under the white cap.

"Sorry I couldn't get here any sooner," Würdemann shouted. Though he could see only Hartenstein's aquiline nose and the hollow, bearded cheeks with the cheek-bones sticking out, he could guess how tired his friend was. "How many rescued in your boat?"

"Two hundred and sixty-three."

"Splendid. I'll take one hundred and thirty-two, one over half—that seems fair? But only give me Italians. We'd best keep the British separate."

Now the submarines were side to side for the trans-shipping operation. Sometimes they moved apart despite the hawsers and gaffs holding them, so it was quite a business. The rescued were not too skilful in jumping from one ship to the other, and they kept having to wait till the gap narrowed.

At last, at 1 p.m., Hartenstein could send a first message to the Commander-in-Chief:

7721—meeting with U-506. Trans-shipped 132 Italians, keeping 131 shipwrecked.

Two minutes later Würdemann also reported:

Trans-shipment completed. Going to area of wreck.

The two submarines separated at once and went in search of other survivors.

At 4:12 p.m. Hartenstein discovered a boat so low in the water that its sides barely came above the surface. He headed for it, and at first sight it looked empty, but then he saw some men lying in the waterlogged bottom, perhaps unconscious. They were frozen stiff, and so weak and spent that if the boat had been found an hour later it would have contained only corpses. The sailors lifted them out of it, took them aboard, removed their soaking clothes, rubbed them down with towels, and gave them hot drinks. Meanwhile their waterlogged boat was emptied, the crack in it blocked, and it was then tied to the submarine's stern behind the other boats. The whole operation took an hour, and those working on it, under a grilling sun, buffeted by the swell, returned on board exhausted.

At the end of the afternoon Hartenstein took a tally: he had fifty-five Italians and fifty-five British, including five women. The numbers on board changed often, with able-bodied men being put back into the boats while the injured came on board for treatment.

At 7:43 p.m. he had filled the last boat for towing, given food and drinking water to the British and Italians in it, and then let them go. He noted all these details in his log, after reporting to the Commander-in-Chief by signal. His last messages gave his position at 9 p.m., 4°46′ south by 11°50′ west, and reported a last boat found at 9:50 p.m.

Finally, at 11:24 p.m., he signalled: "Hove to."

After separating from U-156 Würdemann made for a boat which seemed to be in difficulties, with over a hundred survivors crammed into it. He approached it, and one of his

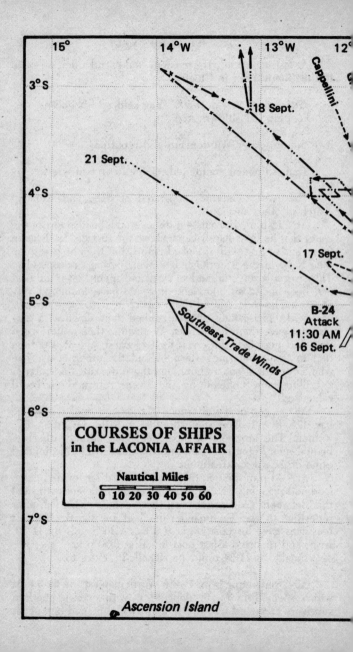

15° 14°W 13°W 12°

Cappellini

3°S

18 Sept.

21 Sept.

4°S

17 Sept.

5°S

Southeast Trade Winds

B-24
Attack
11:30 AM
16 Sept.

6°S

COURSES OF SHIPS
in the LACONIA AFFAIR

Nautical Miles
0 10 20 30 40 50 60

7°S

Ascension Island

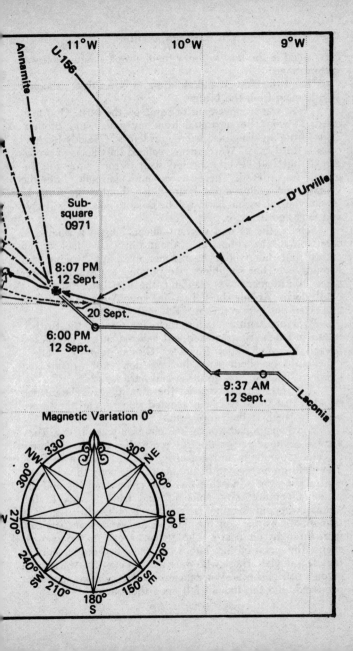

crew stood in the bow to throw them a rope as soon as it was within range.

"Send the women and children on board first," shouted Würdemann from the bridge.

There was a movement of panic on the boat. One man cried: "I won't be separated from my wife," and another: "Nor I from my daughter. You're murderers." "Bloody Jerries!" came a third voice. Würdemann realized the effects of propaganda, but had never expected such terror. "Stop the engines," he ordered. The boat was now alongside. "Put the women and children on board," he shouted in English. "Calm yourselves, no harm will be done to you. We will give you food and drink."

Schulz, the second warrant-officer, helped a woman to come on to the submarine. About thirty, she looked half crazed with her wild eyes and her unkempt, soaking hair hanging over her shoulders. He pointed towards the tower where Würdemann was standing, the iron ladder she must climb down. At this she fell on her knees, wrung her hands and cried out between sobs: "Kill me! Kill me!"

Everyone within hearing, including some of the British, began to laugh. Embarrassed and half reassured, she picked herself up, and Chief Engineer Glasow told her with a chuckle in excellent English: "We don't kill women and children, madam. You go down and have a rest."

This incident had relaxed the atmosphere. The British decided that these Germans seemed sincere, and they were ready to laugh at their own fears.

Würdemann had woman and children taken below. They were accommodated in the tiny petty-officers' cabin. Glasow directed operations and organized the distribution of food. The children were soon beginning to run along the crowded central gangway. A mischievous little girl of twelve found the whole adventure most amusing, and tried to talk to the sailors, who put together a few words of English learnt at school. Meanwhile, on the deck, more British and Italians were brought on board. The Italians were in the poorest shape; the worst off for clothes too: most had only a shirt in rags or a singlet. Those who were naked below the waist were given a pair of shorts. Würdemann had big plates of macaroni prepared, and the Italians fell upon them avidly.

Despite the submarine's reduced speed, water was coming in between the two hulls, sometimes even submerging the bow, so that the rescued had to cling to anything which came to hand. Würdemann made them go below for the night, then he continued to sail over the wreck area, pulling out a few more survivors here and there. The next morning U-506 had over two hundred people on board.

On the afternoon of the 15th, shortly after two, U-507, travelling at fifteen knots, sighted a boat under sail, and was heading for it when a second boat was sighted: they were the rearguard of Buckingham's convoy of four. By 2:35 the submarine had come alongside the first, which contained thirty-five Italians, twenty British and four Poles. Some of the British were armed, and Schacht guessed there had been a struggle between British and Italians at the time of the sinking. The British showed an understandable fright on seeing the submarine.

Schacht ordered the boat's occupants to come aboard. Rather apprehensively they set foot on the U-boat's deck. Soup and cigarettes were distributed among them, and the injured were dressed and treated. The Italians were in a pitiful state, but they showed signs of wanting to take it out of the Poles, and Schacht had to intervene to restore order. He saw he would have to establish an iron discipline, and first of all separate the former prisoners from the rest. He ordered the Italians to go below, the British and Poles to stay on deck. Lieutenant Scherraus with his very good English took down their names and began questioning the British on conditions at the time of the sinking; but he could get nothing out of them at all. Schacht had the liberated prisoners given some clothes from his own men.

Meanwhile the boat had been baled out and taken in tow. A third boat came in sight, as Schacht was heading for the second one, and he thought he could make out two women in it. He reached it, and there were indeed two women—Mrs. Davidson and Mrs. Walker—with twenty-four other British and thirty-one Italians. He told the women: "You can go back into your boat with the others; I've taken it in tow. Or you can stay in the submarine tonight, and I would advise you to do this, because the sea is going to get rough."

They were hesitating when Smith, the R.A.F. officer, said: "Yes, you'd do better to stay on board. I will myself, if they let me."

Ahlfeldt helped them to slide through the small round hatch and climb down the vertical ladder. They were installed in the officers' berths, and soon afterwards Schacht came to see them, accompanied by a sailor, who he said would be at their disposal. "First he will see to getting your clothes dried. You will be given soap to wash with, a comb for your hair, some bars of chocolate. You have only to ask. Anything we can do for you will be done... a large rescue-ship has been alerted, and will be taking you shortly." He was about to leave them, then turned and, noticing their peeling noses and red cheeks, said: "I will see you are given some cold cream for your faces."

Finding him so very considerate, Mrs. Davidson asked: "I lost my daughter when we were escaping from the ship. I'm sure she managed to get into a boat. She isn't on board here, is she?"

"No, she is not in my submarine. But I will ask the people in the boats and let you know if I get any news of her."

Soon the two women, having washed and combed their hair, could lie down comfortably and make up for lost sleep.

The other two boats in Buckingham's convoy had by now been reached and taken in tow, and Buckingham—in the fourth—was glad the submarine was at least German, not Italian. For that morning he had seen a submarine two miles to starboard and made for her at full speed. When she was only a mile away, he thought she was Italian by her lines, and felt convinced of it when he saw on the bridge her officers' uniforms and white caps. His heart beat fast: he had eighty-six Italians round him, and they must not suspect that an Italian ship was near. Despite his desire to be given supplies, he sighed with relief when the submarine moved away. (In fact it seems almost certain that he was wrong, and that this was one of the German submarines, for the *Cappellini's* log records no boat sighted before 8:30 a.m. on the 16th.)

A little later on he heard a noise of plane engines. He looked up at a cloudless, whitish-blue sky, but could see nothing, and the noise died away to the north-west. He wondered what nationality the aircraft was. Hardly German or Italian, it would be too far from its base. British, surely, and looking for the German submarines or the *Laconia's* survivors, perhaps both. The pilot must have seen them and signalled their presence. So Buckingham felt he had been right to head north-east, and now he had new hopes of being saved.

That morning he had had all the boats in sight, but by noon he could only see one, very far behind him. It was about four in the afternoon when the British signalman sighted a submarine aft. She was heading for them, and moving fast. On the bridge an officer made a gesture signifying: lower your sail and stop. Buckingham pretended not to understand, but this show of resistance did not get him far. The submarine passed him, and went across his course. There was nothing for it: he lowered the sail. This time it was definitely a German submarine, and she was towing three boats filled with shipwrecked people. A young bearded lieutenant—it was Scherraus—at once gave him orders in English: "Everyone is to come aboard this submarine."

When the eighty-six Italians and three British were collected in the stern, they were first searched and then sent forward, where they were served with hot soup from big coppers. Everyone had a mess-tin full; soup had never tasted so good before. The Germans noticed the Italians' thinness, their wild eyes, their hollow cheeks, blue with sprouting beards, their cropped heads suggestive of escaped convicts.

On the submarine's deck Buckingham recognized several people from the *Laconia* rescued before him. He was swallowing his soup avidly, when he felt a hand touch him on the shoulder. "You are an officer from the *Laconia*, the commander wants to see you. Come on to the bridge."

He never found out how the Germans guessed he was an officer, seeing that all he had on was a pair of linen trousers in very poor condition. To his surprise he noticed that the German, who spoke perfect English, was wearing a British battle-dress. Later on he learnt that the man's name was Feldmann, and that he was an engineer.

"How did you come to know I was an officer?" Buckingham asked, forgetting for a moment that he was a prisoner. Feldmann did not answer. He climbed by the iron ladder to the conning-tower, and there found the commander, a man of medium height, leaning casually against the tower, the white linen cap pushed back over big ears. Buckingham noticed his irregular, slightly mocking lips. The nonchalant appearance, however, was at once belied by Schacht's sharp tone and words.

"We know you were an officer on the *Laconia*, which was transporting Italian prisoners. Some of them have complained of maltreatment at your hands. Is that correct?"

"I have no knowledge of it. In any case, I can assure you they have been treated with humanity, as prisoners of war."

"Some have told me that the Polish guards, under your responsibility, fired on them and used bayonets on them to stop them getting out of the holds."

"The guards can't have fired on them, they didn't have any ammunition."

"We will look into the matter later on. My function here is to rescue all survivors of the *Laconia* without distinction of nationality. What was her position when she was torpedoed?"

"I don't know exactly, but I can try to work it out approximately from the position of my boat and the time I took to reach the point where you found me."

"Right. I'll take the same way as you came by, to reach the area of the wreck."

Meanwhile the sailors were bringing on board the survivors from a fifth boat. There was now a big crowd on the submarine, with people calling to each other in four languages: English, German, Polish, Italian. The Italians, considered and treated by the German sailors rather like children, made the most noise. They shook their fists at their former guards and abused them, but were very ready to be helpful with the British women and children. Some of the Poles spoke bad German, and some of the crew from Upper Silesia spoke bad Polish. Everyone started to talk to one another, aided by gestures.

At 5:55 p.m. Schacht signalled to the Commander-in-Chief that he had one hundred and fifty-three survivors on board: one hundred and forty-nine Italians and four British—two women, an R.A.F. officer and the *Laconia*'s gunnery and navigation officer (Smith and Buckingham respectively).

Buckingham had stayed at the top of the tower with the German officers. He was provided with a pair of binoculars, and Scherraus told him: "Report to us any isolated survivor, any raft."

It was then that one of the boat's hawsers broke, and Buckingham saw the commander's face change. Schacht seemed very irritated by the occurrence, which caused the submarine to heave to while a new one was being fixed. A quarter of an hour later she got under way again, at reduced speed.

"What are you going to do with us?" Buckingham ventured to ask.

"Put you on to another ship."

"What ship?"

There was no answer. Buckingham turned to Scherraus. "We heard aircraft engines this morning."

"Yes, it's a plane attached to one of our ships."

Disappointed, Buckingham gave up his fruitless questions. Anyhow, he decided, it was probably true about the plane, because clearly there was no look-out to watch what might be happening in the sky.

In fact, though Buckingham was not to know this, Schacht had already acted very rashly by overloading the submarine and concerning himself solely with rescue work. He might be unable to submerge, and could easily have been attacked and sunk. All these "passengers," women as well as men, were swarming everywhere, not only on the deck but from the engine-room to the control-room—where there was barely room to move. Seeing them "running wild" like this, Schacht realized the danger. It was 6:38 p.m. when the hooter sounded for a practice dive. All those on the bridge or decks went below, and were squashed together even more tightly. Schacht warned the people in the boats what he was doing, and cast off the boats. The dive went well, thanks to the skill of the young Hamburg chief engineer, Peter Ahlfeldt. The submarine surfaced, and took the boats back in tow. After this the evening and night passed without incident.

14

ATTACK FROM THE AIR

In the house on the Boulevard Suchet there was an atmosphere of gloom and tension. Admiral Dönitz and his officers sat in the overheated operations room, with its big map of the Atlantic, on which tiny models of the submarines involved were moved as each new message came in. They all watched each other like members of a family anxiously awaiting bulletins on a seriously ill relative; and, indeed, at any moment the telegraphist might bring in a sheet of paper announcing a fatality. They were doing their utmost to get aid to Hartenstein, and were in constant touch with the French to hear the position of their ships, which must now be speeding towards the rendezvous. Meanwhile, there was a gathering of submarines in mid-Atlantic, with the enemy knowing their position: no wonder Hessler called the whole thing suicidal.

Dönitz was inflexible in his decision. For one thing, he insisted, once an operation is started, it shouldn't be broken off till it is completed, which in this case would be when all the rescued were on the French ships. For another thing, it would be highly destructive of his submariners' morale to order them to throw the survivors back into the sea, including the women and children. And yet, and yet . . . he knew the harsh laws of war, which demanded that the enemy be destroyed at any time or place.

During the night of September 15th–16th a second telephone call came from the Führer's headquarters, increasing the Admiral's gloom and anxiety. Commander von Puttkamer, attached to the Führer, repeated his previous order: "If you continue the rescue operation, you must not risk a single submarine." As if I could do one without the other! Dönitz thought, oppressed by the weight of his responsibility. Only the arrival of the French could free the ships involved. But a lot might happen before then.

Just before three on the morning of the 16th Hartenstein received a message from H.Q. with instructions for meeting the French ships on the following day.

An hour later a valve on one of the diesels developed a fault, and although Polchau did a temporary repair the submarine's speed was reduced. Hartenstein signalled to H.Q. that he needed a new valve head, and at the same time rectified the position of rescue operations, which had changed with the movement of the boats; he also gave his own position, and said he had covered fifteen miles on the 15th.

At 8 a.m. he sighted another boat, at a bearing of 340°, went towards it, and took it astern with the three boats already in tow. He still had the same numbers on board the submarine: fifty-five Italians and fifty-five British (including five women).

The sea glittered that morning, the sky was a cloudless blue. Hartenstein leant against the top of the conning-tower and lit another cigar, which he smoked nervously, in short quick puffs. Without taking it out of his mouth, he raked the horizon with his Zeiss at regular intervals, but saw no more isolated survivors. Since the torpedoing of the *Laconia* he had saved the lives of four hundred people. He was impatient to hand them over to the French, so that he could at last get some sleep. His eyes hurt, he could hardly keep them open. He felt he couldn't go on much longer.

Suddenly, at 11:25 a.m., a look-out reported a noise of engines, and everyone on the bridge directed their binoculars at the sky. It was definitely an aircraft, at 70°, and was now clearly visible with its four engines. British? American? It was too soon to tell. Perhaps it was coming to help, or would it just fly over them to locate the boats in the area and radio Allied ships? In any case Hartenstein wanted the aircrew to be in no doubt of the situation or of his peaceful intentions.

"Clear a space round the forrard gun," he ordered, "and have the gun covered with the Red Cross."

Immediately a sailor unfurled a white sheet six foot square with a muslin red cross sewn on it, and spread it over the 105-mm. gun; Hartenstein had had the flag made on September 13th when he began the rescue operations. As ordered, crew and passengers moved away from the gun, which looked like a coffin covered with a flag before being dropped overboard. In the boats astern British, Italians and Poles looked up and waited. All the German sailors lay down behind the tower in the "winter garden." It was impossible to miss seeing that Red Cross over the gun, with no gunners there, everyone lying down, and the four boats in tow. Suspense grew. The throb of the plane became more and more deafening, as it circled briefly above the U-boat. They recognized it as an American Liberator.

B-24 Liberator

Hartenstein ordered a signalman to send a message in Morse: "Signal in English: Here German submarine with British shipwrecked on board. Is there rescue plane in sight?"

The message was transmitted at once, but the pilot did not answer. After some minutes a British officer dashed up to the bridge: "Let me send a message, sir. They'll understand me better."

"All right, but you'll transmit what I tell you to say."

And so something happened probably unique in the annals of naval warfare: a British officer on board a German submarine sent a message to an Allied plane. The message said:

R.A.F. officer speaking from German submarine, *Laconia* survivors on board, soldiers, civilians, women, children.

The pilot still did not answer, but flew off south-westwards.

Everyone on board was sure the plane would return with a rescue ship. They must wait again, be patient. Half an hour passed. The plane was heard coming back, or else a second Liberator. Good, it would probably be dropping drugs, food and a promise of help. The time was 12:32 p.m.

The Liberator dived from about two hundred and fifty feet towards the submarine. Suddenly Hartenstein was horrified to see the bomb bay doors opening. Incredible—it was going to bomb them! They all saw it, the men on the deck and bridge and the survivors in the boats on tow. Two bombs left the hatch and began falling. There were cries of terror.

"Everyone to the bow!" Hartenstein yelled.

The order was at once obeyed, raising the submarine's stern, so that the four boats in tow also had their bows lifted by the readjustment of the tow-rope. Some panic-stricken survivors jumped into the sea. Three seconds later two bombs fell near the submarine, causing two high jets of water which covered the deck. Germans, British, Italians hurled abuse. Hartenstein manoeuvred calmly, trying to escape from the plane. Neither the submarine nor any of the boats had been hit. Still flying low, with its engines slowed down, the plane wheeled above them, preparing for a second attack.

"Cut the tow-rope," shouted Hartenstein.

A sailor with an axe was there already, waiting for the order. With a single stroke he sliced through the rope. The boats thus released collided just as another bomb was falling. This time one boat was blown up, its fragments scattered amidst a column of water.

"We must fire!" cried Mannesmann.

"No!" Hartenstein shouted. "Not a man goes near the gun!"

Meanwhile the plane had released a fourth bomb, which fell in the water two hundred yards from the target. It climbed, wheeled, and was preparing to fly over the submarine again for a further attack. Still smoking his cigar, Hartenstein took stock of the damage: one boat destroyed, another overturned. The shipwrecked in the sea. Some of his crew were running on to the "winter garden."

"Keep calm," Hartenstein called out to them, and took a puff at his cigar.

The plane returned. Hadn't it released all its bombs?

Apparently not. Two last ones left its open belly.

"Hard to port!" cried Hartenstein.

Too late. One of the bombs fell near the submarine, and disappeared in a wave. With a few seconds' delayed action it exploded directly beneath the control-room, and the conning-tower disappeared in a mushroom of black water. Below, women and children screamed with terror, some dashing to the only ladder opening on to the control-room. There Polchau stood, calm too, more worried about these panic-stricken passengers than about the submarine. He wondered what the commander would do: submerge with all these people on board, or evacuate them?

"All hands to don life-jackets," Hartenstein ordered.

Mannesmann pushed through the crowd to make a rapid inspection. "Control-room and forward compartment making water," he reported. Hartenstein realized he had been wrong. He ought to have fired and destroyed the plane. It was now cruising round quite serenely, about two hundred and fifty feet above him. His men couldn't understand that their commander, "the mad dog," was letting this American escape.

He made a quick decision. His ship must be ready to submerge and fight. This was his first duty, which he had badly neglected. At least the British survivors must be sacrificed.

He had the submarine go back nearer to the lifeboats, which by now had drifted some way away. But he couldn't afford to wait till they were alongside again. "All British to leave the submarine at once," he shouted down into the conning-tower. "Open hatches forrard and aft." The British, even the women, came up quite calmly, and jumped into the sea.

Then Polchau reported that the batteries were beginning to give off gas. Hartenstein realized he must evacuate the Italians also; in any case he had no escape apparatus to give them.

The Italians, picturing themselves swimming amidst the sharks once more, screamed and entreated, and force had to be used on some. But soon there was nobody in U-156 but the crew, and the narrow craft seemed empty. All the hatches were closed again and water-tight.

Polchau reported on the damage. "Air-search periscopes jammed. Seven battery cells dud and others doubtful. Diesel-cooling flange torn off. Wireless not working. Sounding gear and hydrophones out of order."

They all got to work at once, and at 1:45 p.m. Hartenstein wrote in his log: "First-class repair job by technical personnel." He ordered a trial dive.

At 4 p.m., while the submarine was two hundred feet below the surface, and holding, he noted: "Damage has been repaired as far as the facilities on board permit."

At 9:42 p.m. he gave the order to surface. The night was

fine, and now he could breathe again, alone with his officers and crew. He took a westerly course.

At 11:04 p.m., the wireless being repaired, he could at last report to U-boat Command:

> Hartenstein. While towing four lifeboats, in clear weather and displaying large Red Cross flag from bridge, was bombed by American Liberator. Aircraft dropped five bombs. Have transferred survivors to lifeboats and am abandoning rescue work. Proceeding westwards. Repairs in hand.

The signal was received at U-boat Command in Paris at 12:40 a.m. on September 17th. U-156, heading west, took no further part in rescuing the *Laconia*'s survivors.

Those of the survivors who were in the four boats towed by U-156 had passed swiftly from the hope of being saved to the fear of almost certain death from the plane's bombs. Dr. Large, then a sailor in the R.N.V.R., was in the first boat, and has given this account:

> The weather was calm and the visibility perfect when the Liberator appeared for the first time about midday. The most short-sighted of pilots could not have failed to appreciate the facts: a U-boat with a big improvised Red Cross flag spread out on the deck, her crew a long way from her guns, the survivors all round the conning-tower, an R.A.F. officer signalling with an Aldis lamp to the plane, which was flying at about 100 feet.[1] The message must have confirmed to the pilot the evidence of his eyes: here was a submarine with four boats full of survivors in tow, the first about twenty yards away from her.
>
> The Liberator then went away, and either it, or another Liberator, returned a few minutes later, opened its bomb racks and made three attacks all within the same radius, all at reduced speed, all

---

[1] Hartenstein, who gave the plane's altitude as 250 feet, was more probably correct.

deliberate and at a very low altitude. The submarine's guns and machine-guns were not used at all. The two depth-charges were well away from their target, but a second burst hit the water six feet away from me, killing several survivors. Meanwhile, a German sailor had dashed up and cut the tow-rope. From my upturned boat, keel in air, I could see the third attack: depth charges shook the submarine and apparently caused her some damage, for oil was escaping from her sides.

In Doris Hawkins's account:

the submarine shivered and shook, and one end compartment was damaged. It was a dreadful sensation; we knew one direct hit would send us to the bottom. The explosions through the water were tremendous.

The German captain decided, naturally, that he must submerge at once. As he could not do so with all of us on board, he was forced to put us off in the shark-infested water . . .

We could scarcely see the boats when we were in the water, owing to the heavy sea. One of the English officers helped Mary, and Squadron Leader Wells again helped me. I am a poor swimmer, and he—a magnificent one but now a sick man—gave of his best to get me into a boat. We swam for nearly fifty minutes, and part of that time he towed me and swam for both of us. He would not abandon me, and finally, telling me to keep going slowly, he swam off with speed and gained a boat, telling them to come back for us. The boat had only one oar, so they signalled to a second boat, whose occupants slowly made towards us. Utterly exhausted but very thankful, Mary and I were helped into the already crowded boat. Wells got into another boat eventually, and, as I learnt a long time afterwards, died ten days later—a very gallant gentleman.

Mary and I now found ourselves the only two women with sixty-six men (all British except for two Polish cadet officers) in a 30-foot boat. Most of the

others who were in the submarine failed to reach a
boat and perished there in the Atlantic when rescue
was almost at hand...

15

THE *CAPPELLINI* IN ACTION

At 8:28 a.m., on the 16th Commander Revedin took
bearings for the *Cappellini:* 4°08′ south by 11°58′ west.

Very soon after this he saw for the first time a boat under
sail; the sail being red, it could be seen a long way off. The
Cappellini approached, and found about fifty men in it, all
British. They seemed well organized, and their boat was in
good condition. They had a compass, a map, and even a small
transmission set, worked by pedal. "Do you need anything?"
Revedin asked them.

"Yes, water."

He had them passed some full water-bottles and some
bottles of wine.

"Are there any other shipwrecked in the area?"

"Yes, several boats and rafts in the direction you're
going, towards the south."

The British saw someone filming them from the deck of
the submarine—for propaganda purposes? They gave a half-
ironical Fascist salute, and shouted their thanks for the
supplies. The submarine moved away.

Comandante Cappellini

At 10:32 a.m. (4°20' south by 11°57' west) Revedin saw another red sail, and headed for it. This boat was damaged and had practically no equipment. It contained forty-one men, all British, eighteen women and twenty-five children. All the children were under six, and two only a few months old. When the submarine was within hearing, the women shouted emotionally, pointing to the children. One of them held in her hands a box of drugs, showing the Red Cross painted on the lid.

The sea was rough, the barometer low, and the boat was in bad shape. Revedin made his decision. "Don't be afraid! We shan't do you any harm!" he called out. "I am going to take on board women and children. As to the men..."

He thought there were too many of them, and he was worried about his submarine's balance.

A woman in the boat stood and called in Italian: "I'm Venetian." Revedin himself was from Venice. He was about to answer when she went on: "I'm married to an Englishman."

"What can I do for you?" he asked.

"The women here would rather stay in the boat with their husbands—but we need blankets for the children, water, and if possible something hot."

The Italians had no spare blankets, but they gave water, three mess-tins of hot soup, wine, biscuits, chocolate and cigarettes. They were pleased to do anything they could.

"Can you give us a chart and a compass?" one of the men asked, with the woman from Venice interpreting.

"I'm afraid not," said Revedin; but he indicated the direction of the coast—seven hundred and eighty miles away!

The men in the boat told him the approximate position of six boats which they said were full of Italians. Here again some of them gave the Fascist salute, and shouted: "Up the Duce!" As the *Cappellini* moved off, one of them cried: "See you after the war."

By the late afternoon the *Cappellini*, heading south, had reached the area where she could hope to find the boats full of Italians. Her look-outs scanned every wave, and at 4:53 p.m. the first boats were sighted. Two were half submerged, and surrounded by hundreds of black dots, apparently survivors struggling to keep above the surface. Some made no movement and floated like balloons. The *Cappellini* approached at high speed. The sea was strewn with wreckage and corpses, some with hands cut off and others half eaten by the sharks. But there were about a hundred men still alive, and when they saw the submarine they made desperate efforts to swim a few strokes towards her, and called for help—in Italian!

The two first men picked up were no sooner on deck than they dashed up to the commander, desperate to talk about their terrible ordeals. Revedin learnt that, out of the 1,800 prisoners locked up in the *Laconia's* holds, some 1,400 had sunk with the ship, unable to get through the bars. Only those in a single hold, about 400, had managed to force a way through. Some of these had struggled in the water with British survivors to take their life-belts, others had swum up and seized a boat and thrown the occupants in the sea. In the other boats British, New Zealanders and Poles had defended themselves by slashing at the hands of the Italians who tried to hang on.

Now to save as many of these poor people as could still be saved. Revedin let the submarine drift towards the points where the shipwrecked were most numerous. He realized that he must always be ready to dive, which limited the numbers he could take on board to thirty or perhaps forty; he soon found he couldn't keep to any such limit. The first Italians pulled out were taken below to be revived and have their wounds dressed. There were some British among them, and Revedin left these on deck to be dealt with later. If an Allied plane came, he would just have to dive, and bad luck for *them*.

The submarine came up to a boat full of water and about to sink. Revedin had ten of its occupants come on board, leaving the rest more room to pump the water, bale it out and get the boat back afloat.

A little farther away, another boat, very low in the water, at first sight seemed abandoned. Then a man in the bow, a Neapolitan who had seen the submarine approach, stood up and called desperately. In the stern another Italian was laughing and plunging his hands in the water, as if at some bizarre game; he took no notice of the submarine. The sea was rough, and she couldn't come too close. About fifteen yards away the crew threw little rubber bags for the survivors to hang on to and keep afloat till they could be pulled out. The Neapolitan understood, jumped into the water and caught on to one of these "buoys." The other man got hold of one, looked at it for a moment, then threw it back into the sea laughing wildly. He was mad.

Revedin felt near madness himself. By letting the submarine drift towards the boats, he had collected an accumulation of corpses against her hull.

He took bearings: 4°46' south by 12°05' west. Night came, and his maximum numbers were far exceeded. There were forty-nine Italians below, and a lot of British and Poles on deck. Everyone who could sheltered behind the conning-tower, or else clung to the rails or anything else they could find, for the swell was making the submarine roll heavily.

On the morning of the 17th Revedin counted those who had stayed on deck during the night: there were only nine-teen, including two officers, and they were all soaked to the skin and stiff with cold. The others had let go, or been carried off by the waves. He had hot soup, biscuits and cigarettes distributed among the survivors.

There was no room at all for anybody else below. It was more like a hospital than a submarine. Treatment was being given a Milanese who had had his ankles severed by sharks. Two of the most serious cases died; their bodies were put in a sack and thrown overboard, with military honours. They were not to be the only ones.

When the two British officers had been revived, they were questioned. One was Pilot Officer Frank Penman, of the Royal New Zealand Air Force, the other was Lieutenant A. E. Boyett, R.N.V.R.

Revedin learnt from some Italian survivors that they had been picked up by a German submarine, which with four or five boats in tow had been bombed by a Liberator. One boat had been destroyed, the U-boat had disappeared.

He soon had the news confirmed by a signal received at 11:30 a.m.:

> Bordeaux to *Cappellini:* Reporting attack already undergone by other submarines. Be ready submerge for action against enemy. Put shipwrecked on rafts except women, children, Italians, and make for *sotto-quadratino* 56 of *quadratino* 0971 where you will land remainder shipwrecked on to French ships. Keep British prisoners. Keep strictest watch enemy planes and submarines. End of message.

That evening Revedin hove to, preparing to remain there till next day amidst the boats. Many had hoisted jury sails, others just drifted.

16

SCHACHT TAKES OVER

From dawn on September 16th Buckingham watched the life of a submarine with interest. He had never seen one except from a distance, and now he was in one of the German U-boats he would have tried to sink had she come within range of the *Laconia's* guns.

He watched the five boats in tow being pulled alongside the submarine, at present hove to, and the sailors filling their tanks with the drinking water they had missed so badly, distilled sea-water. This operation took time and effort, and required great exertions from the German sailors, since the people in the boats were still too tired to give much help. But by 8 a.m. Schacht was able to sail slowly ahead, towing the procession of boats.

"By noon we'll be at the place where the *Laconia* was sunk," he told Buckingham, who had taken over the commander's Zeiss to scan the waves. He could see no swimmer or raft; in this sector the sea was deserted.

At 11:05 a.m. a raft came in sight, and they approached. On it was a solitary woman, stretched out with her face to the planks, perhaps unconscious or dead. When the submarine was within twenty yards, two of the crew jumped in, watched by everyone on deck, and swam vigorously towards these few planks streaming with water, supporting a body. After a while they brought back the woman half conscious, and she opened her eyes to look at them blankly. Her dress was in shreds and exposed her swollen belly, for she was pregnant. She was extremely weak, and had to be carried aboard and below, whimpering softly. Schacht lavished all his care on her, no doubt thinking of his wife and two little girls. He had her laid on his own berth and stayed a good quarter of an hour with her before going back on to the bridge.

As he was walking past the wireless-room, a sailor there made a gesture to detain him. The man seemed so intent on the message he was recording that Schacht leant over him and looked at the transcript, which was a detailed account of the bombing of U-156 and Hartenstein's consequent evacuation of his passengers. Schacht read on with mounting fury and amazement.

"There was a previous message, sir," the wireless operator told him. "I passed it to Lieutenant Scherraus, as you were busy with the Englishwoman."

Schacht asked for the transcript of the first message, received at 11:25 a.m.

Shortly before arrival of other boats, sighted four-engined aircraft with American markings, bearing 70°. As proof of my peaceful intentions displayed large Red Cross four yards square on bridge facing line of aircraft's flight. Aircraft flew over once, then cruised in vicinity for some time. Made Morse signals: "Who are you?" and "Are there any ships in sight?" No response. Aircraft flew off in southwesterly direction, then returned for a few moments half an hour later.

So Hartenstein, with all the shipwrecked on board and with his boats in tow, had been bombed by a four-engined American plane flying calmly at 250 feet—and he hadn't shot it down! Letting out a vehement oath, Schacht swept through the control-room up the ladder and on to the bridge. He found Scherraus there talking to Buckingham. "Read this," he said, handing Scherraus the second message.

Buckingham watched the lieutenant read it, saw his face grow pale, and guessed some very bad news had been received. At last Scherraus told him: "A submarine's been bombed by an American plane. Attacked while rescuing your people, survivors from the *Laconia*, and with a big Red Cross spread over her bridge."

Not bothering about Buckingham, who didn't speak German, Schacht summoned his officers for a council of war. It still seemed impossible to put back into the sea the women and children they had saved. Eventually he decided to continue the rescue operation and go on towing the boats towards the rendezvous with the French ships, which must now be very near. But he took the precaution of reducing speed, posting a sailor with an axe bear the tow-rope, and doubling the look-outs. Attack might come again from the sky.

With these dispositions made, he set about interrogating Buckingham. Buckingham tried to answer evasively, but in the end was obliged to come out with information as to the numbers of crew and of British and Italian passengers on board the *Laconia*. Schacht carefully recorded all this in his log, and went on with the report he had started:

> According to the Italians' statements, there was a bitter struggle to get into the lifeboats. Some of their men were killed by gunfire. The Italians also say they received bayonet blows from the Poles. The Italians were very thin, and had recently had only bread and water. According to the British, this was punishment for having broken into a hold with stores and smoked against orders. The prisoners' clothing was very bad, most of them being almost naked...

Schacht came up on deck, walked round among the half-naked Italians, who were smoking their cigarettes—freely at last. Then he made sure that the look-outs and the man with the axe were standing by, climbed down into the control-room for a word or two with Ahlfeldt; on the way he clapped a friendly hand on the wireless operator's shoulder, and passed on to the galley. In his overheated cubby-hole the cook was pouring with sweat, surrounded by dixies and dishes, with a crowd coming in and out like people in a bar parlour.

Here was a woman whose eye was hurting. Schacht stopped and looked at the lid and cornea, red and inflamed. He had her given an eye-bath and some ointment. Then there was another Englishwoman begging him to let her go and look in the boats to see if her daughter Molly was there. He told her that all the women were now on board the submarine; no, he hadn't seen the girl.

The woman with the eye-trouble was Mrs. Walker. With her and Mrs. Davidson was an Indian woman, Mrs. Nagle, a British officer's wife, who had come aboard from one of the boats in tow. Schacht told their "orderly" to get something for them to eat and drink, and they were brought German black bread, butter, jam and tea. "Eat—eat plenty," he advised them. Before leaving the "women's mess," as it had become, he noticed that they had no towels or handkerchiefs; these too were brought, and Mrs. Nagle was given a bottle of lavender water.

There was now great sympathy for all these women and for the children. The sailors vied with each other to give them all they might need, finding the situation very strange and "unwarlike." It was as if in peacetime they had rescued the survivors from a big liner which had gone down. The evening before, these bearded sailors had sung songs in German and even in English to their British passengers, their fine deep voices beguiling the women and making them forget they were in an enemy submarine.

At 2 p.m. Schacht turned to Buckingham, handed him a pencil and a sheet of paper, and said: "Go below and take the names of the British survivors."

Buckingham hesitated.

"They'll send the list to the International Red Cross," Schacht told him.

For the first time Buckingham went below. Sliding down the vertical ladder, he put his feet on bodies. There were so many shipwrecked, all exhausted and half asleep, that he couldn't take a step without moving them aside. The smell was bad.

A sailor called to him: "The British are over here, amidships."

It took Buckingham several hours to complete his task. After getting the names of the people in the submarine, he had to do the same for those in the boats, going from one boat to another. Women and children were in despair; many had lost their whole family in the disaster. A little girl knew nothing of her parents or her two brothers.

When he went back on deck, U-507 was going alongside another two boats, and she hove to so as to give them supplies, then tied them to the others astern, and continued on her way towards the rendezvous. Dorothy Davidson recognized a friend of hers in one of the boats, Mrs. Gibson, and the two women waved joyfully to each other.

According to Buckingham, there were fifteen women and children on the submarine, and one hundred and sixty-three Italians. The seven boats contained three hundred and twenty British and Poles. Schacht also took a tally, and reached a very different figure. But he decided it was not important; this was no time for roll-calls and check roll-calls. U-507 continued on her course north-eastwards, and the night of September 16th–17th began.

Schacht and his officers had given up their berths to the women, the hammocks were all used by the passengers, and none of the officers or crew got much sleep during the night. The air was thick with the smell of packed humanity.

At dawn Buckingham returned to the bridge; Schacht decided to make use of him to watch for further survivors. "If a plane appears," he warned Buckingham, "you are absolutely forbidden to make the slightest signal. We shall show no mercy if you disobey. This evening we should reach our rendezvous with a large warship which will take you all on board."

"What nationality?"

Schacht did not answer.

"Will you let me tell the women and children?"

"Yes."

When he went below, Buckingham saw sailors grinning self-consciously as they carried receptacles which had been used as chamber-pots for the children. Ahlfeldt, who had become more or less ship's doctor, was treating a little girl.

Everyone on board now knew that an American bomber had attacked a German submarine, that a lifeboat had been capsized, and that some of the shipwrecked had been killed. Dorothy Davidson wondered anxiously whether Molly had been in the attacked submarine.

The device for distilling sea-water was not working properly and had to be repaired; there was a shortage of fresh water on board after the boat's tanks had been filled. Progress was very slow with all the boats on tow, and in one of them a quarrel broke out between a Pole and an Italian; Scherraus had to go and restore order. Schacht had a good deal to worry him, not least the reactions of headquarters to what he was doing.

At 1:25 that morning the Commander-in-Chief's message
to Hartenstein had been picked up:

> Stop rescue. Check fuel, torpedoes, supplies and
> equipment, then report.

A quarter of an hour later, there was a signal to all the
submarines in the *Laconia* sector:

> The Tommy is a swine, the submarine's safety must
> in no circumstances be risked even if rescue opera-
> tions have to be stopped. Remember that protection
> of submarines by enemy is completely ruled out.
> Schacht and Würdemann give your positions.[1]

So Dönitz was making a distinction between U-156,
which must stop rescue operations at once, having been
attacked and hit, and the others, which must continue without taking the slightest risk—as if that were possible.

At 3:05 a.m. Schacht replied, giving his position and
going on:

> 129 Italians, 1 British officer, 16 children, 15 women
> on board, 7 boats with 330 survivors, including 35
> Italians. We are prepared to trans-ship them.

At 3:30 a.m. Würdemann replied, giving his position,
and saying he had one hundred and forty-two Italians on
board, nine women and children; no plane in sight.

At 5:50 a.m. Schacht and Würdemann received another
order practically impossible to carry out:

> U-boats will at all times be kept in instant readiness
> to dive, and must retain at all times full powers of
> under-water action. You will therefore transfer to
> the lifeboats any survivors you have aboard. Only
> Italians may be retained aboard your U-boats. Pro-
> ceed to meeting point and hand them over to the

---

[1] The first part of the signal, "The Tommy is a swine," which all the operators
heard and was recorded in their logs, was omitted in the official telegrams destined
for history. Cf. F. T.00/19/A (Nuremberg Trials).

French. Beware of enemy countermeasures, both
from the air and by submarines.

Schacht could imagine Admiral Dönitz's anxiety, irritation and even disapproval; a signal the previous day had told
him and Würdemann: "Don't send me whole novels on the
details." If I have the submarine evacuated, Schacht thought,
I'll be able to go faster, reach the rendezvous, and let the
French know where I left the seven boats. He re-read this
latest message. "So I'm to keep the Italians on board," he
murmured to himself. "All right. That's clear enough."

The British on board were warned they were to be
turned into the boats. Buckingham was made responsible for
carrying out the operation, and he managed it expeditiously
despite his weariness: soon they had all jumped into the
boats. To his secret satisfaction Buckingham was last to leave
the submarine. He shook hands with Schacht, and thanked
him for all the care given to everyone. The tow-rope was
released, as Schacht shouted final instructions to him: "Above
all, don't move. If night comes, light the hurricane lamps and
hoist them to the mast-head." Then the sailors threw a few
packets of cigarettes and boxes of matches into the seven
boats, which had nothing to do but wait for the mysterious
rescue ship. Left on their own in a deserted ocean, they
began to doubt her reality.

"At any rate we *can* wait now," Buckingham told his
neighbours. "The boat's stocked with supplies and the water-
tanks are full."

"Those Germans were really very kind," a woman said.

"They were," Buckingham agreed. "Specially as they
had no obligation to save us."

"What are we going to do?"

"Stay here all day, and tonight if necessary. If no ship's
come by dawn tomorrow, we'll set sail towards the coast."

The boats weren't full. There was now space to lie down,
curled up. The survivors could hope to sleep. Many hadn't
closed their eyes in the four days since the *Laconia* went
down. But for a while some of them talked to each other from
boat to boat, expressing individual opinions and reactions,
bringing up their hopes and fears.

Before two hours had passed, a man shouted: "A submarine!" The lines of a U-boat were unmistakable, and it was

"theirs," U-507. "Schacht has forgotten something," joked a British sailor.

The U-boat was heading for them fast, and they were a bit alarmed at this unexpected return. Scherraus was in the bow with some of the crew. He cupped his hands to shout: "Buckingham, Buckingham!"

Buckingham stood up at once and waved his arms, indicating: "Here I am, what do you want with me?"

The submarine approached. "Buckingham, the commander has news for you. Come up on board."

It must be something important, to do with the boats of which he, Buckingham, was in charge. As soon as his boat was alongside the submarine, he jumped on to her deck.

"The commander wants to see you, he's in the tower."

Buckingham saw Schacht's white cap emerge from the top of the tower. He climbed up there, followed by Scherraus. But what was going on? The submarine's engines suddenly started up again, and she moved away from the boats at full speed. He looked uneasily at Schacht, who did not leave him time to speak.

"I'm sorry to act like this," said U-507's commander, "but since I left you, I've received orders to take two prisoners. And I'm very much afraid you're one of them."

Buckingham looked aft. The boats with his companions in them were no more than dots on the horizon. "Could we go back and let them know what's happened to me?" he ventured.

"Impossible."

Resignedly he went below, followed by Scherraus. At a table in the ward-room he found a man in R.A.F. uniform, whom he knew well: it was Flying Officer Smith.

"You here?"

"I'm here all right."

"Why? Any idea?"

"No. We're British officers, that's all the explanation we need."

"Then why did they let me go and then come back for me? They knew I was a naval officer two days ago, they told me so then."

"I should forget about it if I were you," said Scherraus with a smile. "You'll be well treated here, you'll eat with us.

Do you play chess, by any chance? We might have a game some time."

"Yes," said Buckingham. "Meanwhile I'd rather like a wash. Can you give me some sea-water soap?"

"Follow me."

In a few steps they were at Scherraus's berth. Under the bolster Buckingham noticed the butt of a heavy revolver. He raised his eyebrows.

"Given me by a British officer," Scherraus explained. "As a souvenir and in thanks for kindness received. Anyhow he didn't need it any more to maintain order... Well, here's some soap. But be economical with it. Look at me." In the pale gleam of the electric light Buckingham saw the young officer, bearded and hairy as a hermit, and probably as dirty.

U-507, with her two officer prisoners and the Italian ex-prisoners, sailed on towards her rendezvous with the French ships.[1]

---

[1] On her arrival at Lorient U-507 had been a hundred and two days continuously at sea. She was sunk by American bombs three months later, in January 1943, off the Brazilian coast. Lieutenant Scherraus was not in her then—he had been put ashore for an operation—and it was he who gave me the reason for the submarine's return. I was able to pass it on to Buckingham, who thus heard it for the first time eighteen years later.

Scherraus lent me a photograph of U-507. "Look at the tower," he said. "Those white dots are the devices intended to jam radar sets and also warn us that we had been located. Our submarine was then one of the very few to possess this new piece of equipment. After we had let Buckingham go, Commander Schacht thought he had seen the devices, that he knew too much, and if recovered by the British would talk. So on reflection we made him prisoner. If you are in touch with Mr. Buckingham, please tell him why we did it."

Buckingham has acknowledged that he and Smith were well treated in U-507 during the forty-eight days they remained there. They ate in the ward-room with the German officers, and used their berths at night while the officers were on watch. Smith seemed to get on better with the Germans than Buckingham did. He played long games of chess with Scherraus. On being landed, Smith was taken to a camp in Stuttgart, where he later died, perhaps from the dysentery which laid low half U-507's crew on their return to Lorient. Two of them died of it, and many Italians went down with it.

Buckingham was remembered by Scherraus as a great consumer of sea-water soap! He remained in captivity for the rest of the war. He is still at sea today, as Chief Officer with the Cunard line.

Webley Mk. VI

17

THE *LACONIA* ORDER

Tension had mounted in the Paris headquarters since the news of the bombing, and on the night of the 16th–17th Godt and Hessler, their nerves strung to snapping point for three days, were wild with fury. Admiral Dönitz retained his calm with a deliberate effort of will, but it was almost the last straw when Schacht's telegram came in, giving the numbers still on board U-507 and in the boats.

"That's three signals we've sent him," exclaimed Hessler bitterly, "telling him: don't risk your ship. And he goes on keeping the survivors on board and a procession of boats in tow. It's sheer insubordination."

"Suicidal folly too," Godt put in. "He knows Hartenstein's been bombed by an American only a few miles away. I knew it would happen, sir, we should never have gone to the rescue of these British swine in the first place. They've shown no signs of trying to rescue their own people, have they? All they've done is take advantage of the suspension of operations to bomb our submarine and their shipwrecked alike."[1]

The Admiral's thin lips tightened. He made no criticism of Schacht, though he felt the commander was now being rash. After pacing up and down the room for a moment, he sat down and wrote a new signal, which he handed to the operator.

"I'm giving orders to Schacht, and Würdemann too," he told the others, "that they're to clear the submarines of the British survivors and put them in the boats. They'll keep only the Italians, whom they'll hand over to the French ships."

"Which should be there already," murmured Hessler.

"No," said the Admiral. "They had orders not to arrive till the morning. We don't want one of them torpedoed and sunk by mistake. Let us try to be patient and calm, gentlemen."

The time passed very slowly. Every time the phone went, every message that came in, Dönitz expected an outburst of rage from Hitler; but none came. Admiral Fricke must be managing to get across to the Führer the difficulty of breaking off rescue operations once started.

At 5:50 p.m. Dönitz told Hessler to send the submarines another signal giving their position and the state of their reserves. "And warn them that the Red Cross doesn't apply on a submarine, and therefore doesn't give them the slightest protection."

He shook his head, and the others guessed that he was far more anxious than he showed. Again he paced up and down, stopping to stare at the map and at the distance

---

[1] Why did the British *not* come to the rescue of the *Laconia*'s survivors, their own fellow-countrymen and their prisoners? There are three reasons, all justifiable, all no doubt partly responsible.

(a) They did not hear the *Laconia*'s SSS calls, or heard them indistinctly, transmissions being not very audible that day and the ship's wireless faulty.

(b) Hartenstein's appeal for help might have been considered as a trap, since each of the belligerents used all possible means of destroying the enemy.

(c) The British probably did not have any ship available, all shipping being in service for the imminent North African landings.

separating Dakar from the square where the submarines were. How soon would he receive the eagerly awaited message: "All survivors handed over to the French"?

"When the rescue work's finished," said Hessler, as if following his train of thought, "shall we send them towards the Cape to continue Operation Polar Bear?"

"No," answered the Admiral. "Let them return to port. The crews are too tired to fight."

"You know, sir, the same sort of situation might arise: torpedoing followed by rescue. And this *Laconia* affair is not an example to follow. As Chief of Operations, it is my duty to keep the submarines always in a condition to fight and to sink enemy tonnage."

"I agree with you, Hessler. What time is it? Ah, you go and get something to eat now. I need to be alone, to think over an important order I'm going to give all submarine commanders, to relieve them of responsibility in such a case."

When they had gone, Dönitz went to his table, and began scribbling notes, tearing up what he had written and starting again. He was completely absorbed in his task.

At last he read the order out loud for his own benefit:

1. No attempt of any kind must be made at rescuing the crews of ships sunk. This prohibition applies to the picking up of men in the water and putting them in lifeboats, righting capsized lifeboats and handing over food and water. Rescue runs counter to the primary demands of warfare for the destruction of enemy ships and their crews.

2. Orders for bringing in captains and chief engineers still apply.

3. Rescue the shipwrecked only if their statements will be important for your boats.

4. Be harsh, bearing in mind that the enemy takes no regard of women and children in his bombing attacks on German cities.

Admiral Dönitz was satisfied: he felt the order included everything he wanted to say.

He had once commanded a submarine himself, and had had hundreds built, poring over the smallest details, the subtlest new improvements. He had repeatedly warned submarine commanders of the danger of attack from the air, but they always seemed to underestimate that the essence of these attacks was surprise. The U-boats were perfectly safe as long as there was no aircraft in sight; but to give those on the bridge time to get below and then to submerge required a full minute—and in that time an aircraft could cover very nearly four miles.

Rescue operations could start only when an action was over, but modern aviation, supplied with detection devices which were being improved all the time, meant that an action was never over for a submarine. From this it was only one step to forbidding all rescue operations by U-boats at sea. After the *Laconia* experience, Admiral Dönitz took this step, abandoning a fine and long-standing sailors' tradition for the harsh laws of war. At this time the war was at a turning-point; and for the Admiral as a patriot, Germany had to win. Or perhaps he had realized that the curve of the Reich's victories had reached its highest point, that soon it would start going down, that defeat was possible, even probable!

What he didn't know was that in signing the general order he was risking his own life. He had written: ". . . the destruction of enemy ships and their crews"; but did he mean fighting crews or shipwrecked? The prosecutor at Nuremberg said the latter, since the order was given in the context of rescue operations; but this interpretation was not upheld by the international tribunal.[1]

He called back Hessler and Godt, and gave them the order to read.

---

[1] An appendix gives extracts from the Nuremberg trials concerned with the *Laconia* affair and with that of the *Peleus*, which was connected with it in the trials.

On March 13th, 1944, Heinz Eck, commander of U-852, torpedoed the 8,833-ton *Peleus* in the South Atlantic, she sent out no SOS. Wishing at all costs to conceal his presence, he had the boats containing the survivors machine-gunned and then destroyed all the pieces of wreckage. He missed seeing a buoy marked *Peleus*, which was picked u by a destroyer. After thirty-seven days three survivors out of the crew of thirty-five men were discovered and saved by the Portuguese ship *Alexandro Silva*. U-852 was sunk in May 1944 by an R.A.F. squadron off Aden, and among the prisoners taken were Eck and the machine-gunner responsible. They were tried by a court-martial, sentenced to death and executed. U-852's chief engineer claimed that Eck had been acting on the basis of the "*Laconia* order"; but at Nuremberg he admitted that he was lying in an attempt to save his commander's life.

"We'll send it at once," said Hessler promptly.

"No, not yet, not till the *Laconia* rescue operations are completed by the transfer of all the survivors to French ships. Then you can send it to all submarine commanders and have its contents made known in submarine bases."

Even this delay was disappointing to Hessler and Godt, but they had got most of what they wanted and they knew better than to argue with their chief in his most authoritative mood.

18

THE FRENCH ARRIVE

In the *Gloire* the day and night of September 16th passed without incident, and on the morning of the 17th she was speeding through a choppy sea at twenty knots. Commander Graziani had not retired to his cabin since leaving port; he wanted to be on the bridge at once if either a plane appeared in the sky or a ship on the horizon. British or German, for him the danger was the same, or almost the same. To the U-boats, any cruiser in the Atlantic was likely to be British or American, and they might sink her without asking any questions.

At 6:36 a.m. she was sixty miles north-north-west of the rendezvous. Graziani was resting in the chart-house when the call came: "On the port bow—a submarine."

"Send a recognition rocket—it will show our intentions are peaceful."

The rocket went up from the ship's bow, making its little trail in the sky. The *Gloire* slightly altered course and made for the submarine. A red speck!—that couldn't be a submarine. The closer they came, the clearer the details grew. It was a red sail—a lifeboat's sail.

The cruiser was soon alongside the lifeboat. It proved to be a motor boat, in perfect condition and with a wireless set, unsinkable lockers and a Morse lamp. In a heavy sea, rope ladders were thrown from the cruiser's deck, and the shipwrecked began to come aboard one by one. There were fifty-two of them, all British, including one young woman and several of the *Laconia*'s officers. Amongst these were the senior first officer, J. H. Walker; Hurst the purser; Colonel Baldwin; and H. C. Cooper, the third wireless officer. Cooper had spent the night after the sinking on various rafts and boats which had all capsized; this motor boat had picked him up exhausted on the Sunday morning. The crew of the *Gloire* were particularly struck by an immensely tall man without a nose—Ben Coutts.

The survivors abandoned their well-equipped boat almost with regret. "There's a cask of whisky on board," a British officer told Lieutenant Samson, who was on the quarter-deck directing the boat's evacuation. "It would be a sin to leave it."

Samson made a helpless gesture. Already the motor boat and its whisky were far away in the cruiser's wake. It was 7:28 a.m.

Graziani called some of the survivors on to the bridge. "Where are the other boats?"

"We don't know. We've lost contact for forty-eight hours," answered the R.A.F. sergeant, Batchelor.

"They should be towards the west," someone else said.

"More to the north-west," Cooper corrected.

Graziani decided against heading north-west. His orders were to rendezvous with the German submarines and the *Annamite*, and only to alter course if he saw other lifeboats. They were nearing the rendezvous anyhow, and binoculars were fixed on the horizon.

He hoped to see the *Annamite* at about eleven, at 4°52' south by 11°26' west, but she did not appear till twelve-thirty. The two ships hove to and Graziani told Quémard he had picked up the first *Laconia* survivors, and that other boats were vaguely reported west or north-west.

"I've not seen any boat or submarine," said Quémard, "and I've nothing to report." The *Annamite* had actually met a solitary cargo-ship on the morning of the 15th and preferred to keep away. A little later a British corvette escorting another cargo-ship approached and asked the French ship for her identity. Quémard adopted his usual effective method of not replying; he merely altered his course as if making for the

Ivory Coast. The British ship got tired of following and left him, to rejoin her cargo-ship.

"We'll make a search north-west in rake form," said Graziani, taking command of operations.

"Right," said Quémard.

At 1:25 p.m. they got under way again, the *Gloire* keeping the *Annamite* on her starboard side. Soon the sloop was barely visible on the horizon.

At 2 p.m. the look-outs on the cruiser sighted a submarine at six miles. It was really a submarine this time, coming towards the *Gloire* at high speed; the *Gloire* also increased her speed. Graziani was a little uneasy, in case the U-boat did not recognize his signals. He had the tricolour at the masthead, and the first rockets went off according to the established code. The U-boat came on, her stern low in the water; she was now so close that four bearded men could be seen on the bridge. The tallest wore a white cap—probably the commander. By his side, almost motionless, were the officer of the watch and the two look-outs; one had his Zeiss directed at the cruiser, the other gazed out over the submarine's stern.

The submarine replied regularly, but did not give her identity. In fact it was U-507, with only Italians among the survivors; Schacht reported that the boats with British and Poles in them would be forty or fifty miles away, bearing 320°

The *Gloire* at once moved off north-west.

"What about my Italians on board?" asked Schacht.

"Give them to the sloop to starboard," said Graziani. "She's just coming up now. Good heavens, here's another submarine."

Würdemann brought U-506 up and then submerged to keep watch on the *Annamite* as trans-shipment began with U-507.

Quémard observed without surprise that the submerged submarine had her periscope directed at his ship. Naturally the Germans were taking precautions. At the slightest alert or inclination to engage, they would torpedo her. Both sides were on their guard—this was only to be expected.

Quémard knew he must hurry if he was to get three hundred and thirty survivors on to his small ship, with the aid of a few boats, before nightfall. He put Sub-Lieutenant Bonzon in charge of taking the boats to and from the submarines.

On the deck of U-507 Scherraus saw Bonzon come

Annamite

alongside. German and French sailors stared at each other. Scherraus felt rather envious of the French officer, well-shaven, in a spotless white uniform, looking calm and rested, while he, Scherraus, with his beard, his hair curling down to his neck, must have seemed more like a pirate than a naval officer. A few words of English and French were exchanged, and the first survivors boarded the *Annamite's* boats.

Between 3:40 and 5 p.m. one hundred and sixty-four Italians from U-507 were transferred to the *Annamite*. Taking only ten at once, for there were seriously wounded men on stretchers, this meant about fifteen journeys for the boats. The exhausted, sick, injured Italians had to be helped to jump into the boats and supported again when they got to the sloop.

Quémard watched the boats coming and going, saw the second submarine's periscope menacing him, observed Schacht on the bridge of the first. Finally, the last survivor had been put on to a boat, Bonzon and Scherraus saluted each other on one side, Quémard and Schacht on the other.

The submarine seemed very empty now. Commander, officers and crew were glad to be on their own again, to move freely without knocking against a leg or stepping on a foot. Buckingham and Smith, confined below, saw the Italians leave one by one, go up the steel ladder and disappear.

Schacht did not move off; it was his turn to submerge

and keep watch on the *Annamite* while she took on board the survivors from U-506.

To the survivors this activity was almost as agitating as their unnerving experience two days before. Those on deck had seen the submarine suddenly increase speed and go so fast that her stern was submerged, giving an unexpected bath to all the passengers there. "Everyone below," Würdemann ordered at once, and the sailors helped the Italians to get to the tower and go below by the iron ladder.

"Full ahead!" came the order, and U-506 reached eighteen knots, her stern completely submerged, as she made a round of the lifeboats in the vicinity. Only Würdemann, Lieutenant Schulz and two look-outs stayed on the bridge. Rüter was at his wireless, head-phones to his ears, intent, trying not to let himself be distracted by the hubbub of the survivors squeezed together behind him. Ten minutes passed, then the hooter sounded for action stations. What might that mean?

"Funny chap the Old Man is," Rüter commented to Bätz, his leading seaman, sitting on a stool beside him. "With so many people on board, he could surely miss out on exercises."

The submarine dived with her hundred and ninety-eight people.

"Incredible," muttered Bätz.

Suddenly, when the U-boat was in an abnormal submerged position, she was shaken by two heavy explosions quite close. Rüter heard the cries of the Italians behind him. The British women and children had not moved. A plane was bombing her. Half an hour later she emerged unscathed, and sailed on towards the rendezvous, her passengers none the worse except for the scare they had had.

These were the passengers now going aboard the *Annamite*. The U-boat's cook was perhaps the man most relieved to see them depart; one evening he fell on to his range from sheer fatigue.

Before leaving the submarine, a dignified old lady[1] turned to Würdemann and said: "I am a friend of Winston Churchill's, and he'll be the first person I shall visit when I get home. I shall tell him the men of this submarine are not

---

[1] I have not been able to find out who she was.

barbarians, and that I've been very well treated on board your ship." Then she turned to the chief engineer, Glasow, took off an ivory necklace she was wearing and handed it to him. "Here's a souvenir for your wife." Around her all the children were crying "Thank you...thank you..." Rüter, who heard them from his wireless room, was afterwards to say: "These thank-you's were a better reward for us than any decorations."

This was the first boat-load to leave U-506. From 5 to 6:40 p.m. the *Annamite* took on board the submarine's nine women and children and one hundred and forty-two Italians. It took twenty-five journeys with the one boat, which was in very poor shape after the operation was completed.

Night had fallen, and the sloop accommodated the three hundred and fifteen survivors as best she could. They were given clothes, physical help and comforting words. The British children were all girls who had lost their parents. The women had lost both husbands and children. The sick-bay was full of patients, Italians with bayonet wounds, many mauled by the sharks, with heels taken off or ankles sliced away as if with a razor, the tibia bone exposed. They were given all the nursing and treatment the sloop's resources would allow.

Meanwhile the *Annamite*'s searchlights were raking the sea, flooding a circle of water with white light, then plunging it again in the darkness of the tropical night.

All night she patrolled round the point 4° south by 12° west, her look-outs searching for lifeboats. The sea was empty. Only one overturned boat was seen. Quémard made several vain attempts to renew contact with the *Gloire*, which must surely be giving new instructions, another rendezvous. A third of the crew was on watch, another third remained on the alert, and the rest helped in the sick-bay. Nobody slept, and everyone was dead tired.

Meanwhile, the *Gloire* was not wasting her time. At 4 p.m. a group of four boats under sail was sighted eleven miles off, and an hour and a half later she hove to near them. The operation of embarking the shipwrecked started at once in difficult conditions, for the sea was pretty heavy. Because of this and the number of boats, no gangplanks could be fixed up, and the crew of the *Gloire* had to use lines with a loop at the end to "fish out" the people in the boats, who were in a pitiful state. Sub-Lieutenant Vivier saw an Italian pass near him, supported by a French sailor, with one of his bare buttocks neatly scooped out like a blancmange after a spoon has dug into it. An Englishwoman, emaciated, wearing an evening dress in rags, tottered along in high-heeled shoes. Only the children seemed in better shape. Many were in pyjamas. They smiled faintly at the French sailors, and were at once taken or carried to the crew quarters or the sick-bay. The trans-shipment was completed at 6:06 p.m.

Graziani got under way again immediately, and a quarter of an hour later saw a group of seven boats tied together. As before, lines had to be lowered into the boats and loops put over the survivors, who were then hoisted on to the ship one by one. There they were helped to stand. On deck the crew gave singlets to the half-naked men, leant over children or squatted in front of them trying to get them to look or smile. Many of the little girls still had a knotted ribbon in their hair stiff with salt. One young woman sat down behind a capstan and, miraculously finding lipstick and a small mirror, started to make up.

The evacuation of these boats started at 6:54, and by 8:35—it was night—the last had been abandoned, empty, with a piece of metal foil still tied to its mast, as if still calling for help.

Graziani had stayed on the bridge all this time, and had seen a solitary boat in the south-east. Now they had to find it again. He set off in that direction, and the searchlights swept wide spokes of water with their rays.

"Boat sighted, port 30°."

The boat was there all right, loaded almost to sinking. The *Gloire* approached. There were so many people in it they couldn't move. Bringing them aboard the ship took from 9:15 to 10 p.m.

The look-outs thought they could see gleams of light farther to the south-west, so the cruiser set off in that direction. But Graziani soon gave it up. He had arranged a rendezvous with the *Annamite* for one in the morning, and realized he would never reach it if he continued searching in the present sector for too long. He went about and headed north.

At the rendezvous time a look-out thought he saw a light 15° to starboard for the fraction of a second; after that, he said, the sea had become pitch-black again. Graziani had a searchlight shone in the direction indicated—and a boat was seen. The chances were a million to one against its being spotted. Without much hope the survivors in it had seen the cruiser's lights passing in the distance, and a sailor had struck his last match.

There were eighty-four of them, mostly Italians, and by 1:40 a.m. they were all in the *Gloire*. Among them was Middleton, the R.A.F. sergeant, and one woman, Gladys Forster. They were all taken below and given glucosed water to drink.

By a strange coincidence the boat was at the exact point fixed for the rendezvous with the *Annamite*. But the sloop did not appear; later it was learned that she had not picked up the *Gloire*'s message owing to peculiarities that night in radio wave propagation.

Till the morning the cruiser went on searching in a north-westerly direction as far as 2°40′ south by 13°50′ west. None of the crew slept. Everyone was busy finding clothes for the survivors, reviving them, dressing and nursing the wounded.

Graziani realized that the *Annamite* would be heavily overloaded with the passengers given her by the two submarines, and at six he wirelessed a new rendezvous to her for 9:30 a.m., 3°22′ south by 13°06′ west. This time she received the message, and set off north-westwards.

Two American planes gave her a worrying time on the way. First a Liberator circled above for about twenty minutes, not too near, but near enough to embarrass Quémard and make him order all the passengers below to hide them. The plane suddenly came down as if intending to bomb the ship, but the commander decided not to have the very modest anti-aircraft defences manned, and the plane flew off without dropping any bombs.

Five minutes later another appeared on the horizon, came down very low—the American stars were visible—and signalled to the *Annamite* by searchlight: a repeated O . . . O . . . O, the signal for "man overboard."

"Where, where?" the *Annamite* answered, but the plane kept flashing the same signal, probably asking for a reconnaissance signal in answer; and Quémard hadn't the slightest idea what this signal would be. So he changed his tactics, and began signalling indefinitely "Red Cross . . . Red Cross" uncoded—until the plane got tired and flew off. This was a very clever move of his, for if he had answered by one or two letters of the international code, it might have caused unpleasant misunderstandings. While his passengers reappeared on deck, he wondered what would have happened if the two planes had discovered him the evening before, beside two German submarines, during the rescue operations: incomprehension, quite certainly, followed by tragedy.

Despite these alarms the *Annamite* found the *Gloire* at the rendezvous fixed, even a little before 9:30 a.m. At 10:15, with both ships hove to, the cruiser's motor boats began to take over the survivors. The sea was heavy, the gap was two or three yards wide, and for these physically and mentally exhausted people, who had been passed in turn from a boat or raft on to a submarine, then on to a sloop, this transshipment was beyond their strength. Many longed to find a bed, a hammock, some corner where they could sleep for hours and hours and simply forget everything. Among them were sick and wounded who were almost too ill to be moved. Yet this great cruiser, motionless on the sea, inspired confidence in them. Because of the gap gangplanks were again impracticable. As soon as the two ships were alongside, the cruiser's sailors slid down a line on to the sloop, put ropes on to the survivors, wrapped the babies in blankets, and hauled them aboard the *Gloire*. Those already there looked at the new arrivals and started questioning them eagerly on the fate of their own dear ones. There were great shouts of delight as people began to recognize each other.

Dorothy Davidson spotted Gladys Forster, whom she had not seen since the sinking, went up to her and was greeting her joyfully, when she heard a voice say: "Madame Davidson?"

She turned round. A French naval officer was there.

"You are Madame Davidson? Eh bien, your daughter Molly is on board."

Five minutes later mother and daughter fell into each other's arms. Somehow neither had ever doubted that this moment would come, so their joy was less wild than Gladys Forster's, who had despaired of seeing her daughter again; yet Elizabeth too was now on the *Gloire*.

There was sadness as well for those who were missing. Sergeant Batchelor found two of his old bridge four, Middleton and Allen. They brought back to his mind the abandoned card-table on the *Laconia*, with Elliot's gold wrist-watch lying by the dummy hand he had just laid down.

"Elliot's here too, I hope."

"We haven't seen him."

"Oh!" All three looked at each other full of foreboding, which was justified—for Elliot was not on board and did not survive the torpedoing.

The trans-shipment was completed by 12:30, and the *Annamite*, her duty well done, turned and headed for Conakry. Meanwhile, in the *Gloire*, Graziani at once took a tally of his passengers. In addition to his crew of 750, he had 1,041 people on board: 373 Italians, 70 Poles and one Greek, 597 British, including 48 women and children. The British were given quarters forrard, their officers in the crew's reading-room, the Italians aft and in the hangar, the Poles forrard in the starboard wash-house, the women and children amidships along the gangways. It was a terrific squash, but everyone fitted in as best he could. The galley coped manfully with the huge increase of numbers to be fed, and the sick-bay was also worked to its limits. Among its patients a merchant-navy officer died that night, and a merchant sailor the next morning. Their bodies were sewn up in a sack, weighted, and slid overboard on a plank, to the accompaniment of ceremonial piping.

Colonel Baldwin, as senior officer for the troops on board the *Laconia*, took over responsibility for the passengers with his usual calm and authority, as if nothing out of the way had happened. He soon had to deal with complaints from some of the ladies. They agreed that the French officers were being very kind and helpful, but they began to forget they were on a warship and found their quarters too primitive, the sanitary arrangements not what they could have wished, and the food not to their taste. Luckily Colonel Baldwin was a very tactful man with a good knowledge of French. He managed to mediate between the ladies and the ship's authorities, and saw to it that conditions were as satisfactory as possible for all the passengers during the week they spent in the *Gloire*.

The children started playing games on deck and in the gangways, and Freddy Moore could be seen at the head of the little band of urchins turning all the handles within reach, not bothering much what the results might be. One day he got himself up as a French sailor, in a uniform lent him by one of the crew, and gave his pals a demonstration near a torpedo tube—much to the indignation of the women, who found the children really too noisy and undisciplined. After their enforced immobility in the boats and on board the submarine, the children had soon regained their energy and were certainly indulging their animal spirits; later they calmed down a bit.

A petty officer, Mignon, and a young rating called Jean, showed great devotion in looking after women and children, who were full of their praises.

There was not enough cutlery available. The men used empty food-tins as plates, the more ingenious made themselves spoons and forks by cutting and working pieces of sheet-iron. There were also not enough waiters, and it took a long time for everyone to get served; but soon the situation was eased when the petty officers let women and children eat in their mess. It was a pleasant surprise for the women to sit down at table with cutlery which was not of iron, and they greatly appreciated this arrangement.

The Italians also recovered their cheerfulness. They slept in the hangar rolled up in tent canvas. Their N.C.O.s were given sailors' caps as a sign of their rank.

The week did not pass, of course, without a certain amount of malicious gossip, jealousy at examples of alleged favouritism, cross words, and even the beginnings of flirtations. The ladies soon had their peace disturbed by a number of masculine visits. Mignon remedied this on the second day by getting visits authorized only from five to six every evening and with the chief petty officer's approval. The men protested, the women said nothing, except for one who remarked to Mignon with a slight sigh: "Que l'on est tranquille aujourd'hui"—"How quiet we are here today."

The passengers knew little of the anxieties of the handsome, slightly aloof commander whom they often saw in the gangways or on the bridge. Graziani was always afraid that British ships might turn up and demand that he should hand over all his passengers.

But, in fact, although a few planes passed above, including a big sea-plane, the *Gloire* returned to Dakar undisturbed, travelling at seventeen knots. In the morning of September 21st she was safely moored to her buoy in the outer road;

Admirals Collinet and Longaud at once came on board to question Graziani on how the rescue work had gone and about the life of the passengers on board. He was congratulated on having carried out the operation successfully in a heavy sea without loss of life or casualties.

At 3 p.m., after revictualling, the cruiser left again for Casablanca. It was a voyage without incident and everyone on board was full of goodwill and cheerfulness. British, Poles and Italians fraternized as if the war were over. The Poles used to congregate on deck in the evenings and sing Polish folk-songs in their deep, nostalgic voices.

On September 25th the *Laconia*'s survivors saw the white houses of Casablanca in a blur of heat haze. There was at once great animation on board. Everyone collected his or her small belongings, from a handbag or haversack to a piece of soap or comb. The women made up their lips and did their hair. They had on a varied assortment of clothes, mostly still torn, despite the mending done on the *Gloire*.

All the passengers now began to feel a bit worried again. The Italians pictured themselves being handed to the German authorities and sent back to the scorching Libyan desert where they had been taken prisoner: fancy going round Africa, being torpedoed, then rescued, and now coming back to just where they'd started from! As to the British, they knew that an internment camp awaited them, but they remained calm. Some began thinking already of escape into the teeming populace of Casablanca.

The *Gloire* came into port, and Graziani supervised the operation of bringing her alongside a quay, which was guarded by soldiers. Anxious to land, the passengers hurried on to the deck. Then Colonel Baldwin stepped forward and handed Graziani a sheet of paper.

"I want to thank you, Commander," he said, "you, your officers and the crew of the *Gloire*, for all you have done for us British, our Poles and our former Italian prisoners. Allow me to present you with this address signed by all my officers, as a small token of the gratitude we feel."

Commander Graziani took the sheet and read:

We the undersigned, officers of His Majesty's Navy, Army and Air Force and of the Merchant Navy, and also on behalf of the Polish detachment, the prisoners of war, the women and children, wish to express to you our deepest and sincerest gratitude for all you have done, at the cost of very great difficulties for your ship and her crew, in welcoming us, the survivors of His Majesty's transport-ship, the *Laconia*."

The Poles presented Graziani with a drawing which showed the Polish eagle and a small sailing-ship on a rough sea. They had all signed this token of thanks to the French sailors.

After these ceremonies everybody pressed on to the gangplanks, British and Poles on one side, Italians on the other. Then they went down, pushing a bit, till the British officers restored order. They took a last look at the great cruiser and the sailors, with the red pompons on their caps, leaning against the rails. It was one of those moving moments which occur when men had lived together in difficult times, learning to know and appreciate each other, and then have to say goodbye.

Colonel Baldwin was the last to walk down the gangplank. As he reached the quay to join the thousand survivors, he turned and raised his hand as a signal: "Three cheers for the *Gloire*. Hip hip hooray!..."

"Hip hip...!"—it was repeated by all in various accents. Then the little force dispersed towards their new destinies.

Ben Coutts later wrote to Doris Hawkins, telling her of his adventures.

> On arrival at Casablanca, we were all popped into an internment camp—the women and children in one, service personnel in another... When on the third day they held a sick parade they saw my wound, and rushed me off to the local military hospital. Life there was much more pleasant, the only trouble being that, with my big size, they couldn't get clothes for me, especially for my big feet!—and I only had pyjamas and a greatcoat. However, they managed to procure a sackcloth suit; and with some boots of an ersatz material, a shirt and a tie and string socks, I was indeed well off.

The colonel in charge of the hospital arranged for me to go to France to be interviewed by their plastic surgeons with a view to repatriation . . . I was to go on October 20th . . . but God was with me and the ship was full. I eventually left on November 5th, and the ship crawled along the North African coast, and was to put in to Oran Bay, then cross to Marseilles.

On November 8th the Allies made their attack on North Africa, and the night before that I saw a greyhound-looking shape loom alongside and order us to halt; it was a British destroyer . . . I was taken off next day, and put in the senior naval officer's ship . . . From there I was taken to Algiers, which was packed with British shipping—a magnificent sight. The first ship I saw was the one in which we had travelled out as far as Durban—safe and sound, having been home and out again. [This was the *Stratheden*.]

I got a colossal welcome and we were home in eight days. The rest, interned in Casablanca, were released when the Allies landed, and were repatriated, coming back via America.

Coutts was mistaken in some respects. Major Creedon and two other officers, as well as the three R.A.F. sergeants, did in fact escape while in transit from the prison camp to an unknown destination.

19

SOME OTHER SURVIVORS

While the *Gloire* was making for Dakar with her passengers and the *Annamite* was on her way to Conakry, the *Cappellini* was still searching for the French ships. Commander Revedin began to despair of ever finding them.

Before dawn on September 18th he had seen a lighted warship going in the opposite direction. He had tried to reach her by increasing his own speed, but the submarine was too slow. Revedin signalled to the ship by searchlights, but she did not respond. While the submarine was trying to catch up, the rough sea carried off several planks and a searchlight. At dawn Revedin lost heart and submerged, to get greater stability beneath the surface and also to see how the *Cappellini* would behave with a hundred and ten people on board.

The shipwrecked had been questioned. One of them, a sergeant-major, interpreter to a British commanding officer in Egypt, gave useful information on the fortifications of Alexandria and the morale of the British. Revedin was much interested by the almost identical versions of the *Laconia*'s sinking given him by Sergeant Dino Monti and Private Adolfo Sangiorgi, both captured in North Africa; they had both previously told Hartenstein their stories. They had been in the boats towed by U-156 when the Liberator bombed her, sinking her with all hands, or so they thought. They themselves had managed to swim to a boat.

For the Italian survivors their stay in the *Cappellini* was a paradise after the purgatory of the *Laconia* and their shipwreck. "I had the honour to eat spaghetti one hundred and sixty feet under water," Dino Monti was to boast afterwards.

Revedin still could not find the French ships, and wondered if he would have to go all the way to the Cape Verde archipelago to land his passengers. He drafted a note in French in case he met the ships, informing them of the positions of the three boats he had sighted on the 16th and 17th, the times of sighting, and the directions in which they were heading. He hoped this would enable the French ships to find these boats after they had taken over the survivors on the *Cappellini*. On reflection, Revedin did not sign this note, or give the submarine's name.

At the time when the trans-shipment of survivors was starting in the *Gloire*, the *Dumont-d'Urville* was still over three hundred miles away to the north-east. At 8:30 a.m. on the 17th a look-out reported a sail on the starboard bow, and half an hour later she came alongside this boat. It contained fourteen shipwrecked people: they were not from the *Laconia*, but from a 5,000-ton British cargo-ship, the *Trevilley*, which had been torpedoed three days before while making for England with a convoy of forty-six ships. Although badly damaged, the *Trevilley* had not actually sunk until the German submarine finished her off with guns. The British still possessed food supplies and were in fairly good physical condition; they were trying to reach Lagos. After a brief hesitation Thomas Hastings, the *Trevilley*'s captain, decided to be taken on to the French ship rather than undertake an uncertain and perilous voyage under sail. The survivors were berthed in the crew quarters.

After a few vain attempts to find two other of the *Trevilley*'s lifeboats, said to be drifting farther west, Madelin gave it up and put the *Dumont-d'Urville* back on her course towards the rendezvous.

At three in the morning on the 18th she picked up a message from the *Gloire*, reporting to Dakar the results of the first rescue operations. Madelin began to doubt whether his ship, slow as she was, would reach the area in time to be of any use at all. But he kept going most of that day and remained on the look-out for lifeboats.

At 5 p.m., knowing that many of the survivors were safe on board the *Gloire*, he decided to return to Port-Bouet. But on the morning of the 19th both he and Quémard on the *Annamite* received a message from Dakar informing them of the *Cappellini*'s position at one o'clock that morning and giving her course; one of the two ships must go to her and take over forty-seven shipwrecked.

The *Dumont-d'Urville* was nearer to the submarine, and Commander Madelin replied just after noon that he could make contact with her on the morning of the 20th. Approval came through from Dakar at 4:30 p.m., and the *Dumont-d'Urville* changed course to 250°.

At eight the next morning Revedin was on the bridge of the *Cappellini* with the officer of the watch and the look-outs.

"Smoke bearing 30°. Over there, sir."

Revedin focused his binoculars on the point indicated. "Quite correct. Not a very big ship, eh?"

"Perhaps the French."

"We shall soon find out."

The ship was approaching rapidly, clearly making for the submarine.

It was a critical moment for Revedin. When he made the

first recognition signal, the ship facing him did not respond. It might be a British destroyer. She seemed to be heading for the submarine with all the speed her engines could give.

"Stand by to submerge."

Just as he was about to give the order to submerge, the unknown ship at last answered his signal, and hoisted a big French flag to her mast-head.

"What is your name?" signalled Revedin.

"*Dumont-d'Urville*."

The French sloop hove to and put to sea a motor boat and a lifeboat. The sea was rough. A few casualties were taken on board first.

Revedin gave the French officer on the motor boat the note he had drafted earlier, and said: "Ask your captain to manoeuvre so that I'm in the lee."

The *Dumont-d'Urville* acted accordingly, and the trans-shipment continued. At 11:30 a.m. all was finished. The *Cappellini* kept the two British officers and also six of the Italians who seemed to know most about the British; these were detailed to guard the prisoners. After having cruised round the *Dumont-d'Urville* for a while, so as to keep her course secret, the *Cappellini* submerged and went off westwards, to surface out of sight of the French ship.

At 12:30 Revedin saw a ship on the horizon. The *Annamite*? Perhaps. The *Cappellini* submerged for safety's sake. Her hydrophones registered a noise of turbines, and he believed that the *Annamite* used diesel engines. The noise disappeared, and the *Cappellini* surfaced again with only her conning-tower out of the water. Damnation, the ship was still there, as if waiting for him. He did a crash dive, to three hundred feet, and waited for the night before he surfaced. When he did, the sea was deserted. Revedin summoned the two British officers.

"You are prisoners of war. You will be well treated in my ship. You will each have a berth in the forward torpedo compartment. You will have meals in the ward-room. Four times a day you will be allowed to go and smoke a cigarette in the control-room. You will have a man guarding you, a former prisoner from the *Laconia*. I hope not to have to make any complaints about you."

The two officers put a good face on it. For them the war

was over. "In case of action, you'll put us on the bridge?" asked Lieutenant Penman.

"What an idea!" said Revedin, smiling.

At 1:33 a.m. the next day, September 21st, he wirelessed to Bordeaux:

Trans-shipment carried out successfully... Have 83 tons of fuel oil left.

On the 25th the *Cappellini* passed east of the Cape Verde isles, and two days later she arrived back at her base, Bordeaux.

As soon as the forty-two Italians were on board the *Dumont-d'Urville*, her crew began giving them hot drinks, food, clothing and medical treatment where necessary. They were all very tired, with drawn faces, and their extreme thinness showed up beneath their tattered shorts and shirts. Madelin questioned them, but could find out no more than that they had been captured in Libya, put on board the *Laconia*, and torpedoed. When dressing wounds on arms and legs, the ship's doctor noted that these were neat round holes as if made by a punch, from three and a half to four inches in diameter—the bites of small sharks.

At 12:53 p.m. on the 19th, almost directly she had got under way again, the *Dumont-d'Urville* met the *Annamite*, which had also gone about on receiving the message from Dakar, and had sailed through the night to meet the *Cappellini*.

Commander Quémard had a boat put to sea, and went on board the *Dumont-d'Urville* in person.

"I have forty-two Italian survivors," Madelin told him, "and I'm to go to Conakry."

"Hand them over to me," said Quémard. "I'll take them to Dakar."

An hour later the trans-shipment was finished, and the two ships separated. The Italians, though sorry not to have returned to Europe with the *Cappellini*, were glad to see the end of their sufferings at last when the *Annamite* reached Dakar on September 24th, three days after the *Gloire*.

"We were treated wonderfully," Dino Monti wrote in his

diary. "In the few hours we stayed on board the *Dumont-d'Urville* we were given all possible care and attention. Then we were transferred to another French ship, the *Annamite*, and there too French hospitality fully lived up to its reputation."

Commander Madelin did not consider his mission completed, however. The *Dumont-d'Urville* searched for the three boats signalled in the Italian commander's note, and they were found on the afternoon of the 21st between 4 and 8 p.m. at 9.43° south by 14.05° west. They were empty.

Going down into them, the French sailors quickly made an inventory of their contents: life-jackets, oars, sails, lines, tins of pemmican, Horlicks tablets, chocolate, and even some small devices for distilling water by solar energy.

The boats themselves were in good condition.

"Look," said a sailor, discovering a huge tin of butter. "We've not seen that much butter for ages."

"And look at this. Woman's boots, outsize!"

"I bags this—a bra." The sailor began to put the garment on, amidst general laughter, which suddenly stopped dead. They had seen the shadow of sharks prowling round the boats, moving fast and very little below the surface of the water. Where did these boats come from? Did they belong to the *Laconia* or some other torpedoed ship? There was no time to investigate, and when the sailors were back on board, the *Dumont-d'Urville* abandoned the useless boats and headed for Port-Bouet.[1]

Thus ended the rescue mission assigned to the three French ships. The German and Italian governments asked the French sailors to give the names of their relatives or close friends who were prisoners in Germany, promising that these would be released as a token of gratitude. All three ships eagerly made lists, which reached the Germans at the beginning of November 1942. On November 27th seventy-three French ships scuttled themselves at Toulon, while the three "rescue ships" joined the Free French. This jeopardized the liberation of the prisoners, but the French Armistice Commission at Wiesbaden kept tirelessly pressing the matter, using all manner of arguments, notably the very reasonable

---

[1] It is likely that Madelin would have had the boats machine-gunned, deciding that they would be dangerous to shipping; but I have not been able to check on this.

one that the Germans had waited too long to keep their promise of releasing these French prisoners. At last, on June 10th, 1944, while there was fighting in Normandy, 385 French prisoners landed at Compiègne. They were on the list supplied by the *Gloire*, which contained 414 names; in the circumstances this was fairly satisfactory. The lists given by the other two ships were never acted upon.

On September 24th, 1942, his ship having reached Dakar, Commander Quémard wrote in his log: "Everyone in the *Annamite* has given of his utmost, and we are all extremely glad to have contributed to this humanitarian mission. We are also pleased that it may bring us tangible rewards, in the freeing of French prisoners, and we know that it will enhance the prestige of the French Navy." What Quémard wrote could be applied with equal force to the crews of the *Gloire* and the *Dumont-d'Urville*.

For days after the sinking vast areas of the sea, covering many square miles, were like a battlefield when the armies have withdrawn. But here there were no stretcher-bearers to collect the last wounded, no fatigues to bury the dead. There were only corpses floating on the surface, half devoured by the sharks, staved-in lifeboats, scattered oars, useless life-jackets.

Yet two lifeboats crammed with shipwrecked from the *Laconia* were sailing slowly and painfully eastwards, towards Africa. One of them was the boat which Sister Hawkins and Lady Grizel Wolfe-Murray had managed to get into, helped by Squadron Leader Wells and the other British officer. Lady Grizel died on the voyage. The end of *Atlantic Torpedo*, describing the terrible three weeks which followed, is given in an appendix. The survivors landed in Liberia on October 9th, only sixteen being left out of the sixty-eight in the boat when it left the submarine; and one of the sixteen was to die a few days later. They were taken to Freetown, where they were in hospital for six weeks; they returned to England, curiously enough, in the sister-ship of the *Laconia*.

In the final section of *Atlantic Torpedo* Doris Hawkins observes:

> Had essential equipment, especially such things
> as the rockets and flares, medical supplies and wa-

ter, been *secured* in such a way that loss would be impossible in the event of lifeboats capsizing, I feel that many more of our number would have reached safety. There may be good explanations for all this, but I do not know them.

One of the *Laconia*'s lifeboats was still at sea on October 21st. It contained four exhausted men, among them two sailors, A. V. Large and Harry Vines, who had been in the leading boat in tow when U-156 was bombed. Doris Hawkins gives a brief account of this boat too.

> The boat into which Squadron Leader Wells was taken started off towards the coast as we did. There were fifty-one men but no women or children in that boat, which had even less equipment than we had, and only three gallons of water. Their numbers decreased rapidly. They managed to catch plenty of fish, and after three weeks, when they had been three days without water, they had plenty of rain; but they were at sea for thirty days before being sighted by a convoy. There were only four of them alive, naval ratings, and these were picked up and actually reached Freetown before we did, since the rescue ship took them there direct.

So ended the tragic odyssey of the *Laconia*'s shipwrecked. Out of the 2,732 members of the crew and passengers on board on September 12th, 1942, those who survived were the 1,041 taken on board the *Gloire*, the forty-two brought to Dakar by the *Annamite*, the four British officers made prisoner, two in U-507 and two in the *Cappellini*, the six Italians retained on the *Cappellini*, and the twenty in the last two lifeboats—1,111 altogether, several of whom died almost immediately after landing. Of the 1,800 Italians on board the *Laconia* about 450 survived, and seventy-three out of the 103 Poles.

Appendix A

OPINIONS OF THE BRITISH AND ONE ITALIAN ON LT.-COMMANDER HARTENSTEIN

Doris Hawkins (Preface to *Atlantic Torpedo*):

"Reading the account which follows will make it clear that some of the German officers and sailors had not been corrupted by the Nazi policy of brutality which they were constrained to apply in their torpedoings.

"Even in the middle of the war we are obliged to pay grateful homage to the humanity with which the survivors were treated by the crew of the German submarine which picked us up. I shall remain eternally grateful to them, although I know that this German captain, so courteous and humane, was at the same time responsible for our ordeal."

R. M. Miller:

"The U-boat was swinging round while we trans-shipped. The commander showed himself a very humane character, doing his best to keep the lifeboats together and taking the women and children on board during the night, giving them hot soup and chocolate."

Wing-Commander Blackburn:

". . . To our great surprise they treated us well. They took about fifty women and children on board and treated us with the greatest consideration."

Ian Peel:

"Whatever one may think of the Germans—and I would say first that there are good and bad in every race—as regards the U-boat in question and her crew, I can speak only of their kindness towards us."

Molly Lewes (née Davidson):

"The Germans were very nice to us, they gave us their berths and fed us well."

Brigadier Creedon:

"The accounts of the various survivors bring out clearly that the U-boat commander treated the women and children extremely well."

Surveyor Antonio Pochettino:

"Unfortunately I do not remember the name of the U-boat: I don't know if she survived the war or is at the bottom of the sea. Nor do I know the commander's name, but if by some extraordinary chance I should meet him, I should naturally give him a warm embrace. There is the testimony of some two hundred and fifty-nine other Italians: they also owe their lives to the generous and unselfish action of this man who was later to become officially our enemy; but I shall always remember him as a friend."

Appendix B

TWENTY-SEVEN DAYS IN AN OPEN BOAT

(from the end of *Atlantic Torpedo* by Doris Hawkins)

Now we found ourselves only two women with sixty-six men (all British, except for two Polish cadet officers) in a thirty-foot boat. Most of the others who were in the submarine failed to reach a boat and perished there in the Atlantic when rescue was almost at hand.

I was wearing very little clothing when I left the U-boat, but a naval rating immediately removed his vest and gave it to me, and an airman stripped off his shirt and put that on me; in those garments only I remained for many days.

Among our number was the young ship's surgeon, Dr. Geoffrey Purslow. When the ship was torpedoed, Dr. Purslow placed his three hospital patients, together with his first-aid equipment, in a lifeboat, and returned on deck to help get other passengers away. Finally he had to swim away from the ship, and climbed into a lifeboat. This was not his original boat, and so he was separated from his equipment.

Dr. Purslow and other officers checked over the equipment and food in the boat. Much was missing, including the medical chest. There were only five oars, one of which was later used as a mast; some tools and white lead; a compass; and a battery lamp with no spare battery. There were no rockets or flares, no sail, and only two blankets, later used to make a jib. The rudder was also missing.

Dr. Purslow and others made and erected a sail from the tarpaulin cover, lashed to an oar. They called him the navigating doctor—he had done a great deal of sailing in his student days.

The boat... had a leak in one side which necessitated pumping day and night... We were packed so tightly that it was almost impossible even to ease our positions during that first long cold night, as we sat shoulder to shoulder. The next morning, Thursday, we started to sail for the coast, which the U-boat commander had told us was six hundred miles away north-north-east; but we had no skilled navigators or charts. We had only fifteen gallons of water for sixty-eight people, and a minimum of six hundred miles to go...

During the morning an American plane sighted us, circled low over us twice, flashed us a message, which unfortunately no one could read, and flew off. We were jubilant and hope ran high... In a few hours a flying-boat would come and pick us all up; in a day or two a destroyer would be there seeking us, or a convoy would be diverted to rescue us. So the hopeful suggestions ran, and we believed them all in turn. Finally, however, as night came, we settled down and determined to make land.

At first the men rowed in shifts day and night, but after some days rowing discontinued as they became too weak... Two or three days later a U-boat came upon us, and asked if we wanted anything. Dr. Purslow asked for some bandages, and a few were provided; also some water and hot coffee...

Our daily ration of food, dispensed at first by Dr. Purslow and a colonel, was as follows: Morning, four or five Horlicks tablets, three pieces of chocolate (size 1½ in. × ¾ in. × ⅛ in.), no water. Evening, two ship's biscuits (size of petit-beurre, but very dry and hard), one teaspoonful of pemmican, two ounces of water.

After a few nights a place was made where Mary and I could lie side by side, and we tried to keep each other warm by lying very close together. But the wind seemed to blow through us, and sometimes we were soaked as a wave broke over the boat. It was dark in that latitude from about 6:30 p.m. to 6 a.m.

The days passed in a dreadful monotony. Nobody had anything to do. Mary and I used to sit during those days "up forward" behind the sail, where there was a little shade in the mornings; for we were in equatorial waters, and the sun was almost unbearable by 10 a.m.

We all talked of our homes and families and friends—of what we would do when we were rescued and when we reached home. We discussed the things we were going to eat and drink, and spoke of most of the things we had ever eaten in the past. We were unanimous in declaring that water would always be treated with great respect in the future, and that we should never again complain about our food. Mary and I were always confident and our sense of humour persisted.

Strange as it may seem, I never failed to appreciate in those first days the beauty of the ever-changing sea and sky... We saw the most lovely-coloured tropical fish through the transparent blue water, clouds of blue-green flying-fish, their fins shining silver in the sunlight as, leaving the water, they darted through the air, to strike the water again with a little splash. We saw brown gulls and other birds, flying in flocks and excitedly diving, crying and fighting as they came on a shoal of fish. We saw porpoises tumbling through the water. Less pleasant was the sight of sharks' dorsal fins cleaving the surface, often following our boat with uncanny knowledge. One day we saw several whales quite close to us, their great bodies making smooth green patches as they moved near the surface. Suddenly we would glimpse the dark forms half out of the water and from time to time they noisily spouted jets of water into the air.

The sun always set in a blaze of glory, reflected in the sea, and left an afterglow of colours which spread across the sky and lasted till the blue shadows of night stretched across and took their place. Then the moon came up, making a silver pathway across the waves, and stars came out and twinkled encouragingly, looking larger and nearer than those in an English sky.

In the mornings we watched the sun rise, for then occasionally just a very few drops of rain fell...; we liked to feel it on our faces.

One of our number was the fourth engineer of the ship, William Henderson, and he never spared himself... He made a rudder from some pieces of wood, and two of the lads went over the side to fix it. He organized the "pumping squads," himself taking the longest night watch... and if anyone fell out, he was always there, ready to carry on. One day he made one of the doors covering the buoyancy tanks into floor-boards, so that "the ladies" might be a little more comfortable at night, and two more into notice-boards, on which was printed by means of white lead "SOS WATER"—to be held aloft should any aircraft pass our way again. Another day, with great care, he removed the two buoyancy tanks and discovered the position of the worst leak. Then, with the help of two other men, the place was made more or less water-tight by teasing out rope and impregnating it with white lead, then pressing it firmly into the crack.

Several mornings found him blue with cold, and we had to chafe his limbs to bring him back to consciousness. Those of us who finally reached safety must always remember with gratitude Billy Henderson's selflessness and devotion to duty, on what was to prove his last voyage; for one morning we found he was no longer breathing.

In spite of such losses, with each new day came fresh hope. Surely today must be the day? Was there anything on the horizon? Could that be smoke? Yes!—No, only a wisp of cloud. All day we longed for our minute ration, which came

at 5 o'clock. After a time we could quite easily bear the lack
of food, but thirst was a torture. When each water ration was
passed along, everyone peered at it with longing, as it went
from hand to hand. When we received our precious drop, we
took a sip, ran it round our teeth and gums, gargled with it
and finally swallowed it. We repeated this till not a drop nor a
drip was left clinging to the little biscuit tin from which we
drank. After five minutes we could not tell that we had had
any... As we grew weaker, our mouths drier and drier, we
only spoke when necessary. Whenever we had a few minutes
of fine rain in the very early morning, it was a pathetic sight
to see all these people with their dry brown tongues hanging
out, and heads thrown back, trying to catch "just a few
drops."

Our pores closed up completely after a few days and we
did not perspire at all, in spite of the intense heat. We all
became a little lightheaded, and were unable to sleep, but
dozed slightly, and dreamed always of water, cool drinks,
fruit—and of rescue. I saw the cups of tea I had had in
hospital, ice-creams and iced coffees as I had so often enjoyed
them in Palestine; I saw myself in Cairo, with a glass of
pineapple juice at Groppis, and ripe mangoes ready to be
eaten, and once more came the cup of tea. Over and over
again, teasing and tormenting, like a cinematograph show the
scenes passed and re-passed. I thought of the water I had
wasted, of the dripping taps. People were washing up and
cleaning floors with precious life-giving water, unconscious of
our need and our longing. If only...!

We became thinner daily, and we were hollow-eyed. The
men's beards grew until they looked like pirates. All of us
were insufficiently clad, only two having shoes and socks, and
the sun and salt water rotted such clothes as we had. All our
sore areas began to discharge pus, and continued to discharge
all the time... We had no medical supplies at all, no dressings, no drugs, no stimulants, and as a nurse I had never felt
so helpless... Dr. Purslow and I opened septic fingers and
toes with a pen-knife, cleansed in sea water, and tried to
explain the importance of not infecting each other.

Mary became a little weaker every day. She never
suffered acutely, but just faded... She spoke often to me of
her family, never once did she allow the sorrow which must
have been in her heart to depress those round her, and she

kept her keen sense of humour all the time. I remember how, despite our desperate position, something would amuse us, and, catching each other's eye, we would laugh, and then the men up forward would smile too. She was most considerate of others, and grateful for everything done for her.

On September 25th she realized she could not live much longer. She smiled and thanked me for taking care of her, adding: "We've had lots of fun." Quite calmly she repeated her home address, and then seemed to fall asleep... Throughout that night I had my arms round her, in a last effort to keep her warm, but this night she didn't shiver, nothing disturbed her, and at six in the morning she just stopped breathing while asleep. Dr. Purslow held a little service for her, and we tried to sing a verse of "Abide with me," but the effort was pathetic. They lowered her into the water. I felt very much alone—the only woman with some sixty men.

As our journey continued, our numbers decreased... Daily we saw our companions growing weaker, saw they had not long to live, and then sometimes found they were no longer with us. Some, despite all warnings, drank salt water and succumbed, and others became delirious. Their cries and rambling speech and often repeated pleas for water were terrible to hear. One wondered how long one would remain sane.

... With our exceedingly small water ration, it was soon impossible to eat our biscuits or malted-milk tablets... I tried to eat my pemmican ration every day, as I had read that it has high food value, but it often took an hour to swallow one teaspoonful. The Horlicks tablets stuck to the roof of the mouth and stayed there. The chocolate dissolved easily, and I was able to eat the three little squares daily, until the supply ran out.

Some of the men managed to eat at least part of a biscuit by soaking it in sea water. One of the Polish cadets ate his biscuit in this way till the end of the time, and was the only one of the survivors who had no septic sores or boils. He... remained alert, kind and helpful to the end of the voyage, although he spoke no English.[1] When we were exhausted, he could always manage to dip up some water

---

[1] This man, Zdzislaw Uher afterwards came to Britain, where he is still living.

from the sea and pour it over our heads and limbs to refresh us. The other cadets died beside him in the boat.

. . . Until they became too weak, most of the men used to go over the side for a dip twice a day, and they used to pour tins of water over my bare head and shoulders and limbs. Then we would sit during the heat of the day with our clothing soaked in water, and with cloths which we kept perpetually wet tied over our heads. I believe that in these ways water was absorbed through the skin. By night our clothing had dried on us, and burning heat gave way to cold.

One night a small flying-fish came into the boat. It was divided among eight of us and we ate it with relish. We looked with longing at the numerous but elusive fish seen swimming around the boat, through the blue water. The men tried to make hooks and lines, but they had nothing firm enough for a hook, the fish were wiser and stronger than they, and none was caught.

On September 27th we saw quite clearly during the morning a three-funnelled vessel about four miles away. We were terribly excited and made great efforts to attract the attention of the vessel's look-out . . . We all leapt up, several climbed on thwarts and waved anything at hand . . . One man produced a petrol lighter which, miraculously, still worked, and we tore open a kapok life-jacket and set fire to it in our bucket which was held aloft. Someone blew our "boatswain's whistle," lips moved in silent prayer, faces were eager, hopeful, one felt all must now be well. Surely she was turning? No—not yet. "Oh, but she *is* nearer," the forrard look-outs agreed, and we all craned our necks and thought so too. Murmurs of "Rescue," "They've seen us," "Oh boy! Navy rum," were heard excitedly on all sides, and eyes filled with tears; but our hopes were not realized. She moved on and out of sight, and we sank back exhausted, terribly disappointed.

That was a silent day. As the colonel was about to help serve the rations, he spoke to us all. "Listen, everybody," he said, "we've had a big disappointment today, but there's always tomorrow. The fact that we've seen a ship means we are near a shipping route, and perhaps our luck will turn now . . ." But when another day passed and we had sighted nothing further, many people did give up hope. I still felt confident that somehow we should be saved; I was often conscious of the power of the prayers of my family and friends. During the time on the lifeboat there was a universal feeling after God, and a sense of dependence on Him, and one or another of us used to lead "family prayers" at night. For the last ten days or so this was my privilege, and everyone joined in readily. Unfortunately we had no Bible, but we had one Gospel of St. John belonging to an R.A.F. sergeant, and a prayer book.

. . . Dr. Purslow developed a deep infection of his left hand and arm and his right foot and leg. I used a razor blade to open his finger, and this discharged well, but nothing came from his foot. His glands began to swell, and red lines streaked his arm and leg . . . His condition did not improve at all . . . he lay day and night, only moving when necessary, and scarcely speaking at all. More septic places appeared, and it became evident he was suffering from blood-poisoning.

One morning, about nineteen weary days after the ship was torpedoed, I heard voices, and after a while realized that one was his . . . I gathered that, knowing he was a potential source of infection to others, Dr. Purslow had come to a great decision.

I stumbled to where he was sitting and tried to speak to him, but no words came. He was quite conscious, and in a voice stronger than I had heard for many days, he said: "As I cannot be of any further help, and if I am now a source of danger to you all, it is better I should go." As he heaved himself painfully up the side of the boat, I found my voice and said: "Greater love hath no man than this that he lay down his life for his friends." He said "goodbye," and with a long look he took that final step backwards. The sea closed over him.

We were fortunate in having a following wind almost every night, and the sea in our favour. As we grew weaker, we just sat or lay around, with one man keeping watch at the tiller, endeavouring to keep our course. When there was no wind, we felt our limp yellow sail was an enemy; but when, small as it was, it filled out with wind, it was a friend indeed and we hoped we made several knots an hour.

. . . Towards the end of our third week at sea, when I could no longer eat at all because I was devoid of saliva and depended for life on my water ration, we ran out of water; we hadn't enough for the next day's ration. We prayed for rain. Next day we had a torrential downpour, lasting nearly six hours. We caught it in every conceivable kind of vessel, as it ran from the sail, the gunwale, the thwarts and the mast; and how we drank. Never had any of us seen or tasted anything so wonderful. We were soaked to the skin and shivering—and we revelled in it. Our dried-up bodies took new strength, as we absorbed this life-giving water, and drank as we had dreamed of doing for so long. That day I managed to eat two biscuits again, and two or three Horlicks tablets. We collected about six gallons of water in our tanks, which we kept. That which had run from the sail was bright yellow, but who cared? That downpour had saved our lives; our hearts were full of praise and thanksgiving to God, Who had abundantly met our need... We thought of those no longer with us, for by this time the colonel... and indeed all our officers had died; so had many of the men. If only this rain had come before, so many others might have been saved.

Before sunset the rain ceased, and a pale sun came out of an overcast sky. The boat was inches deep in water, and there was nothing dry anywhere, so we set to work to get things as dry as possible before night fell... but we had a rather chilly time that night. Several of us had earache; even that could not depress us now.

... The heat continued, and we had no more rain. There was by this time room for us all to lie down, and so, by means of articles of clothing suspended from the seats, we made a little shade when the sun was at its hottest, and lay full length in the bottom of the boat.

We noticed an occasional *grey* gull now, and new birds; cloudbanks formed on the horizon morning and night, and we wondered whether land was near. Then one day we saw a leaf in the water, and our hopes rose.

On the morning of Thursday, October 8th, one of the British naval ratings sat looking ahead. I was sitting near him, and saw his face brighten. He spoke to an airman. They both looked eager, and I asked what the excitement was. He beckoned to me and said: "Sister, can you see anything over there?", pointing ahead of us. "Don't disturb the others, in case it's nothing, but I think that I can see a ship."

I looked, and was sure I could see something... after a little while we took it to be a destroyer on the horizon. It appeared to come a little nearer, and then we saw other shapes, which we took to be the ships of a convoy. We watched for half an hour, and then, as the ships did not move onwards, we knew that our prayers were answered and our dreams realized, that ahead of us was land. Our eyes smarted as we roused the others, sure now that they would not again be disappointed.

By the end of the day we could make out trees and hills easily ... but there was no sign of habitation. In the morning an off-shore breeze blew us slowly away from land ... We saw our special hill and palm-trees, for which we had decided to steer, growing farther and farther away. However ... towards the afternoon an on-shore breeze sprang up again ... and we made fair progress towards land.

When we were about five miles from the shore, we saw a flying-boat, with a Union Jack painted on its body. We waved and waved, and the plane circled over us. We were seen. It circled again, came lower, and again lower still. We lifted our board with "SOS WATER." Someone waved from the cockpit, and then the plane flew off landwards. We saw them flashing, then back came the plane heading for us once more, and circled round us again. As it flew very low over us, a life-jacket came hurtling through the air, and struck the water just beside us. It was a superb shot. Attached was a linen bag containing some food, but unfortunately it broke loose and was carried away. One of our airmen ... climbed over the boat's side, fell into the water and swam a few strokes. He rescued the life-jacket, and only an apple, a pear and a banana.

On the life-jacket was written: "O.K. Help coming. You are 60 miles south of Monrovia." None of us had any idea where Monrovia was, but we knew what help was, and our hearts sang.

On reaching England, I saw an extract from Captain A. G. Storr's voyage report, as follows:

> 9:10:42. At 1601 we passed over a small craft about five miles off the Liberian coast. Thinking this resembled a ship's lifeboat, I turned, descending, and inspection confirmed that this evidently was a boatload of survivors from a sunken vessel. Due to a south-westerly wind, the boat had slight way on her towards the shore. The occupants, some of

whom appeared to be women, were delighted to see us, and held up a board on which was chalked, "SOS WATER."

We circled for some time, but could find no container in which water could be dropped, so filled a double pillowslip with fresh fruit, and a can of orange juice, also enclosing a waterproof bag containing cigarettes, matches and a note. To this pack was tied one of the kapok life-jackets. A bombing run was made over the boat, and the bundle dropped from the starboard drift-sight hatch. It fell from the boat and was picked up immediately by a swimmer.

On arrival in Lagos Captain Storr again reported that he had sighted a lifeboat whose occupants were obviously in a bad way, and suggested it might be a good idea for flying-boats to carry water-containers for such occasions. They could be fairly small, and fitted with a small parachute to prevent them breaking on striking the water...

When the plane had gone we settled down again... we did not expect any more help that night. We could see waves breaking on the shore and spray being flung all along the coastline, except for one spot. We knew therefore that there must be rocks where the spray flew high and shingle where we saw no spray. Our boat was being blown directly towards the gap in the rocks. A British naval rating at the tiller kept the little boat headed towards the place of safety... Night fell and we went drifting on. We could still see the great white walls of spray. We scarcely spoke, but sat staring fixedly ahead, unmoving, breathing fast. At last, a little before eight, we were washed up on the sand by two great rolling waves. We had beached, and our boat was held firm, on the one spot possible; anywhere else for miles on either side we should have been dashed against the rocks.

We scrambled with difficulty over the boat's side, and promptly collapsed into shallow water. We crawled on hands and knees out of reach of the tide.

The ground seemed to be rocking, rocking, even as our boat had rocked, and this sensation was to bother us for several days. The men brought with them our remaining biscuits and pemmican and a few souvenirs from the boat; and then, wet to the skin, we huddled together on the sand,

and gave thanks to God for the miracle he had wrought for us sixteen survivors out of our original sixty-eight. We had travelled over seven hundred miles in our open boat.

The heavy scent of tropical undergrowth was in the air. Crickets were singing as I had never heard them before. After about twenty minutes we saw a light approaching along the shore. Who could be coming? We wondered if they might be cannibals or untamed savages. Two of our men staggered forward, and found themselves face to face with a crowd of negroes, the leader of whom flung his arms around them and said in English: "Thank God you safe." They had watched our boat for two days, and had come to search for us, rather expecting to find a wreck and no living people.

They came up to us and began talking to us in their excited voices in pidgin English, and in their own language to each other. They searched the boat, taking everything they could carry. I was grieved because Mary's wedding ring had slipped from my thin finger, and it had fallen between the floorboards. I had so much wanted to keep it safely for her husband.

After a short time these men helped us to our feet, supported some of us, and carried three men who were unable to stand. They led us to a native African village some distance away in the bush. We staggered along on our bare swollen feet for some time, and wondered whether we should ever reach a resting-place. Suddenly we heard voices, and came through the trees into a clearing. There, by the light of flares, we saw thatched native houses; all the inhabitants of the village were standing around one house, larger than the rest, where the "priest" lived. Some were laughing, some crying (we *were* a pitiful sight), and some just stood staring stolidly and silently.

The village was near the coast, and also near a trading town, so some of the men spoke English, and the adult men wore European clothes. The women spoke no English... most were draped with cotton cloth, the younger ones wearing only skirts of material or grass. The children wore nothing.

Into this primitive place we had come, and once again I experienced the sensation that all was a dream... They made room for us to sit, and brought us fruit, for which our bodies were crying out: oranges, huge bananas and plums like mangoes. We ate sparingly, fearing to do ourselves harm after our long fast. We asked for hot water, as we knew the water must have come from the creek over which we had passed, and imagined it must be full of germs. We mixed in some of the pemmican and made a drink which was hot and nourishing, even if not delicious. They vied with each other to do something for us, and laughed and cried alternately.

Suddenly one of the women nudged another and pointed to me. I had been in the background and away from the light, but apparently she had just noticed I had no beard. Soon there was some excited conversation between a knot of women, and they pointed to me and said something. I caught the word "Mammy" several times and wondered. Then one of the men said: "She say you lady. Yea?" I answered in the affirmative, and hands went up in horror and sympathy... It was quite understandable that they were not sure of me, for my uncombed hair was curly and too long for a man, but my R.A.F. shirt and army shorts were scarcely feminine... They then wanted to know where my husband was; at that I was a little apprehensive, so I tucked my hand through the arm of one of our men, and they appeared to think all was well...

[The party were soon taken to the near-by trading town, where there were a few Dutch and Syrians, who put them all up and treated them with great kindness. From there they were brought to Freetown, on October 25th, where Sister Hawkins spent six weeks in hospital, "becoming stronger every day."]

... So at last came the morning which I had longed for, yet dreaded. I was taken aboard the sister ship of the one on which I had been torpedoed, and the next journey of three thousand miles in an unescorted ship through submarine-haunted waters had begun. It was a nightmare voyage—every bang made me leap from my bunk. No real rest of mind came by night or day, and a great gale lashed the waves in its fury, so that even the top decks were drenched. Then the good ship rolled and pitched and we knew that no lifeboat could be launched safely in such weather. But at last we sighted the coast of England, and arrived safely in port. Five years before, I had made my outward journey from England to Jerusalem in one week, and this time it had taken me over four months. I reached my own home in the early hours of December 18th.

. . . Many other heroic acts are not recorded in detail in this story. We who survived will remember some whose patience, tact and courage were an inspiration. Amongst others, we think of the man with the broken arm . . . whose only complaint was that he was unable to row and to help with the navigating. He was a most energetic member of the "pumping squad," and always cheerful . . . We think of the Irishman, no longer young, ever optimistic and comforting, and full of ingenuity over the sail and jib. He would sit considering, then, if he thought of an improvement, he would energetically undo work which he had done perhaps only an hour before, and refix sails and ropes, so that we might take fuller advantage of the wind prevailing at the time. He was always giving as many as possible jobs to do . . . The assistant purser inspired the forward end of the boat, and was always among the first to move if there was a job to be done. We were impressed by the quiet, unassuming way in which an R.A.F. corporal helped us in those last days in the boat; it was he who lent his greatcoat to cover Mary at night, when the blanket was taken to make the jib. Only those who have lived through such an experience can know how big the little things seem, and how one word or action, or one person's optimism, can change the atmosphere for everyone.

It is impossible to imagine why I should have been chosen to survive when so many did not. I have been reluctant to write this story of our experiences, but in answer to many requests I have done so; and if it strengthens someone's faith, if it is an inspiration to any, if it brings home to others, hitherto untouched, all that "those who go down to the sea in ships" face for our sakes, hour by hour, day by day, year in, year out—it will not have been written in vain.

Appendix C

AMERICAN SERVICES: ANSWERS ON THE LIBERATOR INCIDENT

1. Letters from Rear-Admiral E. M. Eller, Department of the Navy, Office of the Chief of Naval Operations, Washington.

October 9th, 1959

Dear Mr. Peillard,

Unfortunately a search in Navy Department files and an inquiry to the Department of the Air Force have failed to identify the Liberator aircraft which attacked the U-156 off Freetown on September 16th, 1942. The Germans do make reference to the attack, but, of course, the British were also flying Liberators, and Freetown was primarily a British base.

Construction battalion personnel of the U.S. Navy did assist in the base development at Freetown. Freetown was used as a staging area by the Air Transport Command of the U.S. Army Air Force until September 15th, 1942.

U.S. Naval land-based aircraft are credited with sinking U-156 on March 8th, 1943.

The best of luck with your book.

Sincerely yours,

E. M. ELLER

November 12th, 1959

Dear Mr. Peillard,

This is in reply to your letter of October 21st.

Further research on the incident involving an attack

on U-156 on September 16th, 1942, has established that
if the attacking aircraft was American, it definitely was
not a U.S. Navy plane. In view of this fact, may I suggest
that you address your inquiry directly to the Historical
Section, Department of the Air Force, Washington 25,
D.C. Perhaps this organization will be able to supply the
information you seek.

Again, best wishes for success with your book.

Sincerely yours,

E. M. ELLER

B-25 Mitchell

2. U.S.A.F. Historical Division Research Report. Liberator Attack on U-156, September 16th, 1942.

Problem:

Provide all available information concerning an attack on
German U-boat 156 on September 16th, 1942, by a Liberator
based at Freetown, Africa. Requested by Office of Naval
History.

Findings:

1. No information concerning this attack has been found
in the documents available in the Division's archives. Although the attack may have been made by a U.S. B-24, it
probably was made by an R.A.F. plane.

2. We have found no evidence that the A.A.F. had any
combat unit of squadron or higher echelon based at any of the
fields near Freetown, Sierra Leone, Africa. If any regular
combat operations were conducted by the A.A.F. from Freetown,
they apparently would have been conducted by a detachment
of some unit. Search of documents of units known to have

engaged in anti-submarine operations in 1942 has provided no information about any such detachment.

3. The A.A.F. anti-submarine operations closest to Freetown in September 1942 apparently were those from Ascension Island. On September 16th, 1942, a B-24 flying from Ascension attacked a U-boat about 130 miles north-north-east of the Island. The following day the same pilot, flying in a B-24 from Ascension, attacked a U-boat at 4°50′ south, 12°22′ west. We have no reports on the unit's aircraft for September 1942. The available reports show that the unit had P-39s and B-25s at the end of November 1942 and for several weeks thereafter.

4. At least two fields near Freetown could have been used for B-24 operations. One was Waterloo, which an A.A.F. route manual dated October 5th, 1943, describes as the best in the vicinity. At that time Waterloo was operated by the R.A.F. The other field was Hastings. A route manual dated February 18th, 1943, states that the latter was operated by the R.A.F. and was "not recommended" for B-24s. The manual of February 18th, 1943, does not list Waterloo, but the field is shown in an airport directory dated January 13th, 1943.

5. From December 14th, 1941, to September 15th, 1942, the A.A.F. Air Transport Command used facilities that Pan American Airlines operated at Freetown. We have found no evidence that A.T.C. was directly engaged in anti-submarine operations from West Africa.

6. B-24s often flew across the South Atlantic, and some may have landed at Freetown. It is possible that at Freetown these A.A.F. planes were pressed into service to carry out specific missions against enemy submarines reported in the vicinity.

7. The history of the Africa-Middle East Wing, A.T.C., states that aircraft flying the South Atlantic Route "did not carry depth-charges because of their heavy gasoline loads." A.A.F. crews flying the South Atlantic were, however, instructed to report submarine sightings. Full-time interrogation officers were stationed at Accra, Roberts [Field, Liberia] and Dakar. Major H. R. Turkel, Wing A-2, described the "submarine-sighting situation" in October 1942: "Those sightings which occur within a range of 300 miles of here [Accra] are reported to R.A.F. Takoradi, R.A.F. Freetown, and Rear-Admiral, West Africa. In addition, I send reports of all submarine sightings to W.Z.Q. Boriqueen P.R. for the use of

O.N.I." The history also says that "the R.A.F. and Royal Navy took steps when submarines were reported."

8. Admiralty document C.B. 04050/42 (9), dated October 15th, 1942, gives the number of flying hours for aircraft engaged in anti-submarine operations off West Africa. A chart in the same document shows three aerial attacks on submarines during September 1942 in the area off Liberia and Sierra Leone. No further information on these attacks has been found.

9. Admiralty document C.B. 04050/43 (7), dated August 15th, 1943, contains a map that shows the number of anti-submarine sorties flown in the R.A.F. Freetown sector in May 1943. The next issue of the same document, C.B. 04050/43 (8), gives a similar map. The latter includes data for the number of French flying hours in the Dakar-Bathurst sector.

10. The history of the Africa-Middle East Wing contains the following statement: "In August, 1943, an R.A.F. B-24 was shot down by a German submarine just off Dakar; in September a U.S. B-24 attacked a U-boat and the pilot thought he sank it, though it later turned out that he had not." No other information has been found concerning the latter attack, which apparently took place in September 1943.

11. Air Ministry document A.M.C.O. 12/1946, dated June 1st, 1945, a final assessment of enemy submarine casualties, states that German U-156 was sunk on March 8th, 1943, by "U.S.N. A/U PatRon 53" at 12°38' north, 54°39' west. An Admiralty document, A.F.A. 4305/46, dated June 26th, 1946, lists German U-156 as having been sunk by "U.S.N. A/C PatRon, No. 53 Sq. (D)" at a position "E. of Barbados" on March 8th, 1943.

Appendix D

EXTRACTS FROM NUREMBERG TRIALS DEALING WITH THE *LACONIA* INCIDENT (OFFICIAL TEXT IN ENGLISH)

Monday: January 14th, 1946—Morning Session

COLONEL H. J. PHILLIMORE (*Prosecuting*): My Lord, I turn to the next document... This is the first of a series of orders leading up to the issue of an order which enjoined the U-boat commanders not merely to abstain from rescuing crews, which is the purpose of this order, not merely to give them no assistance, but deliberately to annihilate them.

In the course of my proof of this matter, I shall call two witnesses. The first witness will give the Court an account of the speech made by the defendant at the time that he issued the order, describing the policy, or his policy towards the recovery of allied troops, that it must be stopped at all costs.

The second witness is the officer who actually briefed crews on the order.

This document is an extract from the standing orders of the U-boat Command, and it is signed by the defendant:

"Do not pick up men or take them with you. Do not worry about the merchant ships' boats. Weather conditions and distance from land play no part. Have a care only for your own ship and strive only to attain your next success as soon as possible. We must be harsh in this war. The enemy began the war in order to destroy us, so nothing else matters."

THE PRESIDENT. What is the date of that?

COL. PHILLIMORE. My Lord... it is earlier than May 2nd, 1940. That is a secret order....

It was, however, in 1942, when the United States entered the war with its enormous ship-building capacity, that the change thus brought about necessitated a further adjustment in the methods adopted by U-boats and of the defendant; and the defendant was guilty of an order which intended not merely the sinking of merchant ships, not merely the abstention from rescue of their crews, but their deliberate extermination.

The next document is a record of a conversation between Hitler and the Japanese ambassador Oshima, in the presence of the defendant Ribbentrop, on January 3rd, 1942.

"The Führer, using a map, explains to the Japanese ambassador the present position of marine warfare in the Atlantic, emphasizing that what he considers his most important task is to get the U-boat warfare going in full swing. The U-boats are being reorganized. Firstly, he had recalled all U-boats operating in the Atlantic. As mentioned before, they would now be posted outside United States ports. Later they would be off Freetown, and the larger boats even as far down as Capetown."

And then, after further details:

"After having given further explanations on the map, the Führer pointed out that, however many ships the United States built, one of their main problems would be the lack of personnel. For that reason even merchant ships would be sunk without warning with the intention of killing as many of the crew as possible. Once it gets around that most of the seamen are lost in the sinkings, the Americans would soon have difficulty in enlisting new people. The training of sea-going personnel takes a very long time. We are fighting for our existence and our attitude cannot be ruled by any humane feelings. For this reason he must give the order that in case foreign seamen could not be taken in as prisoners, which is in most cases not possible on the sea, U-boats were to surface after torpedoing, and shoot up the lifeboats.

"Ambassador Oshima heartily agreed with the Führer's comments, and said that the Japanese, too, are forced to follow these methods."

The next document I do not propose to read. It is an extract from B.d.U. War Diary of September 16th, 1942. It records an attack on a U-boat' which was rescuing survivors, chiefly the Italian survivors of the Allied liner *Laconia*.

The next document ... contains four separate documents. The first is a top-secret order, sent to all commanding officers of U-boats from the defendant's headquarters, dated September 17th, 1942.

1. No attempt of any kind must be made at rescuing members of ships sunk, and this includes picking up persons in the water and putting them in lifeboats, righting capsized lifeboats and handing over food and water. Rescue runs counter to the rudimentary demands of warfare for the destruction of enemy ships and crews.

2. Orders for bringing in captains and chief engineers still apply.

3. Rescue the shipwrecked only if their statements will be important for your boat.

4. Be harsh, bearing in mind that the enemy takes no regard of women and children in his bombing attacks on German cities.

Now, my lord, that is, of course, a very carefully worded order. Its intentions are made very clear by the next document on the same page, which is an extract from the defendant's war diary ... personally signed by the defendant Dönitz. It is the war diary entry for September 17th, 1942:

"The attention of all commanding officers is again drawn—and I would draw the Tribunal's attention to the word 'again'—to the fact that all efforts to rescue members of the crews of ships which have been sunk contradict the most primitive demands for the conduct of warfare for annihilating enemy ships and their crews..."

The last two documents on that page consist of a telegram from the commander of the U-boat, Schacht, to the defendant's headquarters, and the reply. Schacht had been taking part in the rescue of survivors from the *Laconia*. The telegram from Schacht, dated September 17th, 1942, reads: "163 Italians handed over to *Annamite*. Navigating Officer of *Laconia* and another English officer on board." And then it goes on setting out the position of English and Polish survivors in boats.

The reply sent on the 20th: "Action as in wireless telegram of 17th of September was wrong. Boat was detailed to rescue Italian allies and not for the rescue of English and Poles."

It is a small point, but of course "detailed" means before the bombing incident had ever occurred.

To sum up these documents, it would appear from the war diary entry of September 17th that orders on the lines discussed between Hitler and Oshima were, in fact, issued, but we have not captured them. It may be they were issued orally and that the defendant awaited a suitable opportunity before confirming them. The incident of the bombing of the U-boats detailed to rescue the one hundred and sixty-three survivors from the *Laconia* afforded the opportunity, and the order to all commanders was issued. Its intent is very clear when you consider it in the light of the war diary entry. The wording is, of course, extremely careful, but to any officer of experience its intention was obvious and he would know that deliberate action to annihilate survivors would be approved under that order.

You will be told that this order, although perhaps unfortunately phrased, was merely intended to stop a commander from jeopardizing his ship by attempting a rescue, which had become increasingly dangerous as a result of the extended coverage of the ocean by Allied aircraft; and that the notorious action of the U-boat Commander Eck in sinking the Greek steamer *Peleus*, and then machine-gunning the crew on their rafts in the water, was an exception; and that, although it may be true that a copy of the order was on board, this action was taken solely, as he himself swore, on his own initiative.

I would make the point to the Tribunal that if the intention of the order was to stop the rescue attempts in the interests of the preservation of the U-boat, first of all

it would have been done by calling attention to Standing
Order 154.

Second, this very fact would have been prominently
stated in the order. Drastic orders of this nature are not
drafted by experienced staff officers without the greatest
care and an eye to their possible capture by the enemy....

My lord, I would call my first witness, Peter Heisig.

*(The witness took the stand, and was given the oath,
which he repeated in German.)*

COL. PHILLIMORE. Peter Josef Heisig, are you an Oberleutnant
zur See in Germany?

HEISIG. I am Oberleutnant zur See in the German Navy.

COL. PHILLIMORE. And were you captured on December
27th, 1944, and now held as a prisoner of war?

HEISIG. Yes.

COL. PHILLIMORE. In the autumn of 1942 what rank did you
hold?

HEISIG. I was senior midshipman at the 2nd U-boat Training
Division.

COL. PHILLIMORE. Were you attending a course there?

HEISIG. I took part in the training course for U-boat officers of
the watch.

COL. PHILLIMORE. Do you remember the last day of the
course?

HEISIG. On the last day of the course Grand-admiral Dönitz,
who was then Commander-in-Chief of the U-boats,
reviewed the 2nd U-boat Training Division.

COL. PHILLIMORE. And what happened at the end of this tour?

HEISIG. At the end of his visit—not at the end, but rather
during his visit—Grand-admiral Dönitz made a speech
before the officers of the 2nd U-boat Training Division.

COL. PHILLIMORE. Can you fix the date of this visit?

HEISIG. I remember the approximate date; it must have been
at the end of September or the beginning of October
1942.

COL. PHILLIMORE. Now will you give the Tribunal—speaking
slowly—an account of what Admiral Dönitz said in his
speech.

HEISIG. Grand-admiral Dönitz said in his speech that the
successes of the U-boats had declined. The strength of
enemy air control was responsible for that decline. New

anti-aircraft guns had been developed which in future would make it possible for the U-boats to fight off enemy aircraft. Hitler had personally given him the assurance that U-boats would be equipped with these anti-aircraft guns before all other branches of the armed forces. It could be expected, therefore, that the successes of former times would be reached again within a few months...

The Allies were having considerable difficulties in manning their ships. Some of their seamen were even trying to shirk a crossing of the Atlantic, so that the Allied authorities were compelled, if it became necessary, to retain the men aboard by force of law... Admiral Dönitz concluded that the question of personnel was a very grave matter for the Allies. The losses in men affected the Allies especially seriously because they had few reserves and also because...

COL. PHILLIMORE. I don't want to interrupt you, but did he say anything about rescues at all?... Will you come to the crucial part of the speech, at the end, and deal with that? What did the Grand-admiral go on to say?...

HEISIG. He continued, saying approximately that under the circumstances he could not understand how German U-boats could still rescue the crews of the merchant ships they had sunk, thereby endangering their own ships. By doing that they were working for the enemy, since these rescued crews would sail again on new ships.

The stage had now been reached in which total war had to be waged also at sea. The crews of ships, like the ships themselves, were a target for the U-boats; thus it would be impossible for the Allies to man their newly built ships; and moreover it could then be expected that in America and the other Allied countries a strike would break out, for already some of the seamen did not want to go back to sea.

These results could be expected if our tactics would render the war at sea more vigorous. If any of us consider this war or these tactics harsh we should also remember that our wives and our families at home are being bombed.

That, in its main points, was the speech of Grand-admiral Dönitz.

NAVAL JUDGE ADVOCATE OTTO KRANZBÜHLER (*Counsel for defendant Dönitz*). Oberleutnant Heisig, did you yourself take part in an action against the enemy?

HEISIG. Yes.

KRANZBÜHLER. On which boat were you, and who was your commander?

HEISIG. I was on U-877, under Kapitänleutnant Finkeisen.

KRANZBÜHLER. Were you successful in action against enemy ships?

HEISIG. The boat was sunk on its way to the area of operations.

KRANZBÜHLER. Before you were able to sink any enemy ship?

HEISIG. Yes.

KRANZBÜHLER. How was the boat sunk?

HEISIG. By depth-charges. Two Canadian frigates sighted the U-boat and destroyed it through depth-charges.

KRANZBÜHLER.... Since you have knowledge of the circumstances, do you maintain that the speech of Grand-admiral Dönitz mentioned in any way that fire should be opened on shipwrecked sailors?

HEISIG. No; we gathered that from his words; and from his reference to the bombing war, we gathered that total war had now to be waged against ships and crews. That is what we understood, and I talked about it to my comrades on the way back to the Hansa. We were convinced that Admiral Dönitz meant that. He did not express it clearly.

KRANZBÜHLER. Did you speak about the point with any of your superiors at the school?

HEISIG. I left the school on the same day. But I can remember that one of my superiors, whose name to my regret I do not recall—nor do I recall the occasion—once spoke to us about this subject and advised us that, if possible, only officers should be on the bridge ready to liquidate shipwrecked sailors, should the possibility arise or should it be necessary.

KRANZBÜHLER. One of your superiors told you that?

HEISIG. Yes, but I cannot remember in which connection and where. I received a lot of advice from my superiors on many things.

KRANZBÜHLER. ... Were you instructed at the school in the standing orders of war?

HEISIG. Yes.

KRANZBÜHLER. Did these standing orders mention anywhere that shipwrecked sailors were to be fired on or their rescue apparatus destroyed?

HEISIG. The standing order did not mention that. But—I think one can assume this from an innuendo of Captain Rollmann, who was then officers' company commander— a short time before that, some teletype message had arrived containing an order prohibiting rescue measures and demanding that sea warfare should be fought with more radical, more drastic means.

KRANZBÜHLER. Do you think that the prohibition of rescue measures is identical with the shooting of shipwrecked sailors?

HEISIG. We came to this . . .

KRANZBÜHLER. Please answer my question. Do you think these two things are identical?

HEISIG. No.

KRANZBÜHLER. Thank you.

Tuesday, January 15th, 1946—Morning Session

(Karl Heinz Möhle took the stand and was sworn in.)

COL. PHILLIMORE. Karl Heinz Möhle, you held the rank of Lieutenant-Commander in the German navy?

MÖHLE. Yes, sir.

COL. PHILLIMORE. In the autumn of 1942 were you head of the 5th U-boat flotilla?

MÖHLE. Yes, sir, for four years.

COL. PHILLIMORE. What were your duties as commander of that flotilla?

MÖHLE. My main duties consisted of the fitting-out of U-boats which were to be sent to the front from home bases, and giving them the orders of the U-boat Command . . . It was my responsibility to see that out-going U-boats were provided with the new orders of the U-boat Command . . . The orders of the U-boat Command were always very clear and unambiguous.

COL PHILLIMORE. Did you personally see commanders before they went out on patrol?

MÖHLE. Yes, each commander before sailing on a mission went through a briefing session at my office.

COL. PHILLIMORE. . . . Do you remember an order in the autumn of 1942 dealing with lifeboats?

MÖHLE. . Yes. In September 1942 I received a wireless message to all commanders at sea, and it dealt with that question. . . .

COL. PHILLIMORE. After you got that order did you go to Admiral Dönitz's headquarters?

MÖHLE. Yes. At my first visit to headquarters after receipt of the order I personally discussed it with Lieutenant-Commander Kuppisch, who was a specialist on the staff of the U-boat Command . . . At that meeting I asked him how the ambiguity contained in that order—or I might say, lack of clarity—should be understood. He explained the order by two illustrations.

The first example was that of a U-boat in the outer Bay of Biscay. It was sailing on a patrol when it sighted a rubber dinghy carrying survivors of a British plane. The mission, that is, being fully equipped, made it impossible to take the crew of the plane on board, although, especially at that time, it appeared especially desirable to bring back specialists in navigation from shot-down crews to get useful information from them. The commander of the U-boat made a wide circle around this rubber boat and continued on his mission. When he returned from his mission he reported the case to the staff of the Commander-in-Chief of U-boats. The staff officers reproached him, saying that, if he were unable to bring these navigation specialists back with him, the right thing to do would have been to attack that crew, for it was to be expected that in less than twenty-four hours, at the latest, the dinghy would be rescued by British reconnaissance forces, and they . . .

COL. PHILLIMORE. I don't quite get what you said would have been the correct action to take. You were saying the correct thing to do would have been . . .

MÖHLE. . . . To attack the air-crew, as it was not possible to bring back the crew or these specialists, for it could be expected that that crew would be found and rescued within a short time by British reconnaissance forces, and in given circumstances might again destroy one or two German U-boats . . .

COL. PHILLIMORE. What was the second example?

MÖHLE. During the first month of the U-boat warfare against the United States a great quantity of tonnage had been sunk in the shallow waters off the American coast. In these sinkings the greater part of the crews were rescued, because of the close proximity of land. That was exceedingly regrettable, because merchant shipping not only consists of tonnage but also of crews, and in the meantime these crews were again able to man newly-built ships.

COL. PHILLIMORE. From your knowledge of the way orders were worded, can you tell the Tribunal what you understood Admiral Dönitz's order (in September 1942) to mean?

MÖHLE. The order meant, in my own opinion, that rescue measures remained prohibited, and moreover it was desirable in the case of sinkings of merchantmen that there should be no survivors.

COL. PHILLIMORE. How did you brief submarine commanders on this order?

MÖHLE. . . . I read them the wording of the wireless message without making any comment. In a very few instances some commanders asked me about the meaning of the order. In such cases I gave them the two examples that headquarters had given to me. However, I added, "U-boat Command cannot give you such an order officially; everybody has to handle this according to his own conscience."

COL. PHILLIMORE. Do you remember an order about rescue ships?

MÖHLE. Yes . . . I do not remember the exact date, but I think it must have been about the same as the order of September 1942.

COL. PHILLIMORE. Do you remember an order about entries in logs?

MÖHLE. Yes, sir. At the time, the exact date I do not remember, it had been ordered that sinkings and other acts which were in contradiction to international conventions should not be entered in the log but reported orally after return to the home port.

COL. PHILLIMORE. Would you care to say why it is that you are giving evidence in this case?

MÖHLE. Yes, sir; because when I was taken prisoner, it was claimed that I was the author of these orders, and I do not want to have this charge connected with my name.

NAVAL JUDGE ADVOCATE KRANZBÜHLER. Lieutenant-Commander Möhle, since when have you been in the U-boat arm?

MÖHLE. Since the end of 1936.

KRANZBÜHLER. Do you know Grand-admiral Dönitz personally?

MÖHLE. Yes.

KRANZBÜHLER. Since when?

MÖHLE. Since October 1937.

KRANZBÜHLER. Do you know him as an admiral to whom none of his flotilla chiefs could speak?

MÖHLE. No.

KRANZBÜHLER. Or was the opposite the case?

MÖHLE. He could be approached by everybody at any time.

KRANZBÜHLER. Have you yourself been a commander of a U-boat?

MÖHLE. Yes, on nine occasions . . . from the beginning of the war until April 1941.

KRANZBÜHLER. How many ships did you sink?

MÖHLE. Twenty ships.

KRANZBÜHLER. After sinking ships, did you destroy the rescue equipment or fire on the survivors?

MÖHLE. No.

KRANZBÜHLER. Did you have an order to do that?

MÖHLE. No.

KRANZBÜHLER. Had the danger passed for a U-boat after the attack on a merchantman?

MÖHLE. No.

KRANZBÜHLER. Do you know that the order of September 1942 was given in consequence of an incident in which German U-boats had undertaken rescue measures?

MÖHLE. Yes, sir.

KRANZBÜHLER. And the U-boats were then attacked by Allied aircraft?

MÖHLE. Yes, sir.

KRANZBÜHLER. You interpreted the order of September 1942 to the commanders in the sense that it should include the destruction of rescue facilities and of the shipwrecked crew?

MÖHLE. No, not quite; I gave the two examples to the

commanders only if they made an inquiry, and I passed them on in the same way as I had received them from the Commander-in-Chief Submarine Fleet, and they themselves could draw that conclusion from these two examples.

KRANZBÜHLER. In which sentence of the order do you see a hidden invitation to kill survivors or to destroy the rescue facilities?... Is it in the sentence: "Rescue measures contradict the most primitive demands of warfare that crews and ships should be destroyed"?

MÖHLE. Yes.

KRANZBÜHLER. Does that sentence contain anything as to the destruction of shipwrecked persons?

MÖHLE. No, of crews.

KRANZBÜHLER. At the end of the order is the phrase "Be harsh." Did you hear that phrase there for the first time?

MÖHLE. No.

KRANZBÜHLER. Was this phrase used by the Commander-in-Chief of U-boats to get the commanders to be severe to themselves and to their crews?

MÖHLE. Yes...

Session of May 9th, 1946

KRANZBÜHLER. Admiral, you have just described the enemy's supremacy in the air in September 1942. During these September days you received the report about the sinking of the British transport *Laconia*. I submit to the Tribunal the war diaries concerning that incident... the war diaries of the commanders of the submarines... which took part in this action, Lieutenant-Commanders Hartenstein, Schacht and Würdemann. I shall read to you the report you received... on September 13th, at 1:25 a.m.

"Wireless message sent on American circuit:
Sunk by Hartenstein British ship *Laconia*."

Then the position is given and the message continues: "Unfortunately with 1,500 Italian prisoners of war. Up to now picked up 90..." Then the details and the end of "Request orders..." Please tell me first what impression or what knowledge you had about this ship *Laconia* which had been reported sunk and its crew?

DÖNITZ. I knew from the handbook on armed British ships

which we had at our disposal that the *Laconia* was armed
with fourteen guns. I concluded, therefore, that it would
have a British crew of at least about five hundred men.
When I heard that there were also Italian prisoners on
board, it was clear to me that this number would be
further increased by the guards of the prisoners.

KRANZBÜHLER. Please describe now ... the main events surrounding your order of September 17th, and elaborate
first on the rescue or non-rescue of British or Italians,
and secondly, your concern for the safety of the U-boats
in question.

DÖNITZ. When I received this report I radioed to all U-boats
in the whole area. I issued the order: "Schacht, Group
Eisbär, Würdemann, Wilamowitz, proceed to Hartenstein
immediately." Later I had to have several boats turn back
because their distance from the scene was too great.
Above all I asked Hartenstein, the commander who had
sunk the ship, whether the *Laconia* had sent out radio
messages, because I hoped that as a result British and
American ships would come to the rescue. Hartenstein
affirmed that and, besides, he himself sent out the
following radio message in English: "If any ship will
assist the shipwrecked *Laconia* crew, I will not attack
her, provided I am not being attacked by ship or air
force." I gained the impression from the reports of the
U-boats that they began the rescue work with great zeal.

KRANZBÜHLER. How many submarines were there?

DÖNITZ. There were three or four. I received reports that the
numbers of those taken on board by each U-boat were
between one and two hundred ... The reports spoke of
the crew being cared for and taken over from lifeboats ... of
the touring of lifeboats by the submarines. All these
reports caused me the greatest concern, because I knew
for certain that this would not end well.

My concern ... was expressed in a message to the
submarines, radioed four times. "Detailed boats to take
over only so many as to remain fully able to dive." It is
obvious that if the narrow space of the submarine—our
U-boats were half as big as the enemy's—is crowded
with one to two hundred additional people, the submarine is already in absolute danger, not to speak of its
fitness to fight. ... That my concern was justified was

clearly evident from the message which Hartenstein
sent, which said that he had been attacked by bombs
from an American bomber. . . .

KRANZBÜHLER. The message from Hartenstein reads: "Bombed
five times by American Liberator in low flight when
towing four full boats in spite of a Red Cross flag, 4
square metres, on the bridge and good visibility. Both
periscopes at present out of order. Breaking off rescue;
all off board; putting out to west. Will repair."

Admiral, would you tell us now what measures you took
after Hartenstein's report?

DÖNITZ. I deliberated at length whether, after this experience,
I should not break off all attempts at rescue; and beyond
doubt, from the military point of view, that would have
been the right thing to do, because the attack showed
clearly in what way the U-boats were endangered.

That decision became more grave for me because I
received a call from the Naval Operations Staff that the
Führer did not wish me to risk any submarines in rescue
work or to summon them from distant areas. A very
heated conference with my staff ensued, and I can
remember closing it with the statement, "I cannot throw
these people into the water now. I will carry on."

Of course, it was clear to me that I would have to
assume full responsibility for further losses, and from the
military point of view the continuation of the rescue
work was wrong. Of that I received proof from the U-506
of Würdemann, who also reported—I believe on the
following morning—that he was bombed by an aeroplane.

KRANZBÜHLER. That report, Mr. President, is . . . in the war
diary of Würdemann, an entry of September 17th at
11:43 p.m. He reported: "Transfer of survivors to *Annamite*
completed." Then came details—"Attacked by heavy sea-
plane at noon. Fully ready for action."

DÖNITZ. The third submarine, Schacht's, the U-507, had sent
a wireless message that he had so and so many men on
board and was towing four lifeboats with Englishmen and
Poles . . . Thereupon, of course, I ordered him to cast off
these boats, because this burden made it impossible for
him to dive . . . Later he sent a long message . . .

KRANZBÜHLER. . . . At 11:10 p.m. I shall read the message:
"Transferred 163 Italians to *Annamite*. Navigation officer

of *Laconia* and another English officer on board. Seven
lifeboats with about 330 Englishmen and Poles, among
them 15 women and 16 children, deposited at Quarter
FE 9612, women and children kept aboard ship for one
night. Supplied all shipwrecked with hot meal and drinks,
clothed and bandaged when necessary. Four other boats
anchored to a buoy in square FE 9619."

DÖNITZ. Because I had ordered him to cast off the lifeboats
and we considered this general message as a supplemen-
tary later report, he was admonished by another message; and from that the prosecutor wrongly concluded
that I had prohibited the rescue of Englishmen. That I
did not prohibit it can be seen from the fact that I did
not raise objection to the many reports speaking of the
rescue of Englishmen.

Indeed, in the end, I had the impression that the
Italians did not fare very well in the rescue. That this
impression was correct can be seen from the figures of
those rescued. Of eight hundred and eleven Englishmen
about eight hundred were rescued,[1] and of one thousand and eight hundred Italians four hundred and fifty.

KRANZBÜHLER. The *Laconia* was torpedoed on September
12th . . . The rescue took how many days altogether?

DÖNITZ. Four days.

KRANZBÜHLER. And afterwards was continued till when?

DÖNITZ. Until we turned them over to the French warships
which had been notified by us.

KRANZBÜHLER. Now what is the connection between the
incident of the *Laconia* which you have just described,
and the order which the prosecution charges as an order
for destruction?

DÖNITZ. Apart from my great and constant anxiety for the
submarines and the strong feeling that the British and
Americans had not helped despite the proximity of
Freetown, I learned from this action very definitely that
the time had passed when U-boats could carry out such
operations on the surface without danger. The two bombing
attacks showed clearly that in spite of good weather, in
spite of the large numbers of people to be rescued who
were more clearly visible to the aviators than in normal

---

[1] See footnote to Admiral Dönitz's similar statement in Appendix E.

heavy sea conditions when few people have to be rescued, the danger to the submarines was so great that, as
the one responsible for the boats and the crews, I had to
prohibit rescue activities in the face of the ever-present
tremendous Anglo-American Air Force. I want to mention, just as an example, that all the submarines which
took part in that rescue operation were lost by bombing
attack at their next action or soon afterwards. The situation in which the enemy kills the rescuers while they are
exposing themselves to great personal danger is really
and emphatically contrary to ordinary common sense and
the elementary rules of warfare.

KRANZBÜHLER. In the opinion of the prosecution, Admiral,
you used that incident to carry out in practice an idea
which you had already cherished for a long time, namely,
in future to kill the shipwrecked. Please state your view
on this.

DÖNITZ....The whole question concerned rescue or nonrescue;
the entire development leading up to that order speaks
clearly against such an accusation. It was a fact that we
rescued with devotion and were bombed while doing so;
it was also a fact that the U-boat Command and I were
faced with a serious decision, and we acted in a humane
way, which from a military point of view was wrong. I
think, therefore, that no more words need be lost in
rebuttal of this charge.

KRANZBÜHLER. Admiral, I must put to you now the wording of
that order from which the prosecution draws its con-
clusions.... In the second paragraph it says: "Rescue is
contrary to the most primitive laws for the destruction of
enemy ships and crews." What does that sentence mean?

DÖNITZ. That sentence is, of course, intended to be a justification. Now the prosecution says I could quite simply have
ordered that safety did not permit it, that the predomi-
nance of the enemy's air force did not permit it—and as
we have seen in the case of the *Laconia* I did order that
four times. But that reasoning had been worn out. It was
a "much-played record"... I was now anxious to state to
the commanders of the submarines a reason which would
exclude all discretion and all independent decision of the
commanders. For again and again I had the experience
that... a clear sky was judged too favourably by the

U-boats and then the submarine was lost; or that a commander, in the role of rescuer, was in time no longer master of his own decisions, as the *Laconia* case showed. Therefore, under no circumstances did I want to repeat the old reason which again would give the U-boat commander the opportunity to say: "Well, at the moment there is no danger of an air attack." That is, I did not want to give him a chance to act independently... I did not want an argument to arise in the mind of one of the two hundred U-boat commanders. Nor did I want to say, "If somebody with great self-sacrifice rescues the enemy and in that process is killed by him, then that is a contradiction of the most elementary laws of warfare." I could have said that too. But I did not put it that way, and, therefore, I worded the sentence as it now stands.

KRANZBÜHLER. The order of September 17th was for you the end of the *Laconia* incident?

DÖNITZ. Yes.

KRANZBÜHLER. To whom was it directed?

DÖNITZ. According to my best recollection, only to submarines on the high seas. For the various operation areas we had different radio channels. Since the other submarines were in contact with convoys and thus unable to carry out rescue measures, they could simply shelve the order. But I have now discovered that the order was sent out to all submarines, that is, on all channels; it was a technical matter of communication which, of course, could do no harm.

KRANZBÜHLER. You said that the fundamental consideration underlying the entire order was the overwhelming danger of air attack. If that is correct, how could you in the same order maintain the directive for the rescue of captains and chief engineers?

DÖNITZ. There is, of course, a great difference between rescue measures for which the submarine has to stop, and men have to go on deck, and a brief surfacing to pick up a captain, because while merely surfacing the submarine remains in a state of alert, whereas otherwise that alertness is completely disrupted.

However, there was a military purpose in the seizure of these captains, for which I had received orders from the Naval Operations Staff as a matter of principle... and in pursuit of a military aim, that is to say not rescue work but the capture of important enemies, one must and can run a certain risk. Besides, I knew that in practice that addition brought very meagre results, I might say no results at all. I remember quite clearly having asked myself, "Why do we still pick them up?" It was not our intention, however, to drop a general order of that importance. But the essential points are, first, the lesser risk that the state of alert might not be maintained during rescue and, secondly, the pursuit of an important military aim.

KRANZBÜHLER. What do you mean by the last sentence in the order, "Be harsh"?

DÖNITZ. I had preached to my U-boat commanders for five and a half years that they should be hard towards themselves. And when giving this order I again felt I had to emphasize to them in a very drastic way my whole concern and grave responsibility for the submarines, and thus the necessity of prohibiting rescue activities in view of the overwhelming power of the enemy air force. After all, it is very definite that on one side there is the harshness of war, the necessity of saving one's own submarine, and on the other the traditional sentiment of the sailor!

KRANZBÜHLER. You heard the witness Lieutenant-Commander Möhle state in this Court that he misunderstood the order in the sense that survivors should be killed, and in several cases he instructed submarine commanders in that sense. As Commanding Officer, do you not have to assume responsibility for the misunderstanding of your orders?

DÖNITZ. Of course I am responsible for all orders, for their form and their contents. Möhle, however, is the only person who had doubts about the meaning of that order. I regret that Möhle did not find occasion to clarify these doubts immediately, either through me, to whom everyone had access at all times, or through the numerous staff officers who, as members of my staff, were either also partly responsible or participated in the drafting of these orders; or... through his immediate superior at Kiel. I am convinced that the few U-boat commanders to

whom he communicated his doubts remained quite unaf-
fected by them. If there were any consequences I would,
of course, assume responsibility for them.

KRANZBÜHLER. You mentioned before the discussion with the
Führer, during which the problem whether it was permissible to kill survivors was examined, or at least touched
on by the Führer. Was tha question re-examined at any
time by the Commander-in-Chief of U-boats or the
Naval Operations Staff?

DÖNITZ. When I had become Commander-in-Chief of the
Navy . . . ?

KRANZBÜHLER. That was in 1943.

DÖNITZ. I think in the summer of 1943 I received a letter
from the Foreign Office in which I was informed that
about eighty-seven per cent of the crews of merchant
ships which had been sunk were returning home. I was
told that was a disadvantage and was asked whether it
was not possible to do something about it.

   Thereupon I had a letter sent to the Foreign Office in
which I wrote that I had already been forced to prohibit
rescue because it endangered the submarines, but that
other measures were out of the question for me.

KRANZBÜHLER. The decisive point of the entire letter seems to
be in Heading 3: "A directive to take action against lifeboats
of sunken vessels and crew members drifting in the sea
would, for psychological reasons, hardly be acceptable to
U-boat crews, since it would be contrary to the inner-
most feelings of all sailors. Such a directive could only be
considered if by it a decisive military success could be
achieved."

   Admiral, you yourself have repeatedly spoken about
the harshness of war. Are you, nevertheless, of the
opinion that psychologically the U-boat crews could not
be expected to carry out such an order, and why?

DÖNITZ. We U-boat men knew that we had to fight a very
hard war against the great sea powers. Germany had at
her disposal for this naval warfare nothing but the U-boats.
Therefore, from the beginning, already in peace-time, I
trained the submarine crews in the spirit of pure ideal-
ism and patriotism.

That was necessary, and I continued that training throughout the war and supported it by very close personal contacts with the men at the bases. It was necessary to achieve very high morale, very high fighting spirit, because otherwise the severe struggle and the enormous losses... would have been morally impossible to bear. But in spite of these high losses we continued the fight, because it had to be; and we made up for our losses and again and again replenished our forces with volunteers full of enthusiasm and moral strength, just because morale was so high. And I would never, even at the time of our most serious losses, have permitted that these men be given an order which was unethical or would damage their fighting morale; much less would I myself have ever given such an order, for I placed my whole confidence in that high fighting morale and endeavoured to maintain it.

KRANZBÜHLER. You said the U-boat forces were replenished with volunteers, did you?

DÖNITZ. We had practically only volunteers.

KRANZBÜHLER. Also at the time of the highest losses?

DÖNITZ. Yes, even then... during the period when everyone knew that he took part in an average of two missions and then was lost.

KRANZBÜHLER. How high were your losses?

DÖNITZ. According to my recollection, our total losses were six hundred and forty or six hundred and seventy.

KRANZBÜHLER. And crew members?

DÖNITZ. Altogether, we had forty thousand men in the submarine force. Of these, thirty thousand did not return and only five thousand were taken prisoner. The majority of the submarines were destroyed from the air in the vast areas of the Atlantic, where rescue was out of the question.

July 16th, Morning Session

KRANZBÜHLER. I am now coming to the second basic charge of the prosecution—intentional killing of shipwrecked crews. It is directed only against Admiral Dönitz, not Admiral Raeder. The legal basis for the treatment of shipwrecked crews, for those ships which are entitled to the protection of the London Agreement of 1936, is laid down in the agreement itself. There it says that, before the sinking, crews and passengers must be brought to safety. This was done by the German side, and the difference of opinion with the prosecution concerns only the question already dealt with, namely, which ships were entitled to protection under the agreement and which were not.

In the case of all ships not entitled to protection under the agreement, sinking should be considered a military combat action. The legal basis, therefore, with regard to the treatment of shipwrecked crews in these cases is contained in the Hague Convention concerning the application of the principles of the Geneva Convention to naval warfare of October 18th, 1907, although it was not ratified by Great Britain. According to this, both belligerents shall after each combat action make arrangements for the search for the shipwrecked, as far as military considerations allow this. Accordingly, the German U-boats were also bound to assist the shipwrecked of steamers sunk without warning, as long as by doing so, first, the boat would not be endangered, and secondly, the accomplishment of the military mission would not be prejudiced.

These principles are generally acknowledged ... This situation was changed through Admiral Dönitz's order of September 17th, 1942, in which he forbade rescue measures on principle. The decisive sentences are:

The rescue of members of the crew of a ship sunk is not to be attempted. Rescue is contradictory to the most primitive demands of warfare, which are the annihilation of enemy ships and crews.

It has been disputed by the prosecution that this actually prohibits rescue. It looks upon this order as a hidden provocation to kill the shipwrecked, and it has gone through the Press of the world as a command for murder. If any accusation at all has been refuted in this trial, then it seems to me to be this ignominious interpretation of the order mentioned above.

How was this order brought on? Beginning with June 1942, the losses of German submarines through the

Allied air forces rose by leaps and bounds, and jumped from a monthly average of 4 or 5 during the first months of 1942 to 10, 11, 13, finally reaching 38 boats in May 1943. Orders and measures from the Command of Submarine Warfare multiplied in order to counter these losses. They were of no avail, and every day brought fresh reports of air attacks and losses of submarines.

This was the situation when, on September 12th, it was reported that the heavily armed British troop-transport *Laconia*, with 1,500 Italian prisoners of war and an Allied crew of 1,000 men and some women and children aboard, had been torpedoed. Admiral Dönitz withdrew several submarines from current operations for the purpose of rescuing the shipwrecked, no distinction being made between Italians and Allies. From the very start the danger of enemy air attacks filled him with anxiety. While the submarines during the following days devotedly rescued, towed boats, supplied food and so forth, they received no less than three admonitions from the Commander-in-Chief to be careful, to divide the shipwrecked, and at all times be ready to submerge. These warnings were of no avail. On September 16th one of the submarines displaying a Red Cross flag and towing lifeboats was attacked and considerably damaged by an Allied bomber; one lifeboat was hit and losses caused among the shipwrecked. Following this report the Commander-in-Chief sent three more messages with orders immediately to submerge in case of danger and under no circumstances to risk the boat's own safety. Again without avail. In the evening of that day, September 17th, 1942, the second submarine reported that it had been taken unawares and bombed by an aeroplane.

Notwithstanding these experiences, and in spite of the explicit order from the Führer's headquarters not to endanger any boats under any consideration, Admiral Dönitz did not discontinue rescue work, but had it continued until the shipwrecked were taken aboard French warships sent to their rescue. However, this incident was a lesson. Due to enemy air reconnaissance activity over the entire sea area, it was simply no longer possible to carry out rescue measures without endangering the submarine. It was useless to give orders over and over again to commanders to undertake rescue work only if their own boats were not endangered thereby. Earlier experiences had already shown that their human desire to render aid had led many commanders to underestimate the danger from the air. It takes a submarine with decks cleared at least one minute to submerge on alarm, while an aircraft can cover 6,000 metres in that time. In practice this means that a submarine engaged in rescue action when sighting a plane has not time enough to submerge.

These were the reasons which caused Admiral Dönitz, directly after the close of the *Laconia* incident, to forbid rescue measures on principle. This was motivated by the endeavour to preclude any calculation on the part of the commander as to the danger of air attack whenever in individual cases he should feel tempted to undertake rescue work. . . .

How then can the prosecution consider this order an "order to murder?"

Grounds for this are said to be furnished by the discussion between Hitler and the Japanese ambassador Oshima, in January 1942, in which Hitler mentioned a prospective order to his U-boats to kill the survivors of ships sunk. This announcement, the prosecution infers, Hitler doubtless followed up, and Admiral Dönitz carried it out by the *Laconia* order. Actually, on the occasion of a report on U-boat problems, which both admirals had to make in May 1942, the Führer suggested that in future action should be taken against the shipwrecked, that is, to shoot them. Admiral Dönitz immediately rejected this action as completely impossible, and Grandadmiral Raeder unreservedly agreed with him. Both admirals specified the improvement of torpedoes as the only permissible way to increase losses among the crews. In the face of the opposition of both admirals Adolf Hitler dropped his proposal, and following this report no order whatever was given concerning shipwrecked crews, let alone concerning the killing of the shipwrecked by shooting. . . .

The testimony of Lt.-Commander Möhle must be taken much more seriously because he had . . . hinted to a few submarine commanders that the *Laconia* order demanded, or at least approved of, the killing of shipwrecked. Möhle did not receive this interpretation either from Admiral Dönitz himself, or from the Chief of Staff, or from his chief assistant Lt.-Commander Hessler, that is to say from none of the officers who alone would have been qualified to transmit such an interpretation to the chief of a flotilla.

How Möhle actually arrived at this interpretation has in my opinion not been explained by the trial . . . One thing at any rate has been proven, namely, that Admiral Dönitz and his staff had not caused this briefing to be given, nor did they know anything about it.

JUDGMENTS October 1st, 1946

War Crimes:

Dönitz is charged with waging unrestricted submarine warfare contrary to the Naval Protocol of 1936, to which Germany acceded, and which reaffirmed the rules of submarine warfare laid down in the London Naval Agreement of 1930. . . .

It is also asserted that the German U-boat arm not only did not carry out the rescue and warning provisions of the Protocol, but that Dönitz deliberately ordered the killing of survivors of shipwrecked vessels, whether enemy or neutral. The prosecution has introduced much evidence surrounding two orders of Dönitz: war order Number 154, issued in 1939, and the so-called *Laconia* order of 1942. The defence argues that these orders and the evidence supporting them do not show such a policy, and has introduced much evidence to the contrary. The Tribunal is of the opinion that the evidence does not establish with the certainty required that Dönitz deliberately ordered the killing of shipwrecked survivors. The orders were undoubtedly ambiguous and deserve the strongest censure.

The evidence further shows that the stipulations on rescue work were not observed and that the defendant ordered that they should not be observed. The argument of the defence is that the security of the submarine, as the first rule of the sea, takes precedence over rescue, and that the development of aircraft made rescue impossible. This may be so, but the Protocol is explicit. If the commander cannot rescue, then under its terms he cannot sink a merchant vessel, and should allow it to pass unharmed before his periscope. These orders, then, prove that Dönitz is guilty of a violation of the Protocol.

In view of all the facts proved, and in particular of an order of the British Admiralty announced on May 8th, 1940, according to which all vessels navigating at night in the Skagerrak should be sunk, and in view also of Admiral Nimitz's statement that unrestricted submarine warfare was carried on in the Pacific Ocean by the United States from the first day that nation entered the war, the sentence on Dönitz is not assessed on the ground of his breaches of the international law of submarine warfare...

VERDICT

The Tribunal finds Dönitz not guilty on Count One of the Indictment, and guilty on Counts Two and Three.[1]

SENTENCE BY THE PRESIDENT

"In accordance with Article 27 of the Charter, the International Military Tribunal will now pronounce the sentences on the defendants convicted on this indictment.

... Defendant Karl Dönitz, on the Counts of the Indictment on which you have been convicted, the Tribunal sentences you to ten years' imprisonment."

---

[1] Count One: Conspiracy.
Count Two: Crimes against peace.
Count Three: War Crimes.

Appendix E

THE *LACONIA* ORDER[1]

In the German Navy, in conformity with the Geneva Convention of October 1907, assistance to the shipwrecked was authorized and ordered when the operation did not endanger the German vessel or risk preventing the accomplishment of her mission. Consequently rescue work, an obvious moral duty, presupposed the end of an action. So rescue must not even be thought of as long as the battle was in progress, or even while other naval actions remained possible.

The decision as to whether an action was to be considered as finished, and whether the vessel's safety allowed rescue work to begin, was left to the sole discretion of each unit commander.

The same principles applied in the fleets of other powers.

Following this line of conduct German submarines, during the first years of the war, often went to the rescue of the shipwrecked.

In 1942, however, the situation in the Atlantic for German ships had taken an abrupt turn for the worse: it was becoming impossible to consider a naval action as definitely over, for almost everywhere you had to be constantly expecting the sudden appearance of enemy aircraft. This was a specially grave danger for a submarine, unless it was seen in time, that is to say, at the extreme limits of visibility. Moreover, a submarine can submerge quickly only when she is under way and when the number of sailors on the bridge or the deck is

---

[1] Statement made to the author by Admiral Dönitz. [I leave it to the reader to form his own judgment on this.]

small enough to allow them to go below quickly. In other words, when a submarine has surfaced and stopped her engines, which is unavoidable if she is going to rescue the shipwrecked, and has a large part of her crew in the open, she is not in a state of alert. She is therefore at the mercy of attack from the air.

During the second half of 1942, the growing intensity of aerial surveillance in all maritime sectors was causing me grave concern. In my War Diary for August 21st, 1942, i.e. very shortly before the *Laconia* incident, I reported this growing danger and concluded: "If this aggravation of our difficulties at sea should continue, it is bound to lead to intolerably high losses, besides reducing our successful actions and thereby our chances of winning a decisive victory through submarine warfare."

The danger to which submarines were liable, having to expect attack at any moment, also comes out in other passages of the War Diary: e.g. from September 2nd to 14th, 1942, there are repeated references to air attacks on our submarines, enemy aircraft seen by our look-outs and loss of vessels through bombing. These passages were quoted by my counsel at the Nuremberg trials.

This situation meant the end of the phase when any action could be considered as definitely over. Nevertheless, it was left to the unit commander's judgment, as in the past, whether there was a chance to rescue the shipwrecked.

It was in such conditions that the *Laconia* was torpedoed in the Atlantic, south of the Equator, on September 12th, 1942. She was a troop-transport, armed with fourteen guns, according to a handbook we possessed on British armed ships. The torpedoing itself was, therefore, justified, and in any case has never been criticized. There were 811 British on board, including servicemen on leave accompanied by wives and children, and 1,800 Italian prisoners of war guarded by 103 Poles.

After the torpedoing, the submarine commander, in conformity with the traditional code, asked himself whether the action could be considered as over, and whether he had the right and the chance to undertake rescue work. Having answered these questions in the affirmative, he started a rescue operation and informed me of having done so.

For my part, having greater experience and a better

overall view, I was by no means sure the engagement was really over. It was for me to decide either to forbid rescue work, which would have been justified from a purely military standpoint, or else to approve it and give it my best support. Having opted for the second alternative, although this obliged me to give up several other missions, I undertook an operation which was to save the lives of about 800 of the 811 British[1] and 450 of the Italians. I suspended a long-planned operation off Capetown, and had the submarines detailed for it directed instead to the area of the torpedoing. I also sent there other submarines stationed in the South Atlantic.

My wireless messages were, as always, recorded by the Naval Operations Command, and were thus automatically made known to the Führer's G.H.Q. The Admiral-in-Chief, while approving my decision, informed me that in no case must the submarines engaged in rescue work be exposed to any danger whatever. Hitler himself declared that the mission for the submarines off the Cape must be neither put off nor stopped, and that the submarines involved in rescue work must not run any danger.

Using the international wave-lengths, we informed the whole world, en clair, of the rescue work undertaken by the submarines, and called for extra help.

Concerned for the safety of the submarines engaged in this perilous operation, and fearing that the indispensable condition—the cessation of all enemy action—was by no means fulfilled, I sent several wireless messages ordering the rescuing submarines at all costs to remain ready to submerge.

These repeated warnings were to prove ineffective. The first of the submarines involved had already taken on board 260 survivors, a really terrific number, and several boats in tow, equally overloaded. On September 16th an enemy aircraft dropped bombs on the submarine and in the middle of the boats. One of these capsized, and several survivors were drowned. The submarine was damaged, although it escaped destruction.

---

[1] The number of British survivors is clearly very much overestimated, even if it includes those picked up by Hartenstein who died as a result of the bombing of U-156. But Admiral Dönitz made an identical statement at Nuremberg, which was not confuted by the prosecution. It was doubtless a genuine mistake, due to misinformation.

When I was informed, it seemed to me that from the military point of view I should really have had the right to stop the rescue operation completely. Several members of my staff suggested this solution, justifiably enough. But I couldn't bring myself to adopt it, since you could not decently, to use my own words, "throw back into the sea people you have just pulled out." So I ordered rescue work to be continued, though realizing that the loss of a single submarine would certainly, and very logically, cost me my place on the War Council. I again ordered the submarines to remain ready to submerge at any time.

The course of events was to prove me wrong. On September 17th a second submarine, after taking on board 142 survivors, including women and children, was bombed by an enemy aircraft. Only the look-outs' vigilance enabled the vessel to escape destruction: the three bombs exploded when the submarine had already reached a depth of 200 feet. After this attack our submarines transferred the survivors on board to two French warships.

From this affair I could draw at least one conclusion: never again must submarines be exposed to the dangers of a rescue operation. The ubiquitousness and behaviour of enemy aviation made it at present absolutely impermissible. The period when an isolated action could be considered as over was indeed gone for good. I could no longer leave it to each individual commander to assess the conditions of safety. Too often experience had proved that they underestimated the danger from the air. They were apt to feel safe while an enemy aircraft was not in sight, only to find the situation desperate a moment later when a single plane appeared. Consequently, security from the air, presumed or real, could no longer decide the question whether the shipwrecked should be rescued or abandoned.

Since I was obliged to withdraw from commanders the right of individual assessment, I had to give them the reasons for this. I had to explain to them that it was illogical to destroy an enemy ship and her crew, and then make great efforts to save that crew, although the action had by no means ceased and the rescue operation exposed the submarine herself to the gravest dangers—in short, to act contrary to the principles accepted in all navies at war.

It was to this end that I promulgated what is today called

"The *Laconia* Order." In this order, the phrase "destruction of enemy ships and their crews" applies to ships having their crews on board.

It is beyond doubt that the crews of Allied merchant vessels were combatants, that they were, therefore, naturally and legally made the object of attack. Merchant ships were fitted with guns and depth-charges, their sailors had received special instructions for fighting the submarines they met, in agreement and collaboration with marines specially attached to the ship. Moreover, merchant ships were completely integrated with the enemy's military dispositions. (In the war on land, a civilian who offered active resistance would be treated as a *franc-tireur.*)

Other countries had anyhow adopted an identical attitude towards the problem of rescue work. In the Nuremberg trials, Admiral Nimitz, Commander-in-Chief of the American Navy, made the following deposition: "Generally, United States' submarines refrained from rescuing the shipwrecked as soon as this operation exposed them to needless additional risks, or again when rescue work stopped them carrying out another mission." Now, quite obviously, the American submarines were running far less danger in the much vaster expanses of the Pacific, and against the much less powerful Japanese Air Force, than German submarines in the comparative confinement of the Atlantic and against the terrific air strength of the two principal maritime powers, which was directed very vigorously against the German submarines.

It was not the commanders of German submarines who gave a false interpretation of the "*Laconia* Order," but the prosecution at the Nuremberg Trials, which claimed that this order was aimed at the massacre of the shipwrecked. Such an interpretation, however, was not upheld by the International Court.

In any case, out of thousands of actions undertaken by the German submarines, there was not a single instance when a commander did attack the shipwrecked, except for the *Peleus* affair. Even there, according to Commander Eck's formal deposition, it was not the "*Laconia* Order" which made him act as he did, but the desire to prevent his vessel being discovered. With this objective he "liquidated" the wreckage of the torpedoed ship, an objective which meant in his judgment that he could not spare the survivors.

On this subject I refer to the documents presented at Nuremberg. They establish quite certainly that even after the *Laconia* incident I refused to have the shipwrecked attacked. I also believe that the morale of the German submariners could not have remained as high as it did until the end of the war, if I had asked them to commit criminal acts. All foreign works with any claim to be taken seriously do justice to this exceptionally high morale. Churchill, in the last volume of his memoirs, finishes the chapter devoted to the submarine war with the phrase: "Such was the greatness of soul of the German submariners."

As to the *Laconia* incident more particularly, Captain S. W. Roskill, British naval historian, tried to justify the attitude of his fellow-countrymen who, instead of helping in the rescue, bombed our submarines. Then he added: "In this affair, Dönitz and his crews were doubtless largely in the right." (*Sunday Times*, February 1st, 1959: "Mystery of U.S. Planes' Attack.")

One last proof that the danger from the air was immense, that the time had gone when an action could be considered as over, that the order not to rescue the shipwrecked was necessary in order to protect our own submarines: the three submarines which took part in rescuing the *Laconia*'s survivors were all attacked by enemy aircraft on their next mission and were sunk with their crews.

Appendix F

LIST OF PASSENGERS AND CREW OF THE *LACONIA* MENTIONED BY NAME

Allen, Sergeant, R.A.F.

Baker, Geoffrey
Baldwin, Lieutenant-Colonel

Batchelor, Sergeant, R.A.F.
Blackburn, Wing-Commander
Boyett, Lieutenant A.E., R.N.V.R.
Buckingham (senior third officer)

Cooper, H.C. (third wireless officer)
Coutts, Captain Ben
Creedon, Major (now Brigadier)

Davidson, Dorothy
Davidson, Molly (now Mrs. Lewes)

Elliot, Sergeant, R.A.F.

Forster, Elizabeth
Forster, Gladys

Gibson, Mrs.

Hall (army officer)
Hall-Clucas (junior first officer)
Hawkins, Sister Doris
Henderson, William (fourth engineer officer)
Hurst (purser)

Jones (member of crew)

Large, Able Seaman (Dr.) A. V.
Lester, Petty Officer
Liswell, Lieutenant-Colonel

Middleton, Sergeant, R.A.F.
Miller, R.M.
Moore, Mrs.
Moore, Freddy

Nagle, Mrs.

Peel, Lieutenant Ian
Penman, Pilot Officer Frank, R.N.Z.A.F.
Purslow, Dr. Geoffrey (ship's doctor)

Riley (member of crew)
Rose (senior second officer)

Sharp, Captain Rudolph, C.B.E., R.D., R.N.R.
Sime (engineer in the Merchant Navy; a passenger)
Smith, Flying Officer
Sollace (member of crew)
Steel, Chief Officer George
Stokes, Second Officer

Tillie, Lieutenant John, R.N., D.S.C. and bar

Vines, Leading Seaman Harry

Walker, Mrs.
Walker, J. H. (senior first officer)
Wells, Squadron-Leader H. R. K.
Wolfe-Murray, Lady Grizel